Web Standards Creativity: Innovations in Web Design with XHTML, CSS, and DOM Scripting

Cameron Adams
Mark Boulton
Andy Clarke
Simon Collison
Jeff Croft
Derek Featherstone
Ian Lloyd
Ethan Marcotte
Dan Rubin
Rob Weychert

friendsof

DESIGNER TO DESIGNER™

an Apress® company

Web Standards Creativity: Innovations in Web Design with XHTML, CSS, and DOM Scripting

ISBN-13 (pbk): 978-1-59059-803-0

ISBN-10 (pbk): 1-59059-803-2

Printed and bound in China

9 8 7 6 5 4 3 2 1

Trademarked names may appear in this book. Rather than use a trademark symbol with every occurrence of a trademarked name, we use the names only in an editorial fashion and to the benefit of the trademark owner, with no intention of infringement of the trademark.

The White Pages® Online screenshots (Chapter 9, Figures 9-3 and 9-4) have been reproduced with the permission of Sensis Pty Ltd.® Registered trade mark of Telstra Corporation Limited.

Distributed to the book trade worldwide by Springer-Verlag New York, Inc., 233 Spring Street, 6th Floor, New York, NY 10013. Phone 1-800-SPRINGER, fax 201-348-4505, e-mail orders-ny@springer-sbm.com, or visit www.springeronline.com.

For information on translations, please contact Apress directly at 2560 Ninth Street, Suite 219, Berkeley, CA 94710. Phone 510-549-5930, fax 510-549-5939, e-mail info@apress.com, or visit www.apress.com.

The source code for this book is freely available to readers at www.friendsofed.com in the Downloads section.

Credits

Lead Editor	**Assistant Production Director**
Chris Mills	Kari Brooks-Copony
Technical Reviewer	**Compositor**
Molly Holzschlag	Diana Van Winkle,
	Van Winkle Design Group
Editorial Board	
Steve Anglin, Ewan Buckingham,	**Proofreader**
Gary Cornell, Jason Gilmore,	Lori Bring
Jonathan Gennick, Jonathan Hassell,	
James Huddleston, Chris Mills,	**Indexer**
Matthew Moodie, Dominic Shakeshaft,	Brenda Miller
Jim Sumser, Keir Thomas, Matt Wade	
	Interior Designer
Project Manager	Diana Van Winkle,
Kylie Johnston	Van Winkle Design Group
Copy Edit Manager	**Cover Designer**
Nicole Flores	Kurt Krames
Copy Editors	**Manufacturing Director**
Marilyn Smith, Nicole Flores	Tom Debolski

Contents at a Glance

Contents

About the Technical Reviewer

Molly E. Holzschlag is a well-known Web Standards advocate, instructor, and author. She is Group Lead for the Web Standards Project (WaSP) and an invited expert to the HTML and GEO working groups at the World Wide Web Consortium (W3C).

Through each of these roles, Molly works to educate designers and developers on using web technologies in practical ways to create highly sustainable, maintainable, accessible, interactive, and beautiful websites for the global community.

Among her 30-plus books is the *The Zen of CSS Design*, coauthored with Dave Shea. The book artfully showcases the most progressive csszengarden.com designs. A popular and colorful individual, Molly has a particular passion for people, blogs, and the use of technology for social progress.

Acknowledgments

Mark Boulton

I'd like to thank Khoi Vinh for the grid background technique, and Phil Wright for his constructive feedback and for being just about the best design writer I know. Of course, the Britpack members deserve a mention, talented bunch that they are. Last, but certainly not least, to thank is my wife, Emma, for her unwavering patience as I prattle on about design. Every. Single. Day.

Andy Clarke

I wish that I had invented all of the techniques that I used to create the WorrySome.net site design and that you will be re-creating throughout the pages of my chapter. Instead I invented a machine that reads brainwaves and projects them onto a large screen in my secret laboratory. With this machine, I stole the thoughts of the many people who came up with these remarkable solutions.

I would like to thank all of the hundreds of designers and developers who dreamed up and then shared their ideas, albeit unwittingly and in their sleep. I am sorry that in some cases my early experiments in thought extraction have led to your madness. Don't worry—working in this industry, who is going to notice?

Special thanks go to editor Chris Mills and to my scooter-riding, parka-wearing colleagues in the Britpack for their friendship and inspiration. Thanks also to those jolly Johnny foreigners who ask me to design, code, and speak to them at conferences and workshops from San Francisco to Southend to Sydney.

My love goes to my family. My chapter is for my son Alex, 14 years old and already twice the man that I will ever be.

Simon Collision

I must thank Agenzia for allowing me to feature the Dirty Pretty Things website, and also Creation Management and Vertigo Records for allowing me to go on and on and on about what I've done for the band. Images of the band are by Roger Sargeant and Max Vadukul, and the source artwork for the website is by Hannah Bays. The website is built with the incomparable ExpressionEngine content management system, handling 35,000 Dirty Pretty fans admirably, and is managed by the lovely administrators Kirsty and Kirsty.

Jeff Croft

Thanks to everyone who helped make this book possible, and there are a lot of you.

To Chris Mills for giving me this wonderful opportunity, and to all of my coauthors, who are a constant source of inspiration. It has been an honor to work with each and every one of you, and I hope it's not the last time.

To everyone else at Apress and friends of ED, you've all been a joy to work with.

To Jeffrey Zeldman, for being the guy who got me—and a heckuva lot of other people—on board with this whole Web Standards thing. And to all the great minds in the Web Standards community who share their discoveries and wonderful personalities with us through blogs, books, and other resources. I can't name you all here, but you know who you are. I never cease to be amazed at the inspiration you guys and gals provide.

To all of my friends at World Online who are among the smartest people I've ever met and have given me the opportunity to do what I love to do every day instead of "going to work."

To my girlfriend Michelle, who never gets frustrated with all the time I spend working on projects like this instead of tending to her. I love you, Meesh.

To my entire family, especially my mom and dad, who supported me in countless ways instead of balking when I dropped out of college to pursue "this Internet thing." I love you guys more than I could ever possibly explain.

To my incredible daughter Haley, who is the reason I do everything I do.

And of course to you, for reading.

Ian Lloyd

Thanks to all the people who commented on my blog about the original proof-of-concept that I put together, and particularly to those who suggested improvements and fine-tuning. Thanks also to beer and junk TV, which always have the uncanny ability of compressing a reasonable time scale for writing into the usual last-minute panic. But I wouldn't have it any other way!

Dan Rubin

Many thanks to Lee Hammond and Geffen/Universal Media for giving the OK to use this project as a case study (not to mention hiring me to do it in the first place), and for being such a wonderful client to begin with. Thanks are also due to Lifehouse and the band's management, to Mike Rundle (aka "phark") for the image replacement technique I use every day, and to Mike Davidson, Shawn Inman, Tomas Jogin, and Mark Wubben (collectively "The sIFR Gang") for creating and improving the only way to accurately control live text rendering on sites built with Web Standards.

To Chris Mills and the Apress/friends of ED team, I leave my—wait, wrong document—thanks for the late and oh-so-sleepless nights; the complimentary cricket bat made it all worthwhile. Special thanks to Kristina Horst for making me look astonishingly dashing in my headshot. Oh, and let's not forget good old mum and dad; my brother Alex for the constant support he provides (in and out of the office); and, of course, Larry, the lizard who lives in my closet, for his completely random but curiously comforting and almost omniscient presence and countenance.

Getting Creative with Web Standards

"Not another Web Standards book!" I hear you cry, "I already own a copy of *CSS Mastery*, so why would I need anything else?" Well, if you can give me a couple of minutes, I'd like to explain why you should buy this book.

Web Standards have come a long way since the first glimmer in W3C's eye. In the early days, CSS was the preserve of coders and gained a reputation of being "boxy but good." Pioneers like Jeffrey Zeldman and Eric Meyer helped popularize the use of standards and inspired designers like Douglas Bowman and Todd Dominey to create some of the first commercially successful standards-based sites around (see Figures 1 and 2).

Figure 1. Wired News was redesigned in October 2002 by Douglas Bowman. This was one of the first major commercial sites to adopt Web Standards and prompted many companies to follow suit.

Figure 2. Designed by Todd Dominey in 2003, the 85th PGA Championship website showed that standards-based designs could be as beautiful as their table-based counterparts.

However, it was Dave Shea's Zen Garden that showed a whole new generation of web designers that standards-based design could be sexy and fun (see Figures 3, 4, and 5). Out went the boxy layouts and in came experimental pieces more at home in a graphic design portfolio.

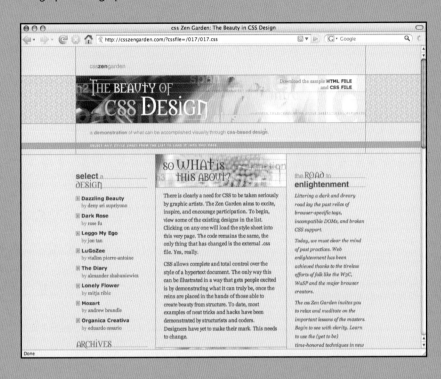

Figure 3. One of the very first Zen Garden designs was "Golden Mean," a beautiful study of typography and composition from Douglas Bowman.

Figure 4. Another early addition to the garden, but still as beautiful as the day it was created, is Mike Picks' "What Lies Beneath."

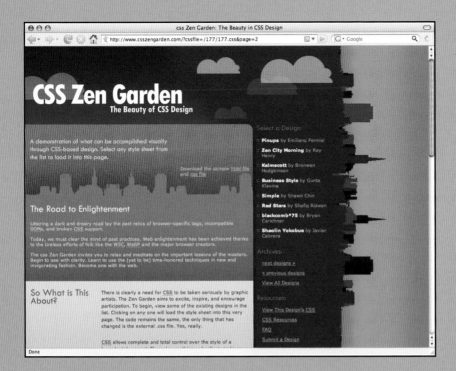

Figure 5. The Zen Garden is still going strong, as demonstrated by this recent submission from Ray Henry of REH3design.

Designers ran with this new freedom, and we now see beautiful CSS designs appearing every day. If you don't believe me, just check out the likes of Stylegala, CSS Beauty, CSS Thesis (see Figure 6), and the million or so other CSS design galleries that have sprung up over the last couple of years.

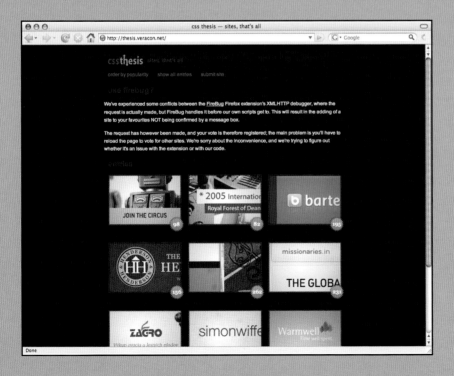

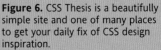

Figure 6. CSS Thesis is a beautifully simple site and one of many places to get your daily fix of CSS design inspiration.

The basics of CSS are relatively easy to master, but the problems start when you try to turn your designs into reality. Knowing how to mark up the document, applying the right CSS techniques, and working around browser inconsistencies become key. This information comes with experience and cannot be learned from reading the CSS specification alone. With *CSS Mastery*, I tried to bridge this gap and show people some of the latest tips, tricks, and techniques. At the end of my book, all this information was put into practice through two amazing case studies from Cameron Moll and Simon Collison.

There is nothing like learning from the masters, and this is where *Web Standards Creativity* comes in. This book picks up where my book left off, with a series of advanced case studies for you to dissect. Here, some of the best standards-based designers in the world will show you how they take a project from inception to completion (be it an entire website design or a cool technique or widget they've developed).

Each chapter is like sitting down with a design master for a private lesson. They will share with you their unique processes: how they look at a design, deconstruct it, and then reassemble it using XHTML and CSS (and sometimes JavaScript, too, or even other technologies!). Along the way, you'll learn some fantastic tricks that you can start using on your projects immediately. Hey, even I learned a few new tricks while reading this book.

Yes, I mentioned JavaScript in the previous paragraph. Scripting is also a big part of this book. For many years, JavaScript was used to create superfluous effects that added little to the overall user experience. We saw effects that did things like scroll the text or shake the browser window. The code required for these effects was often bloated and inaccessible, going against the new philosophy of separation. This led to a backlash, and JavaScript fell out of fashion for a long time. Then along came Ajax, and everything changed.

People started to develop a renewed interest in JavaScript, as pioneers like Jeremy Keith advocated new ways of separating content and presentation from behavior (see Figure 7). Developers rediscovered the power of the Document Object Model (DOM), and JavaScript became cool again. By using JavaScript in a responsible manner, web developers are now able to add advanced interactivity to their web pages—interactivity that can help improve the user experience and make better websites. As well as covering XHTML and CSS, *Web Standards Creativity* contains a whole part dedicated to modern JavaScript techniques for web design.

If you ever wanted a crash course in practical standards-based design, this book is for you. So stop reading the introduction, turn to page 1, and start getting creative with Web Standards.

Andy Budd
Brighton, England, October 2006
Author, CSS Mastery

Figure 7. Check out *DOM Scripting: Web Design with JavaScript and the Document Object Model* by Jeremy Keith, for more information on this subject.

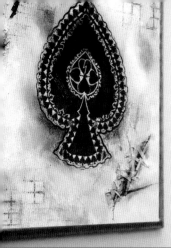

Layout Magic

Welcome to Part 1 of our journey into advanced standards-based web design! Unsurprisingly, the first part deals with advanced layout techniques, so the focus is mainly on CSS. The final choices for inclusion here (as for all of the book) were made because the authors have something a bit interesting and out of the ordinary to say. Let's face it, how many tutorials have you seen on the Web dealing with CSS layout techniques?

The authors have really pulled something special out of the hat here. Simon, Ethan, and Andy show different ways of achieving beautifully designed sites raised on a strict diet of lean, semantic markup, with clever use of class values, positioning out of the box, and more.

Dan shows how you can still make a great-looking site, even if you are constrained by content fed from a content management system. He also throws in some Flash image replacement and a small amount of DOM scripting for good measure.

Jeff focuses on using transparent PNGs, along with your CSS and HTML, to create some truly awesome design effects on your site.

The authors talk about browser-support inconsistencies when they apply, and explain how they got around those problems. The beautiful layouts you see here were achieved without having to resort to many hacks!

Have fun on your travels . . .

Semantic Structure, Dirty Pretty Presentation

simon *collison*

www.collylogic.com

Before starting Erskine Design in 2006, **Simon Collison** was lead web developer at Agenzia (www.agenzia.co.uk), where he worked on numerous web projects for record labels. Simon passionately ensures everything he builds is accessible and complies with current Web Standards.

Simon coauthored *Blog Design Solutions* and *CSS Mastery* (both published by friends of ED). His first solo book, *Beginning CSS Web Development* (www.csswebdevelopment.com), was published by Apress in 2006.

Away from the office, Simon runs the popular blog Colly Logic (www.collylogic.com), and he is an active member of the so-called Britpack—a collective of laid-back designers and developers who all share a passion for responsible web design. When prized away from the laptop, Simon can most likely be found in the pub or at a gig, waffling incessantly about good music, football, or biscuits.

Simon has lived in many cities, including London and Reykjavik, but has now settled back in his beloved Nottingham, where the grass is green and the girls are pretty.

4

The brief

Building a website compliant with Web Standards for a record company is a challenge. For years, Flash has been the essential tool for band websites. Plus, there are unfathomable navigation challenges, jukebox widgets, frames, questionable color palettes, and the ever-present Loading bar. While much of the Web looks current, in the music industry, it is still 1999. The situation is getting better, as Dan Rubin will illustrate in Chapter 2 of this book, but good sites are still few and far between.

For the Dirty Pretty Things website (www.dirtyprettythingsband.com), I and my fellow designers at Agenzia had the opportunity to build on the impact we had made with the relaunched Libertines (www.thelibertines.org.uk) site in the summer of 2004 (see Figure 1-1). We built the Libertines site with Web Standards, using Flash elements in a responsible way. We were hell-bent on keeping content separate from presentation to capitalize on the growing number of users accessing the site through mobile devices, and to ensure longevity for the core content, regardless of future redesigns. As it happens, the great hopes of UK rock and roll disbanded amidst a maelstrom of excess and bad behavior, but the site lives on with an ever-growing community of users.

Fast-forward 18 months, and Libertines cofounder Carl Barat has formed a new band, and there is major anticipation from the music press and fans alike. With celebrity ex-Libertine Pete Doherty all over the tabloids for all the wrong reasons, it is up to Carl and company to bring joy back to the thousands of fans who sold their souls to the Libertines. From the outset, it is clear that any new website is going to be on the popular side, and armed with our experiences from the Libertines site, it is easy to convince the record company that Web Standards are the only way forward.

A mass of original artwork created for the band by Hannah Bays is thrown our way, and although distinctive and cool, none of it seems to lend itself to a web design. In fact, getting a design together becomes a long and drawn-out process, and is put on the back burner while we begin building the core content of the site using just XHTML and PHP/MySQL.

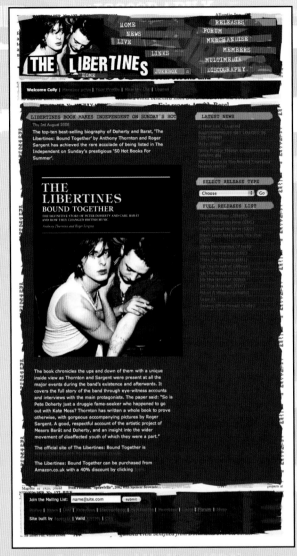

Figure 1-1. The final version of the Libertines website (www.thelibertines.org.uk)

This chapter will join the process as we complete the XHTML and database and return to the presentational approaches, looking at how this was achieved with a separate layer using CSS. The focus will be on applying the presentational visual touches, such as custom backgrounds, headers, and other widgets with CSS, leaving the core content uncompromised. Figure 1-2 shows the final version of the website.

Figure 1-2. The completed Dirty Pretty Things website (www.dirtyprettythingsband.com), launched in January 2006

Semantic structure

We're flying the flag for Web Standards here, so we need to be sure that the document (XHTML plus content) is separated from the presentation (CSS and decorative images). By applying all decorative presentational richness using an external style sheet, the document (the XHTML) remains pure and focused. With all presentational material kept separate from the markup, site-wide style changes can be made with little or no fuss. We just need to amend a single CSS file, rather than having to update every page in the site, making wholesale redesigns a veritable breeze. Equally important is the facility for users to take control of the content themselves by applying their own style sheet to the website, if desired.

An important step is to give any divisions (divs) added to the core content meaningful names, rather than presentational ones. For example, the masthead is called masthead, the main column is called content_main, and so on. This approach is also applied to smaller details, such as IDs and classnames used to change the color or emphasis of an element. There is no point in creating a class called green_heading if that might be used later as a hook for the CSS to render that heading in blue. Instead, the class is given a name that describes the role of the element rather than its style, such as date_heading. In most cases, such hooks are not even needed, as descendant selectors in the style sheet are used to select elements that are the children of others. You'll see how that works in the "Contents" section later in this chapter.

Figure 1-3 shows a screenshot of the website as styled by the browser's own default style sheet. The site is a fully functioning, database-driven site that completes the first stage of the build and demonstrates that everything can function perfectly well, even if a style sheet is not available.

With this stage of the build over, the team can now start thinking seriously about the presentation, and how the core content can be used as a framework for the look and feel of the site. Time to get dirty, and a little pretty.

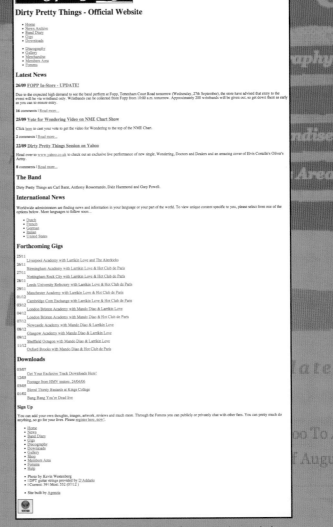

Figure 1-3. The document (XHTML plus content) as styled purely by the browser's default style sheet

Dirty pretty presentation

When building purely with XHTML, it is sensible to have a good idea of what the layout of the site will be. Naturally, we will be thinking in terms of columns and core areas, such as masthead and footer, and often this will be informed by a Photoshop layout (or even a sketch using pencils and paper!) from a designer on the team. With the Dirty Pretty Things site, this was not the case, as none of us had yet arrived at a layout that we ourselves could agree on, never mind the folks at the record company.

By applying an external style sheet to the fully functional XHTML site, we approached the problem organically. This means that, as we were bereft of an agreed-upon design, we began working up a look and feel through experimentation with the CSS. We tested everything from layout (fluid, fixed, or elastic) to font choices by creating and modifying CSS rules. This approach is slow, and demands having Photoshop open at all times to create and tweak background images that may or may not make it into the final design, but it is an exciting process that removes the restraints of a delivered, cast-in-stone design.

Armed with all the original artwork from Hannah Bays, and slowly developing parameters such as heights, widths, margins, and padding, a satisfying design will soon begin to materialize. As the style sheet is applied to all pages of the site, it is easy to see what is working site-wide. What areas of the artwork will work as backgrounds? Can certain areas be used as background tiles? Is a common color palette for text and core elements achievable from the collected source material?

The next step is to discuss the design with colleagues, involving much chin-stroking and coffee, before making sure the client is happy with the progress so far. Then we hone the ingredients bit by bit and tighten the design, before throwing it out for usability testing. Finally, the site is launched and the collected Agenzians can hit the pub.

Background images

Perhaps the most dramatic change from XHTML to carefully styled prettiness happens where the main background image meets the masthead and its descendants. A lot of careful Photoshop work is applied using a succession of background images, as illustrated in Figure 1-4.

Figure 1-4. Split into several layers, various background images are juxtaposed.

Before you start going hell-for-leather with background images, it is important to consider how this will affect the end user. Although less important than it used to be, you still need to realize that some folks are downloading web pages using really slow modems. A typical web page might contain something like 15KB of text and therefore download pretty quickly. Add 35KB of background images to that, and you are reducing the speed of the visitors' viewing experience significantly, at least until the browser has cached the images. Keep image use light, and go overboard only when it is really necessary or when you are designing for an audience you know will be using super-fast broadband connections.

Under no circumstances do we use background images to convey important information when no alternative is available if the images do not display or are manually disabled by a user. For example, we don't use a background image to show the title of the website, any navigation items, or any kind of flattened text content, unless we also provide this information with standard text if images are turned off. Background images are decorative adornments and certainly not to be considered "content," which is why they are referenced in the style sheet as separate presentation elements.

Background, masthead, and menu

We'll begin with how the three main layers—background, masthead, and main menu—are styled on the existing XHTML.

One inline image is present already: the main Dirty Pretty Things logo. The logo (Figure 1-5) is an animated GIF, which spells out the band name letter by letter when the page first loads. This logo is in the flow of the document, sitting top left within the masthead.

Figure 1-5. The Dirty Pretty Things logo becomes an animated GIF, with a jagged background.

Looking at the XHTML for this section, you'll see that the band name is also specified within the <h1> element, which is hidden using display:none. This is to ensure that if images and CSS are disabled, the site is still branded.

```
<div id="wrapper">
  <div id="masthead">
    <a href="home"><img src="logo.gif" alt="Dirty Pretty Things" /></a>
    <h1>Dirty Pretty Things - Official Website</h1>
  </div>
  ...rest of content...
</div>
```

Background

Next, we apply the main background image (Figure 1-6) to the <body> element. Although much larger than ideal, the JPG image will work as a tile. I would have preferred to use the GIF format for background images, but the level of detail and image gradation used for this large background image demanded the greater flexibility of the JPG format.

Figure 1-6. The main background image, which will be placed in the center and tiled horizontally

We use background shorthand in the CSS to place the tile in the center, at the top, and ensure it tiles only horizontally. Looking at the CSS for the body selector, you'll see that alongside the main font rules and other items, all rules for background are combined using CSS shorthand, with the order background-color, background-image, background-position, background-attachment, and background-repeat.

```
body {
    margin: 0;
    padding: 0;
    font-size: 95%;
    font-family: Georgia,'Lucida Grande',Verdana,sans-serif;
    text-align:center;
    color: #333;
    background: #C6C2B6 url(images/background.jpg) center top fixed repeat-x;
}
```

As the image is repeating horizontally (repeat-x), this takes up the whole width of the site, no matter how wide the browser window is. However, the page background-color is sampled on the flat color at the base of the background tile. The image combined with this color will complete the whole background and give the impression of a much taller background image.

Within the shorthand, we used background-attachment:fixed to prevent the background from scrolling with the rest of the page, and background-position:center top to make sure that the midpoint of the first background image tile appears in line with the midpoint of the browser's window. All other tiles needed to fill the width will be placed left and right of this initial centered image.

Masthead

The next task is to take control of the wrapper and the masthead. The masthead background image (Figure 1-7) was created in Photoshop with a flattened version of the logo in place. Prior to exporting the image, the logo was removed and replaced by a flat black color. We know that as long as no padding is applied to the masthead, the animated logo will appear top left on top of the masthead background.

Figure 1-7. The masthead background image

Now some key rules can be defined for the template. With the body selector already defined, and setting all elements to align centrally (text-align:center) so that our content area is centered, it is important that the next major element (defined with the ID wrapper) is set to text-align:left, a value that all descendants will inherit. The margin values (0 auto 0 auto) will ensure that the wrapper has equal margins to the left and right, no matter what the browser window width might be.

```
#wrapper {
    width:779px;
    margin:0 auto 0 auto;
    text-align:left;
}
```

Now, based on the width and height of the masthead background image, equal values are specified in the masthead declaration. The margin values are specified using trial and error to align the masthead where we want it on top of the fixed background. By specifying a 15px top margin, we make sure that just enough of the main background image is visible above the masthead to impress as the content begins to scroll over the fixed background. The background-color is sampled from the area of the main background where the masthead sits. This area contains several colors, but a rough match is made so that things look OK if the user is waiting for the masthead image to load.

```
#masthead {
    width:768px;
    height:254px;
    margin:15px 0 0 8px;
    color:#030;
    background: #ECE4D9 url(images/masthead.jpg) no-repeat
}
```

Finally, the main content selector reverts back to `full-width` as defined in the wrapper, allowing for a fresh start for all remaining content, and a new background image is specified. This new image tiles in all directions, although the content area is only wide enough to show it tiling vertically. This tile extends the edging used in the masthead background to give the impression of a long, worn page.

```
#content {
  width:779px;
  background: url(images/content.gif)
}
```

Navigation menu

The next stage is to add the main navigation menu to the masthead (see Figure 1-8 for the various masthe[ad] with before reaching the final decision). At the XHTML stage, we knew that we wanted to split the naviga[tion] had done something similar for the Libertines website and found it to be an excellent way of making the [mast]head space.

Figure 1-8. Various masthead ideas

The markup is as follows. Note that both lists feature an identical number of list items, and that each menu list has a unique ID (m1 and m2).

```
<ul id="m1">
  <li><a href="#" id="nav_a">Home</a></li>
  <li><a href="#" id="nav_b">News Archive</a></li>
  <li><a href="#" id="nav_c">Band Diary</a></li>
  <li><a href="#" id="nav_d">Gigs</a></li>
  <li><a href="#" id="nav_e">Downloads</a></li>
</ul>
<ul id="m2">
  <li><a href="#" id="nav_f">Discography</a></li>
  <li><a href="#" id="nav_g">Gallery</a></li>
  <li><a href="#">Merchandise</a></li>
  <li><a href="#" id="nav_h">Members Area</a></li>
 li><a href="#" id="nav_j">Forums</a></li>
</ul>
```

We also knew that each menu item might feature unique treatment, so each link has its own unique ID that will come in handy shortly.

Without CSS, the two lists will appear in their normal flow, one below the other. Therefore, we use margin values to push and pull each into position. The first (m1) is simply given a left margin of 20px to move it away from the left edge of the masthead. The second (m2) is moved 130px from the left edge of the masthead, and 160px from its natural position. Therefore, m2 is moved to the bottom right of the other menu, and then pulled up enough to line up with it, thanks to the large negative top margin. There is no need for positioning or floats.

```
#masthead ul#m1 {
    margin: 0 0 0 20px;
    padding-top:5px;
}
#masthead ul#m2 {
    margin:-160px 0 0 130px;
}
```

With the unordered lists where we want them, we can start to think about the list items. Each is given a height and width, plus a few other custom values that all will share.

```
#masthead ul li {
    width:135px;
    height:25px;
    list-style-type: none;
    padding-top:4px;
    font-size: 12px;
    letter-spacing:0.07em;
}
```

Next, we select the links within each list item. Most are common link approaches across the various states, but we found it vital to include display:block to prevent the various margin values applied to each link from causing the links to bunch together and cause untold havoc.

```
#masthead ul li a {
    display:block;
    padding-left:11px;
    text-decoration:none;
    font-weight:bold
}
#masthead ul li a:link, #masthead ul li a:visited, #masthead ul li a:active {
    color:#FFF;
}
#masthead ul li a:hover {
    color:#F00;
}
```

With all of that, the two menus are placed exactly where we want them within the masthead, and we can now think about treating each link individually.

Earlier I mentioned that we had given each link its own unique ID. These hooks can now let us have some fun. In Photoshop, I created three different background images, all of which will fit inside the given widths of our <li> elements. We can now randomly apply any of these three backgrounds to each ID, and also set a unique left margin for each, which gives us the slightly random alignment, along with varying backgrounds.

The following CSS shows how three of the ten IDs are defined in the style sheet:

```
#nav_a {;
    background: url(images/buttonback1.gif) no-repeat;
}
#nav_b {
    margin-left:6px;
    background: url(images/buttonback2.gif) no-repeat;
}
#nav_c {
    margin-left:4px;
    background: url(images/buttonback3.gif) no-repeat;
}
...etc...
```

Unless you study the end result closely, it appears that every list item has a unique background, when really we simply alternate the three.

On each template, an ID is added to the `<body>` element with the intention of highlighting the current page in the main menu easily with a smart bit of CSS application.

```
<body id="home">
```

In the CSS, the relationship between the `id` selector in the `<body>` and the `id` attached to each menu link is cemented. The first part, `#home`, targets the action to instances where the element selector is home. The second part, `#m1 a#homebutton`, looks inside the `#m1` list for a link identified as homebutton. If a match is found, the action is performed. Note that only three matches are shown here to save space.

```
/* Highlight the current page */
#home #m1 a#homebutton, #news #m1 a#newsbutton, #diary #m1 a#diarybutton {
  color: #F00;
}
```

Thus, whenever the user views the homepage, the link color will be set to red but will still be white on rollover. From the CSS, it should be clear that the news template uses `<body id="news">` and the diary template uses `<body id="diary">`. The only remaining job is to replicate the CSS for every unique link ID that needs to correspond with a template, grouping the targets into a neat all-encompassing definition.

Content highlights

With the backgrounds, masthead, and main navigation sorted out, we can look a little closer at a few interesting happenings within the main content area. We'll explore the headings, tables, and definition lists.

Headings

The Dirty Pretty Things website makes great use of level 2 (<h2>) and 3 (<h3>) headings. Most notably, level 2 headings are used at the top of both the main content area and the sidebar on all pages, yet have different appearances. This is achieved using descendant selectors in the style sheet.

The following markup reflects a simplified sidebar. Note that the <h2> element in the main content does not have a unique ID or class either.

```
<div id="sidebar">
  <h2>The Band</h2>
  <p>Dirty Pretty Things are Carl Barat, Anthony Rossomando, Didz Hammond and Gary Powell.</p>
</div>
```

Figure 1-9 shows the two background images used for the two <h2> elements.

Figure 1-9. Two jagged background images are used for the two differently sized level 2 headings.

The CSS rules for <h2>, as used in the main content area, are relatively straightforward. Note that blackhead.gif is specified as a nonrepeating background image, and that enough padding is used to ensure the whole background is in view.

```
h2 {
  margin:0 0 2px -10px;
  padding: 6px 0 5px 13px;
  font:14px/165% italic Georgia,Arial,Helvetica,sans-serif;
  letter-spacing:0.2em;
  color:#FFF;
  background: #EAE5D8 url(images/blackhead.gif) left bottom no-repeat
}
```

Now, we move on to the <h2> for the sidebar. The clever part is done with a descendant selector. The selector #sidebar h2 tells the browser to apply these rules instead when the <h2> element is inside the sidebar. If a match is found, a different background image, blackheadside.gif, is used, and the margins and font-size are scaled down.

```
#sidebar h2 {
  margin-top:3px;
  font-size:12px;
  background: #EAE5D8 url(images/blackheadside.gif) left bottom no-repeat;
}
```

Descendant selectors are essential for avoiding the need for extraneous classes and IDs that might otherwise litter an XHTML document. By using descendant selectors, the CSS rules can be made more specific, and there is no limit to how far down the tree a descendant selector will go—the child of a child of a child of a parent perhaps?

Tables

In essence, a table is for tabular data, and tabular data only. Most responsible designers still use tables. You may not be able to avoid them, but it is important to use them only when necessary.

Tabular data cannot be organized by CSS layout alone, or would make little sense if you tried to do so. Many designers have concocted methods of rendering complex tabular data such as calendars, timetables, and so on with pure CSS layout and positioning. That's great, and certainly an achievement of sorts, but remove the style sheet, and everything falls apart. The beauty of the table is that it presents information semantically, provides numerous elements for CSS styling, and still makes perfect sense should the style sheet be made unavailable.

For the Dirty Pretty Things discography, a table is populated with rows of information relating to each song. If a song has lyrics, audio, video, guitar tabs, or images assigned to it, a small check image is placed in the appropriate cell. The markup is fairly straightforward and is bereft of any additional IDs or classes.

```
<table>
  <thead>
    <tr>
      <th>Title</th><th width="11%">Released</th>
      <th><abbr title="Lyrics">L</abbr></th>
      <th><abbr title="Audio">A</abbr></th>
      <th><abbr title="Video">V</abbr></th>
      <th><abbr title="Guitar">G</abbr></th>
      <th><abbr title="Images">I</abbr></th>
      <th>Comments</th>
    </tr>
  </thead>
    <tr>
      <td><a href="if_you_were_wondering/">Wondering</a></td>
      <td>08/05/06</td>
      <td><img src="images/discotick.gif" alt="Y" /></td>
      <td><img src="images/discotick.gif" alt="Y" /></td>
      <td><img src="images/discotick.gif" alt="Y" /></td>
      <td><img src="images/discotick.gif" alt="Y" /></td>
      <td>-</td>
      <td>26</td>
    </tr>
</table>
```

This results in the basic table shown in Figure 1-10.

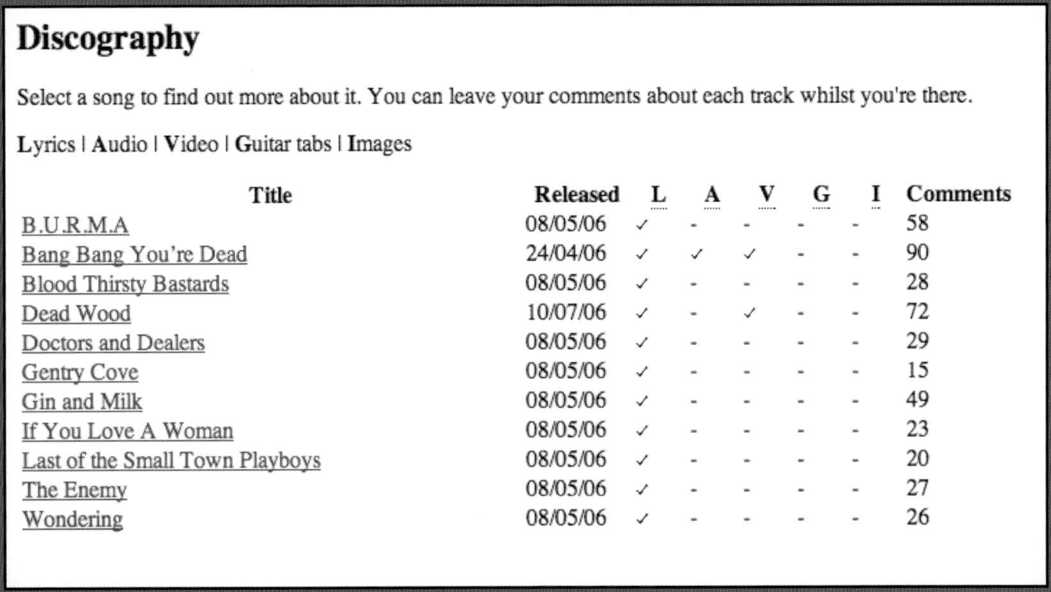

Discography

Select a song to find out more about it. You can leave your comments about each track whilst you're there.

Lyrics I Audio I Video I Guitar tabs I Images

Title	Released	L	A	V	G	I	Comments
B.U.R.M.A	08/05/06	✓	-	-	-	-	58
Bang Bang You're Dead	24/04/06	✓	✓	✓	-	-	90
Blood Thirsty Bastards	08/05/06	✓	-	-	-	-	28
Dead Wood	10/07/06	✓	-	✓	-	-	72
Doctors and Dealers	08/05/06	✓	-	-	-	-	29
Gentry Cove	08/05/06	✓	-	-	-	-	15
Gin and Milk	08/05/06	✓	-	-	-	-	49
If You Love A Woman	08/05/06	✓	-	-	-	-	23
Last of the Small Town Playboys	08/05/06	✓	-	-	-	-	20
The Enemy	08/05/06	✓	-	-	-	-	27
Wondering	08/05/06	✓	-	-	-	-	26

Figure 1-10. The discography's tabular data as styled by the browser's default style sheet

This is radically transformed using some very simple CSS. A lot of the work is already being done thanks to the page background under the table, but it is useful to further define rows and table headings.

First, we take control of the table itself, turning off the default border (border:0), setting the font-size (font-size:11px), and ensuring the table will fill the available space (width:100%).

```
table {
    width:100%;
    margin: 10px 0 20px 0;
    border:0;
    font-size:11px;
}
```

Then we put a dashed border at the top of each row and add specific padding, removing the need for outdated presentational markup such as cellpadding or cellspacing.

```
td, th {
    margin: 0px;
    border-top:1px dashed #999;
    padding: 3px 5px 3px 5px;
}
```

> It is worth noting that there is no reliable CSS equivalent for cellspacing, so many designers still make use of this presentational attribute.

These very simple rules, and the fact that the table is placed over an attractive background, give us the much more interesting table shown in Figure 1-11.

Discography

Select a song to find out more about it. You can leave your comments about each track whilst you're there.

Lyrics | Audio | Video | Guitar tabs | Images

Title	Released	L	A	V	G	I	Comments
B.U.R.M.A	08/05/06	✓	-	-	-	-	58
Bang Bang You're Dead	24/04/06	✓	✓	✓	-	-	90
Blood Thirsty Bastards	08/05/06	✓	-	-	-	-	28
Dead Wood	10/07/06	✓	-	✓	-	-	72
Doctors and Dealers	08/05/06	✓	-	-	-	-	29
Gentry Cove	08/05/06	✓	-	-	-	-	15
Gin and Milk	08/05/06	✓	-	-	-	-	49
If You Love A Woman	08/05/06	✓	-	-	-	-	23
Last of the Small Town Playboys	08/05/06	✓	-	-	-	-	20
The Enemy	08/05/06	✓	-	-	-	-	27
Wondering	08/05/06	✓	-	-	-	-	26
You Fucking Love It	08/05/06	✓	-	✓	-	-	50

Figure 1-11. Thanks to some very simple CSS, the discography table is radically transformed.

Definition lists

To use or not to use a definition list? That is the eternal, ever-present, increasingly dull question. What on earth are we supposed to use them for? Personally, I use them whenever I need a little more structure than a conventional unordered list will give me, but don't need the complexity of a table.

All definition lists consist of two main ingredients: a term and a description. A definition list is built using three essential elements: a container (<dl>), a definition term (<dt>), and a definition description (<dd>). This simple structure lends itself to our needs for the sidebar headlines and tour dates, where a date acts as the definition term, and the headline or venue is the description. The result is logical pairing that provides all the necessary styling hooks.

```
<h2>Forthcoming Gigs</h2>
<dl>
  <dt>25/11<dt>
  <dd><a href="liverpool_academy">Liverpool Academy...</a></dd>
  <dt>26/11</dt>
  <dd><a href="birmingham_academy">Birmingham Academy...</a></dd>
  <dt>27/11</dt>
  <dd><a href="nottingham_rock_city">Nottingham Rock City...</a></dd>
  <dt>28/11</dt>
  <dd><a href="leeds_university_refectory">Leeds University Refectory...</a></dd>
</dl>
```

> *While I feel this pairing is a suitable use of the definition list, be aware that screen readers will precede each item by speaking the label "term" or "definition."*

Figure 1-12 shows the unstyled result in the browser. Each definition term and definition description is separated by a line break and a default left margin.

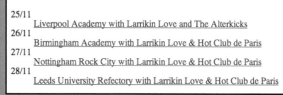

Forthcoming Gigs
25/11
Liverpool Academy with Larrikin Love and The Alterkicks
26/11
Birmingham Academy with Larrikin Love & Hot Club de Paris
27/11
Nottingham Rock City with Larrikin Love & Hot Club de Paris
28/11
Leeds University Refectory with Larrikin Love & Hot Club de Paris

Figure 1-12. The definition list styled by the browser's default style sheet

Now the whole definition list can be styled by using element selectors. Taking the selectors dl, dt, and dd, very similar styles can be applied to bring the whole section together. We found no need to amend the definition list element itself, although we could have added declarations for the dl selector if we had wished. Our first step was to make the definition term work a bit harder. The main job is to float the definition term to the left, which will allow the definition description to be repositioned to the right of it and in-line.

```
dt {
  float:left;
  padding:2px 0 7px 0;
  line-height:130%;
  font-weight:bold;
}
```

Next, the definition description element is styled. Very simply, the key task is to remove the default margin that pushes it away from the left edge of the containing <dl> element.

```
dd {
  margin:0;
  padding:2px 0 7px 0;
  line-height:130%;
}
```

This brings us to a finished, hugely transformed definition list. Note that it is flexible enough to stretch and fit any container we place it in, making it an ideal component for sidebar navigation. The beauty of all of this is that no additional markup is required in the (X)HTML—the CSS takes care of everything. The final result can be seen in Figure 1-13.

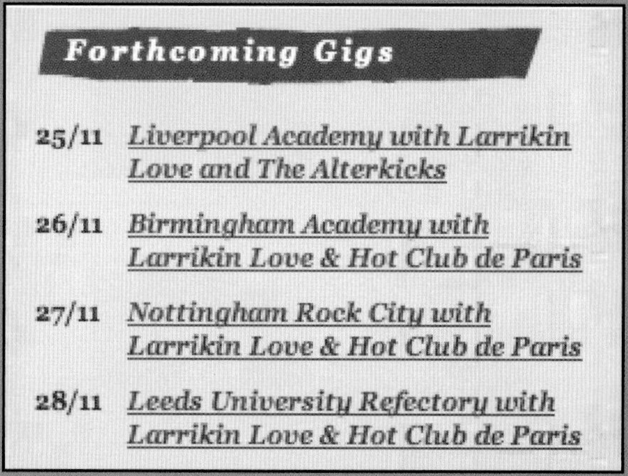

Forthcoming Gigs
25/11 Liverpool Academy with Larrikin Love and The Alterkicks
26/11 Birmingham Academy with Larrikin Love & Hot Club de Paris
27/11 Nottingham Rock City with Larrikin Love & Hot Club de Paris
28/11 Leeds University Refectory with Larrikin Love & Hot Club de Paris

Figure 1-13. CSS to the rescue once more. The definition list is clearer and aligned much better thanks to a few CSS rules.

And with that, the key components of the content area are all wrestled under control thanks to the mighty power of the style sheet. The content itself remains pure and unsullied, and the web designer can sleep soundly.

Conclusion

Of course, building the Dirty Pretty Things website wasn't quite as easy as this chapter suggests, and there were many more issues (both code- and real-world-related) that made life very difficult at times. The important moral of the tale is that thanks to Web Standards, the site is using relatively little bandwidth despite huge user figures (I'm not counting video downloads in that bandwidth), and despite the intricate and all-encompassing decoration, it remains accessible on mobile and print devices.

I would have loved to share many more of my experiences from this build, but there would be no room for the other chaps to tell their stories, so I invite you to view source (note that the code may have changed since I was managing the site) and dig around in the site. There is no better way to figure out how things work, and you are very welcome to explore.

Dirty Pretty Things | Official website

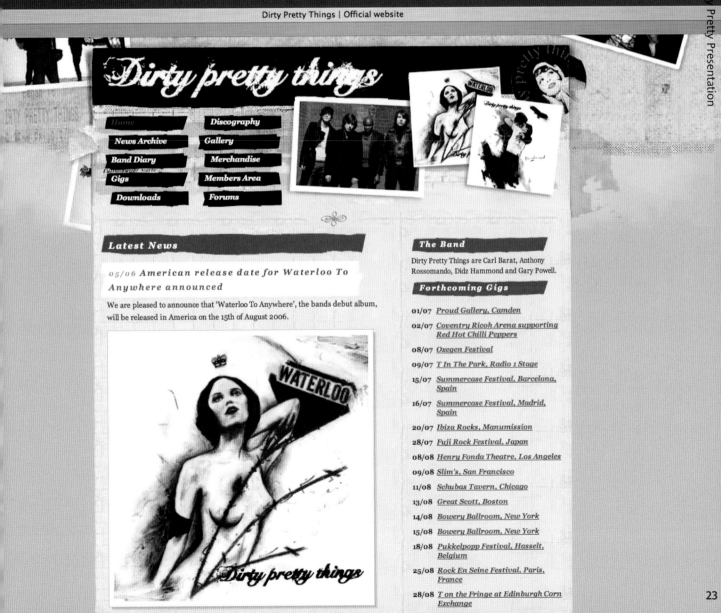

2

Taming a Wild CMS with CSS, Flash, and JavaScript

dan *rubin*

www.webgraph.com

Dan Rubin spends his days blending music, design, and typography with the sunny beaches of South Florida. From vocal coaching and performing to graphic design and (almost literally) everything in between, Dan does his best to spread his talent as thin and as far as he possibly can, while still leaving time for a good cup of tea and the occasional nap.

His passion for all things creative and artistic isn't a solely selfish endeavor either. You don't have to hang around too long before you'll find him waxing educational about a cappella jazz and barbershop harmony (his design of roundersquartet.com is just one example of these two worlds colliding), interface design, usability, Web Standards, typography, and graphic design in general. In addition to his contributions to sites including Blogger, the CSS Zen Garden, Yahoo! Small Business, and Microsoft's ASP.net portal, Dan is a contributing author of *Cascading Style Sheets: Separating Content from Presentation, Second Edition* (friends of ED, 2003), a technical reviewer for *Beginning CSS Web Development* (Apress, 2006) and *The Art & Science of CSS* (SitePoint, 2007), and a coauthor of *Pro CSS Techniques* (Apress, 2006). He writes about Web Standards, design, and life in general on his blog, superfluousbanter.org, and publishes podcasts on livefromthe101.com. His professional work can be found at his agency's site, webgraph.com.

Setting the scene

Your client asks you to redesign the company's site, with one major restriction: you can't customize the markup used to output the content, because it's generated by a *content management system* (CMS). "Wait!" you cry, "isn't a CMS supposed to separate content from its output format?" Unfortunately, it appears that in most cases, and particularly with enterprise-level CMSs, whether through ignorance or careful planning, the templates that define the markup used to render content by the CMS are off limits to designers. "But how can I possibly design something attractive with such archaic restrictions?" While convincing your client to allow customization of the output templates is the best route, the truth is sometimes that isn't possible, and you just have to work with what you're given. It's during these trying times when Web Standards, specifically CSS, along with their dashing side-kicks, JavaScript and Flash, come to your rescue.

This was the challenge presented to me by Geffen/Universal Media when the company asked me to redesign the promotional site for the insanely popular band Lifehouse (www.lifehousemusic.com). I'm going to show you how I used CSS, some smart designing, and a few cool tools and techniques to beat the CMS output into submission. I'll also show you how to use these same real-world methods in your own projects.

Before we begin our journey, let's compare the original site and my redesign (see Figure 2-1). You can see some of the "template mentality" design formula at work in the original.

Figure 2-1. On the left, the original design, including blocks of template content in all three columns

As far as the marketing department is concerned, once we come up with an acceptable design, our work is done. The pixels have been painted on the screen, so there's nothing more to do, right? Ah, but we know better, don't we?

There is, of course, more to creating any site template than just the design. Somehow, we have to get from concept to sketches to visual composites to markup to styles. Then, after a dash of browser testing, we wind up with a finished product. That process is usually enough work on

its own. In this case, I also needed to account for specific markup requirements dictated by the CMS. I'll review each of the steps involved in a moment, but first, a crash course on CMS for the uninitiated. If you're already familiar with the basic functions of a CMS, feel free to hand the book to a nearby colleague in need of some education in this area, and grab yourself a quick cup of tea while he reads the next few paragraphs and looks at the pretty pictures.

A crash course on CMS

In general, CMSs do just what their name implies: they help manage content. In slightly broader terms, they allow content producers to store and organize the content of their site in a database. When a visitor requests a specific "page" within the site, the appropriate content is retrieved from the CMS and displayed in the user's browser.

Usually, a CMS is a secure web application used by site administrators, content creators, editors, or anyone in charge of publishing or editing site content. It can handle text, markup, links, images, audio, video—pretty much any type of content that can be stored in a database.

Typically, a simple CMS might interact with your layout template as illustrated in Figure 2-2.

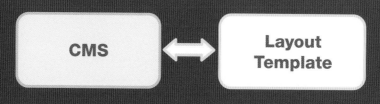

Figure 2-2. A basic CMS in the big picture. In this example, one template defines the layout and pulls content from the CMS.

Some more complex CMSs add extra layers between the stored content and what is displayed to the user, as shown in Figure 2-3.

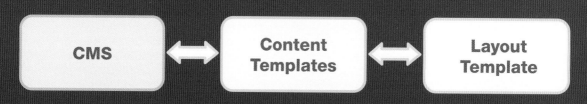

Figure 2-3. This CMS adds an extra layer of templates to define blocks of content separately from page layouts.

This chapter discusses how to work around issues created by this second type of system, with its multiple layers of templates. These layers typically combine to create the basic framework of each page style. The layout templates are usually accessible to designers. The content templates contain chunks of markup for various types of content, and are often off limits to designers. More to the point, those blocks of content often contain markup that is not under your control due to restricted access to the content templates or inflexible output requirements.

The CMS challenge

It doesn't take too much web browsing to find common visual formatting of content on various websites. Such generic patterns are usually dictated by restrictions in the content templates of the particular CMS behind those sites. You can see these common elements on sites managed by popular blog CMSs, sites running expensive commercial packages, and even custom-built systems.

This is the case with the custom CMS used by Geffen/Universal Media to manage its artists' sites. In order to ease mass updates of content formatting, all their sites use the same categories of data, such as News, Media, Photos, Events, and so on. Sites running on this CMS share a single set of content templates. While this makes adjustments to a given block of content much easier to implement, the approach has resulted in many of the sites having a similar look. This is due in large part to the designers' perception that the content *needs* to look the same because the markup can't be customized on a site-by-site basis.

For my Lifehouse site redesign project, Geffen/Universal Media didn't request any specific goals, aside from wanting a design that did a better job of reflecting the band's image and current promotional photography than the existing site. From a design perspective, that's as good as a blank slate, and that's essentially the instruction I was given, with one big restriction: whatever I produced had to work with the existing CMS content templates.

This wasn't the first artist site I had worked on for the company, so I was already familiar with most of the restrictions imposed by the centralized structure of the CMS templates. This meant I already knew exactly what categories and types of content the design had to accommodate, and what restrictions lay ahead of me.

Like my earlier projects, this redesign had a tight deadline and budget, which had previously led to a quick-and-dirty approach to the design process: take the basic set of content and layout templates—a standard two-column layout with header and footer—and skin them to look as un-template-like as possible, while staying within budget. The Lifehouse site redesign would have been the same, if I hadn't become so darned fed up with the limiting effect that approach was having on my designs.

So, faced with the prospect of another boring design project, I proposed an experiment: let me see how much I could massage the content and layout to break out of the basic template mold, without changing the budget or the timeline. After receiving the green light from the client, it was time to get down to business and start designing something—quickly.

Design on a dime

My primary goal was to produce a layout that didn't look like the default CMS layout templates. Of course, since the type of content it had to support would be the same as all the other artist sites, the new layout would need to have some things in common with the default layout. I decided the easiest way to combine these requirements was to use the same elements, but position them a little differently—enough so that, to the casual observer, the site didn't look the same as all the others. This also served as a good starting point for a project that had to be completed in a matter of a few weeks from start to finish.

The visual elements

I had already received the band's promotional source materials from the label's marketing department. Combined with the required content and navigation, these gave me the following visual elements to work into the design:

- The band's logo artwork
- High-resolution photography from the band's latest photo shoot
- Current album cover art
- Primary navigation for ten categories
- Various blocks of content (Events, Videos, News, Mailing List Signup, and so on)

I also decided it would be nice to have a featured article from the News section highlighted on the homepage. Since this was something the CMS did not support, it created another challenge. Thus, armed with this list, a pencil, a sheet of blank paper, and a picture already forming in my head, I proceeded to sketch a few quick thumbnails until I found one that "felt right" (see Figure 2-4).

Figure 2-4. Eenie, meenie, miney, mo!

I feel very strongly that the design process must be organic. Just because we are designing for a technical medium doesn't mean our process must also be cold and calculated. I like to use thumbnail sketches because they are a great way to get my thoughts on paper without worrying about too many details. I start almost every design by spending a few minutes sketching small layouts, and it's the best and fastest way I know to compare multiple layout ideas almost immediately. You can find more design shortcuts like this in "Budget Design," a PDF available from www.sinelogic.com.

The next step was spending some time in Photoshop to turn that sketch into pixels. The color scheme was borrowed from the photograph on the band's most recent album cover, plus a few shades of gray. One session of some intense pixel-pushing later, I wound up with the composite shown in Figure 2-5.

Figure 2-5. The initial Photoshop composite

Some interesting visual elements found their way into the design during this stage:

- A transparent background for the "teaser" article (showing the photo underneath)
- The teaser headline set in the same typeface as the band's logo (Franklin Gothic Condensed)
- A list of recent news headlines in the footer (this may seem like a simple thing to reproduce, except that it wasn't supported by the CMS)
- Vertical text headlines (also rendered in Franklin Gothic Condensed) throughout the layout

By now, you're probably itching to get to the "tips and tricks" part of the story, so feel free to read ahead if markup isn't your bag of chips. But we really need to lay our XHTML foundation before we can start styling.

The markup is but a shell

Since the CMS is in control of the markup surrounding most of the content blocks, the easiest thing to do is to create a shell layout, with <div>s to contain each of those modules of data. The design is essentially two columns plus a footer, with the logo and navigation located within the left column. After tossing in a few bits of sample content, I got this:

```
<!DOCTYPE html PUBLIC "-//W3C//DTD XHTML 1.0 Strict//EN"➡
  "http://www.w3.org/TR/xhtml1/DTD/xhtml1-strict.dtd">

<html xmlns="http://www.w3.org/1999/xhtml" xml:lang="en" lang="en">
<head>
  <meta http-equiv="Content-Type" content="text/html; charset=utf-8" />
  <meta http-equiv="Content-Language" content="en-us" />
  <title>Lifehouse [homepage]</title>
  <link rel="stylesheet" type="text/css" href="c/styles.css" media="all" />
</head>
<body class="homepage">
  <div id="wrapper">
    <div id="content">

      <h1 id="logo">
        <a href="/" title="link to the homepage">Lifehouse</a>
      </h1>

      <div id="content-primary">

        <div id="sidebar-tab"><!-- for presentation only --></div>

        <div id="teaser">
          <h2>latest news</h2>
          <a href="#">
            <img src="p/thumbnail_teaser.jpg" width="122" height="122" alt="" class="fullsize" />
          </a>
          <h3><a href="#">Article heading</a></h3>
          <p>Lorem ipsum dolor sit amet, consectetur adipisicing elit,➡
            sed do eiusmod tempor incididunt ut labore et dolore magna➡
            aliqua. Ut enim ad minim veniam, quis nostrud exercitation➡
            ullamco laboris nisi ut...</p>
          <p class="entry-footer">Published on 5/14/2006 |➡
            <a href="#">Link</a> |➡
            <a href="#">Comments (0)</a>
          </p>
          <a class="readmore" href="#">read more...</a>
        </div><!-- #teaser -->
      </div><!-- #content-primary -->

      <div id="nav">
        <ul>
          <li id="nav-home"><a href="#">Home</a></li>
          <li id="nav-news"><a href="#">News</a></li>
          <li id="nav-dates"><a href="#">Dates</a></li>
          <li id="nav-music"><a href="#">Music</a></li>
```

```
            <li id="nav-videos"><a href="#">Videos</a></li>
            <li id="nav-photos"><a href="#">Photos</a></li>
            <li id="nav-extras"><a href="#">Extras</a></li>
            <li id="nav-links"><a href="#">Links</a></li>
            <li id="nav-forum"><a href="#">Forum</a></li>
            <li id="nav-store"><a href="#">Store</a></li>
          </ul>
        </div><!-- #nav -->

    </div><!-- #content -->

    <div id="sidebar-wrapper">
      <div id="sidebar">

        <div class="module" id="mod-events">
          <h3>events</h3>
        </div><!-- .module -->

        <div class="module" id="mod-videos">
          <h3>videos</h3>
        </div><!-- .module -->

        <div class="module module-alt" id="mod-members">
          <h3>members</h3>
        </div><!-- .module -->

        <div class="module" id="mod-online">
          <h3>online</h3>
        </div><!-- .module -->

      </div><!-- #sidebar -->
    </div><!-- #sidebar-wrapper -->

    <div id="footer-wrapper">
      <div id="footer" class="clearfix">
        <div id="morenews">
          <h2>more news</h2>
          <ul>
            <li><a href="#"><strong>5/14/2006</strong> Article heading</a></li>
            <li><a href="#"><strong>5/14/2006</strong> Article heading</a></li>
            <li><a href="#"><strong>5/14/2006</strong> Article heading</a></li>
            <li><a href="#"><strong>5/14/2006</strong> Article heading</a></li>
            <li><a href="#"><strong>5/14/2006</strong> Article heading</a></li>
            <li><a href="#"><strong>5/14/2006</strong> Article heading</a></li>
            <li><a href="#"><strong>5/14/2006</strong> Article heading</a></li>
            <li><a href="#"><strong>5/14/2006</strong> Article heading</a></li>
          </ul>
          <a class="more" href="#">more...</a>
        </div>

        <div id="extras">
          <h2>extras</h2>
```

```
          <a href="#" class="thumbnail"><img src="p/thumbnail➥
            wallpaper.jpg" width="150" height="112" alt="" /></a>
          <h3>Lifehouse wallpaper - 800x600</h3>
          <p><a href="#">&raquo; Download</a></p>
          <p>5/14/2006 | <a href="#">Link</a> | <a href="#"> Comments (2)</a></p>
          <div id="external-links">
            <a id="logo-geffen" href="http://geffen.com/">Geffen</a>
            <a id="privacypolicy" href="#">Privacy Policy</a>

            <a id="myspace" href="#">visit our <span>myspace</span></a>
          </div>
        </div>
      </div><!-- #footer -->
    </div><!-- #footer-wrapper -->

  </div><!-- #wrapper -->

</body>
</html>
```

This presents fairly well in its raw, unstyled form when viewed in a browser, as shown in Figure 2-6.

The order of content in an unstyled page is important, although not a top priority for this site, because the target audience uses modern browsers on regular PCs. However, all of the content is at least properly formatted without styling, so the site is accessible at a basic level, which is much more than was achieved by the original design.

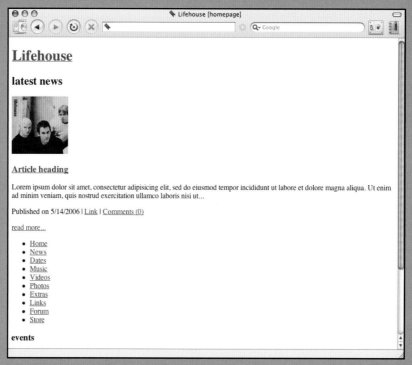

Figure 2-6. The naked lunch . . . er, content

Ever find yourself getting lost in a sea of divs when working with generated markup? If you're stuck working with a CMS that generates as many nested divs as the one discussed in this chapter, you can help make your markup easier to read (for you and others) by commenting the closing tag of each div with the ID or class of its corresponding opening tag. Take a look at the sample markup. See how much easier it is to pair up the closing tags of commented divs compared to the tags without comments?

Notice that the "modules" in the sidebar (conveniently assigned the class .module) are empty. These are just containers, in which the actual CMS-generated content will be dropped shortly, so for now, we leave them alone. The important thing is that they exist, can be targeted individually thanks to their unique IDs, and their order within the document flow is interchangeable.

While most of this markup should be fairly self-explanatory, I'll discuss the handful of .clearfix classes in the next section. Later, in the "Spit and polish" section, I'll review the technique I used to style the unordered list for the main navigation (the navigation wasn't generated by the CMS).

I said that the CMS content templates didn't include a list option, so what's with that <ul> in the footer? Due to the time constraints on the project, I was able to convince the powers-that-be to add a list option to the content templates. This gave me the proper hooks needed to style the list and use more appropriate markup for that styling. It's much better to clean up the markup and then work your CSS magic than to work with messy, crowded markup. That said, the look could also have mostly been re-created using the original non-list markup, it just would have required much more CSS trickery to accomplish a similar result, which would have unnecessarily complicated the project and extended the timeline.

The layout and styles

Now we're getting into the heavy stuff, so you may want to let your family members know they won't be seeing or hearing from you for quite a while, except for bringing you many cups of tea over the course of the next section—you do need your brain fuel, after all. We're not actually going to get into a deep discussion regarding the layout itself—it's not really that snazzy under the hood—but we *are* going to review the basic styles needed to create it.

I find it helpful to organize CSS properties within a rule block, especially when reviewing/tweaking a style sheet during browser testing or when adjustments have to be made after launch. Here's the order I prefer:

- *Display method (display: or float:)*
- *Background settings*
- *Positioning method (position:)*
- *Position (x,y)*
- *Width/height*
- *Margin/padding*
- *Color*
- *Text settings (font/line height/alignment)*
- *Borders*

This is yet another simple time- and aggravation-saver that should make your life a bit easier. Anything that adds some structure and order to your markup or styles will pay you back down the road.

Positioning elements

While we're not trying to accomplish anything groundbreaking with the overall layout, it's worth reviewing how each major element is positioned before we move on to the nitty-gritty. First, clear the floats:

```css
.clearfix:after
{content:".";
display:block;
height:0;
clear:both;
visibility:hidden;
}

.clearfix {display:inline-block;}
/* Hides from IE-mac \*/
.clearfix {display:block;}
/* End hide from IE-mac */"

body {
background:#111 url(../i/bg_body.gif) repeat-x;
margin:0;padding:0;
font-family:'lucida grande',tahoma,sans-serif;
font-size:small;
}

#wrapper {
width:800px;
}
```

#content is set to float:left, causing it to enclose the two floats it contains (#content-primary and #sidebar-wrapper):

```css
#content {
float:left;
}
```

#content-primary is also set to position:relative, allowing #sidebar-tab and #teaser to be positioned absolutely, but within the confines of their containing element. See Doug Bowman's "Making Absolute Relative" (http://stopdesign.com/articles/absolute/) for a good overview of this technique.

```css
#content-primary {
float:left;
background:url(../p/homepage_photo.jpg) no-repeat;
position:relative;
height:549px;
width:520px;
padding:0;
color:#fff;
}

h1#logo {
position:absolute;
```

```
z-index:100;
left:29px;
top:39px;
margin:0;padding:0;
}
h1#logo a {
display:block;
background:url(../i/logo_lifehouse.gif) no-repeat;
width:38px;
height:175px;
text-indent:-5000px;
}

#sidebar-tab {
background:url(../i/bg_sidebartab_events.png) no-repeat;
position:absolute;
right:0;
top:0;
width:20px;
height:194px;
}

#teaser {
background:url(../i/bg_teaser.png) no-repeat;
position:absolute;
left:0;
bottom:0;
width:507px;
padding:20px 0 30px;
color:#EFB32F;
font-family:'lucida grande',verdana;
line-height:1.3;
}
```

#nav is cleared to make sure it falls beneath #content-primary. Similarly, .module is cleared to allow any content within each module to be floated, because each subsequent .module will clear any such floats.

```
#nav {
background:url(../i/bg_nav.gif) repeat-x;
width:520px;
height:53px;
margin-top:0;
border-top:3px solid #111;
clear:both;
}

#sidebar-wrapper {
float:right;
background:#1C1C1C url(../i/bg_sidebar_wrapper.gif) no-repeat left bottom;
width:277px;
margin:0 0 3px;
padding:0 0 10px;
}
```

```
#sidebar .module {
color:#A07029;
padding:15px 15px 15px 0;
border-top:1px solid #111;
clear:both;
}

#footer-wrapper {
background:#1B1B1B url(../i/bg_footer_wrapper.gif) repeat-x;
padding-right:10px;
clear:both;
border-top:1px solid #333;
}
#footer {
background:#262626 url(../i/bg_footer.gif) repeat-x;
padding:20px 0 20px;
}
```

There is nothing really odd about any of this. It's a mixture of container <div>s (or wrappers), some floats for the columns, and a dash of absolute positioning. Since the purpose of this chapter isn't to teach you the basic principles of CSS, I won't go into the details here. I recommend reading Simon Collison's *Beginning CSS Web Development* (Apress, ISBN: 1-59059-689-7), if you feel you're lagging behind in any of the basics.

> *I like to name images based on the convention type_id_label to make it easier to remember the purpose of each image (for example, logo_footer_geffen.gif). Also, file-naming conventions make it easier for a third party or your client to determine the "whats and whys" associated with your design and code. While a style guide can also accomplish this task, often a project's budget or timeline doesn't allow for the creation of a style guide, or if one exists, it might not be available to someone making changes in the future.*

Targeting CSS selectors

The big problem with the generated markup contained within the basic shell markup I showed you earlier is that I have no say in the decision of which markup is used. Where a definition list with nested paragraphs within the description might be most appropriate, I could be forced to deal with a few nested <div>s containing <p>s with <span>s littered all over the place. You can see this for yourself by reviewing the source of the live site. Ugh. Have another (strong) cup of tea to help you get over that mental image.

Thankfully, as bad as that sounds, there is a relatively easy way to dig out of that hole. CSS selectors come in many shapes and sizes. Many designers are used to working with only the basics:

- **IDs:** Appear as #footer in CSS, and as an attribute value on an element in (X)HTML, such as <div id="footer">, where div is the element, id is the attribute, and footer is the value.
- **Classes:** Appear as .readmore in CSS, and as an attribute value on an element in (X)HTML, such as <p class="readmore">, where p is the element, class is the attribute, and readmore is the value.
- **Element selectors:** Target any (X)HTML element. Examples include ul, p, div, body, table, and even html.

However, we have much more at our disposal than those basic selectors, and that's where the shell markup comes into play.

By looking at the markup generated by the CMS, we can create *descendant* selectors that specifically target only the content we want to focus on, while leaving the rest alone. Descendant selectors allow us to style an element nested within a specific hierarchy of our markup. For example, the selector `#sidebar #mod-media img.fullsize` targets any `img` with a class of `fullsize` contained within an element with the ID mod-media that is also contained by an element with the ID sidebar, which is pretty darned specific if you ask me.

Remember the IDs on the sidebar modules? Their purpose will now be made clear. For example, check out this block of markup and content for the videos module in the sidebar, cleaned up a little for this example (but only a little), as generated by the CMS:

```
<h2><a href="/videos/default.aspx"><span>Videos</span></a></h2>
<div class="item summary stream">
  <img src="/images/video.jpg" alt="Blind" class="fullsize">
  <h4>Blind</h4>
  <p class="url">Windows: <a href=➥
    "http://music.yahoo.com/video/24649242/?">300K</a><br /></p>
  <p><span class="subtype">[Videos] </span>"Blind" Music Video</p>
  <p class="byline"><span class="date">10/20/2005</span>➥
    <span class="permalink"> |
    <a href=" /videos/default.aspx?mid=2333">Permalink</a>➥
      </span><span class="comment-icon"> |
    <img src="/images/comment_icon.gif" alt="Comment" /></span>➥
    <a href="/forum/topic.aspx/cid/133/tid/70679">➥
      Comments (197)</a></p>
  <div class="clear"> </div>
</div>
```

Not the *worst* markup you've ever seen, right? A few too many classes for my liking, and the comment icon could be displayed with CSS, rather than using an inline image (and what's that `<br />` doing in there?). But again, the markup that surrounds this content is meant to be used on *every* artist site that is managed by the label's CMS, so the extra hooks make sense in this context. There are better ways to *provide* some of the hooks, but that's a separate discussion altogether.

This markup is completely out of my hands, but I still need to style it. And it's likely—given the generic classnames assigned to the class attributes on the generated `<div>` and `<img>` tags—that my hooks (the classes `item`, `summary`, and `stream`) are used in many other areas throughout the site. That means I need some way to target the classes within this section in order to deal with any specific needs for the videos module. Since those hooks are not provided in the markup generated by the CMS's content template, I create them in the layout template, wrapping them around the code that calls the generated content:

```
<div class="module" id="mod-media">
  . . .
</div>
```

This `<div>` wraps around the markup and provides two important tools:

- `class="module"` will be assigned to each wrapper such as this one, and it allows you to share some basic formatting between each block (margins, borders, and the like).

- `id="mod-media"` allows you to target this block on its own and assign specific styles that are appropriate to displaying this content.

So, let's say that for most modules in the sidebar, I want to style any `<img>` tags assigned class="fullsize" to float to the right within the module, with a 5-pixel margin on the left and bottom and no border. With the new hooks, the generic style should now look like this:

```
#sidebar .module img.fullsize {
float:right;
margin:0 0 5px 5px;
border:none;
}
```

This selector uses the class I've assigned to my wrapper `<div>`, along with `#sidebar`, so that if I decide to use the `module` class anywhere else in the layout, this rule will not apply.

With that taken care of, I can now style the video module to float the image to the left instead of to the right, and adjust the margins accordingly:

```
#sidebar #mod-media img.fullsize {
float:left;
margin:0 5px 5px 0;
}
```

By replacing the class (`.module`) with the ID (`#mod-media`) in the selector, I instruct the browser to apply the generic styles first, and then override the float and margin settings.

> *IDs have higher specificity than classes. See* http://molly.com/2005/10/06/css2-and-css21-specificity-clarified/ *for a thorough explanation of how specificity is calculated, and see* http://stuffandnonsense.co.uk/archives/css_specificity_wars.html *for a more lighthearted overview.*

This same approach will get you out of almost any hole dug for you by CMS-generated markup. While none of us really want to use an ugly selector like body#events #content .item .module .summary #membership p.permalink span {}, if you're in a bind and need to get the job done, combining and layering selectors along with a wrapper `<div>` or two will make your life much less stressful.

The typography

I'm a typography nut, and type usually features prominently in my designs. HTML text is at best difficult to control. Even with CSS, font choices are limited to those installed on a user's operating system, and typographical control really isn't possible. Yet my design uses headings set in the band's typeface of choice, Franklin Gothic Condensed. I don't want to hinder the basic accessibility of the site. I'm not shooting for perfection in that area, but at the same time, it would be irresponsible to shut people out entirely by using bad markup. But somehow I need to get that type to display. Enter CSS image replacement for fixed headings, and sIFR for text that needs to change regularly, such as article headings generated by the CMS.

Let's start with the vertical text headings. They are the most obvious candidate for special treatment, as there isn't any way to mimic them using HTML text alone.

Creating the illusion of vertical text

The headings that should be vertical are all static. Since they don't need to be regularly updated, I can use images rendered in Photoshop. The vertical text effect isn't easy to reproduce any other way. I could do it with Flash, but it's *easier* with this method, as the sIFR approach (discussed next) doesn't support rotated text, and Flash items can be more difficult to position. I could just use the CSS `background-image` property to assign each image to a container `<div>`, but there's no actual heading within the HTML file, and that's not an ideal situation if the markup is to be accessible, even if on a basic level.

The good news is that it's just as easy to make an HTML heading (`<h1>`, `<h2>`, and so on) do exactly what I want, and for somewhat obvious reasons, this approach is called *image replacement*. There are about as many ways to handle image replacement as there are versions of Internet Explorer with weird CSS bugs, but I prefer a method devised by Mike Rundle dubbed the Phark method (after his personal site, `http://phark.net`). Let's use one of our sidebar headings (wrapped in a module `<div>`) as an example:

```
<div class="module" id="mod-videos">
  <h3>videos</h3>
</div><!-- .module -->
```

> For more on image replacement techniques, Dave Shea has compiled a nice comparison for you to bookmark and reference: `http://mezzoblue.com/tests/revised-image-replacement/`.

Without any specific styling, this heading will display just as you would expect. But the idea is to hide the default text output and replace it with the text image created in a graphics editor, and the following CSS rule is all I need:

```
#sidebar .module h3 {
background:url(i/header_module_events.gif) no-repeat;
width:18px;
height:58px;
margin:0;
text-indent:-5000px;
}
```

This rule handles the following:

- Set the background image and instruct the browser to not tile the image.
- Define the dimensions (set here to equal the width and height of the background image).
- Kill the margins. It's a good idea to zero your margins when replacing headings, and then position them as needed.
- And, finally, the slick part: indent the text –5000 pixels to the left of the heading's position. This is important, because otherwise the heading's text would still display above the rendered background image.

Figure 2-7 shows the heading before, during, and after applying the CSS rule.

So that takes care of the vertical text, which at first glance, may seem like the more challenging of the two replacement cases. However, the reality is that the second case—using a specific typeface for text that must remain editable—is actually more of a challenge, as you'll see next.

Figure 2-7. The heading in its default state (left), after the background image is applied (middle), and after setting `text-indent:-5000px;` (right)

sIFR me timbers

When you're dealing with content generated by a CMS, it's a given that a large portion of the content on every page is constantly changing. In this particular instance, it's not fair to assume the band members would be willing or able to create a custom, graphical text heading for every news item they post to the site via the CMS. And yet as a designer, I would much rather have the main article heading on the homepage rendered in the same typeface as the band's logo (Franklin Gothic Condensed). Fortunately, due in no small part to the extraordinary efforts of a few talented programmers, sIFR came to my rescue.

sIFR stands for Scalable Inman Flash Replacement (*Inman*, as in Shaun Inman, who conceived the original DOM replacement method that inspired sIFR). In the words of Mike Davidson, one of sIFR's creators and all-around web-typography-quality evangelist, sIFR is "a method to insert rich typography into web pages without sacrificing accessibility, search engine friendliness, or markup semantics." Phew. More simply put, sIFR is a way to use specific typefaces to replace HTML text when viewed in a modern, visual browser, using a combination of Flash and JavaScript. It doesn't hinder accessibility, and visitors without Flash (or with JavaScript turned off) will see normal HTML text, with CSS applied. Oh, and did I mention it's *free*?

To take advantage of sIFR developers' selfless generosity, you must first have the following at your disposal:

- Macromedia (now Adobe) Flash version 6 or newer (the full version, not the plug-in)
- A font you would like to render using sIFR
- Some free time

Once you've fulfilled those requirements, the process of incorporating sIFR into any project is fairly simple:

1. Download the latest release (2.0.2 as of this writing) from www.mikeindustries.com/sifr/.
2. Read the documentation, at http://wiki.novemberborn.net/sifr/.

OK, so it isn't *that* simple, but all the steps are outlined in the documentation. If you follow the instructions, it will work smoothly. Nonetheless, I will give you a brief overview, along with an example.

The first step, after selecting your typeface, is to export the Flash (.swf) file. The creators of sIFR have kindly included a Flash document (.fla) with the rest of the files, so you simply open that file in Flash, double-click the text box in the center of that file, and specify the typeface. Export the file (in this example, the file is named franklingothiccondensed.swf). This concludes the Flash portion of our exercise.

The sIFR download also includes two CSS style sheets—one for screen and one for print—and a JavaScript file (this is where the magic happens). You can copy and paste the styles into your own screen and print style sheets, as suggested in the sIFR documentation, or just link to them, along with the JavaScript file, in the <head> of your document:

```
<link rel="stylesheet" type="text/css" href="sIFR/sIFR-screen.css" media="screen" />
<link rel="stylesheet" type="text/css" href="sIFR/sIFR-print.css" media="print" />
<script src="sIFR/sifr.js" type="text/javascript"></script>
```

Now you have to call sIFR from within your HTML file, and tell the script what to replace. You can also place these "replacement statements" within the JavaScript file itself; see the sIFR documentation for details.

```
<script type="text/javascript">
if(typeof sIFR == "function"){
  sIFR.replaceElement(named({sSelector:"#teaser h3",➥
    sFlashSrc:"/sIFR/franklingothiccondensed.swf",sColor:"#EFB32F",➥
      sLinkColor:"#EFB32F", sFlashVars:"offsetLeft=0&offsetTop=0",➥
      sWmode:"transparent"}));
};
</script>
```

The first argument defines the CSS selector so the script knows which text to replace. The next argument tells the script where to find the Flash file for the typeface. Next comes the color of the text (one for a heading without a link and another for a heading with a link—the same color in this instance), the position of the replacement text, and a setting to make the background of the Flash text transparent. Note that for the sFlashSrc argument, I use a root-relative URL for the .swf file. You may need to experiment with root-relative or absolute URLs to get things working properly. For this project, I used a relative URL for local development, but it stopped working when uploaded to the server, requiring an adjustment to the URLs.

Before we reach the show-and-tell stage, let's first have a quick reminder of the markup we're using for this replacement, taken from the live site:

```
<h3><a href="/news/default.aspx/nid/8514" target="_self">
   Norfolk Virginia</a></h3>
```

This is the actual line as generated by the CMS, and is nested within the #teaser <div>. If you're curious about the rest of the surrounding markup, just view the source on the homepage of the live site, but it doesn't affect the sIFR use.

Only one step remains, and that's the process referred to by the sIFR creators as *tuning*. This is where you specify the "decoy" styles that the sIFR script uses to determine the size and spacing of the final rendered text, using the font-size, letter-spacing, line-height, and height CSS properties. It works, but you should be ready for some trial and error, and perhaps even the occasional bout of swearing at your text editor of choice, until your replaced text looks properly sized and spaced. The tuned CSS for our example looks like this:

```
.sIFR-hasFlash #teaser h3 {
   visibility:hidden;
   letter-spacing:0;
   font-size:24px;
   line-height:22px;
}
```

And finally, we have our end result, as shown in Figure 2-8.

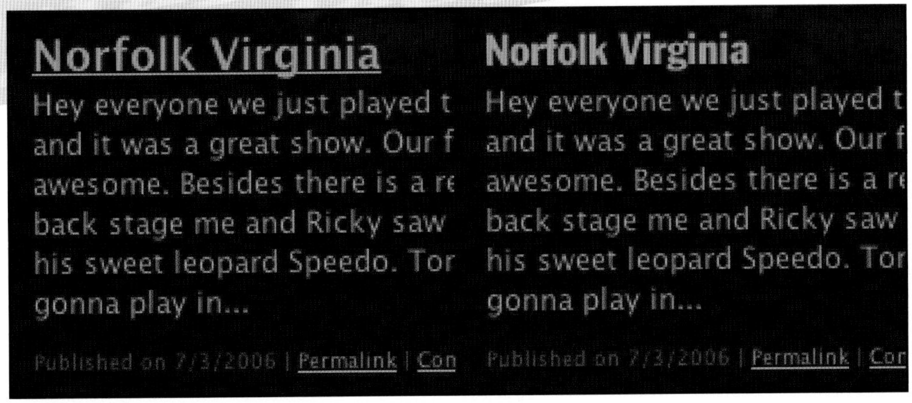

Figure 2-8. On the left, the regular HTML heading (also what users without Flash will see), and on the right, the beautiful sIFRized version

Image replacement and sIFR have their place. They provide us with ways to improve the typography of a design, without sacrificing accessibility. But you must use them with discretion, particularly image replacement. On large sites, creating a custom image for every heading may not be practical, especially if those headings change often.

Spit and polish

There are a few extra details that could go unnoticed if I don't mention them specifically. For example, the logo at the top left of the layout could have easily been included in the main band photo, reducing the number of images needed to produce the page. However, making the logo a separate image file allowed me to set it as the background of the <h1> tag, and make the tag (and thus the logo) a link to the homepage:

Here's the XHTML:

```
<h1 id="logo">
  <a href="/" title="link to the homepage">Lifehouse</a>
</h1>
```

And here's the CSS:

```
h1#logo {
position:absolute;
z-index:100;
left:29px;
top:39px;
margin:0;padding:0;
}
h1#logo a {
display:block;
background:url(../i/logo_lifehouse.gif) no-repeat;
width:38px;
height:175px;
text-indent:-5000px;
}
```

Et voilà, I now have a clickable logo.

Using Firefox? You have probably noticed that this image replacement technique (Mike Rundle's Phark method, mentioned earlier) causes that browser's dotted link borders to extend all the way to the left edge of the browser window when clicked, which isn't very attractive. Luckily, this can be easily fixed by dropping a {outline:none;} into your style sheet. Figure 2-9 show the before and after effects.

Another item of note is the primary navigation (<div id="nav">...</div>), which gets marked up as a simple unordered list. Luckily, the navigation wasn't generated by the CMS, but could be marked up by hand and included server-side on all pages of the site, since as I mentioned earlier, the CMS output templates didn't include lists. The navigation bar uses a simplified variation of the technique known as the Navigation Matrix (Navigation Matrix Reloaded, http://superfluousbanter.org/archives/2004/05/navigation-matrix/) to create the image-based navigation and hover effects. The entire navigation is created using only one image (nav_matrix.gif) referenced in the CSS, as shown in Figure 2-10.

lifehouse
link to the homepage
lifehouse
link to the homepage

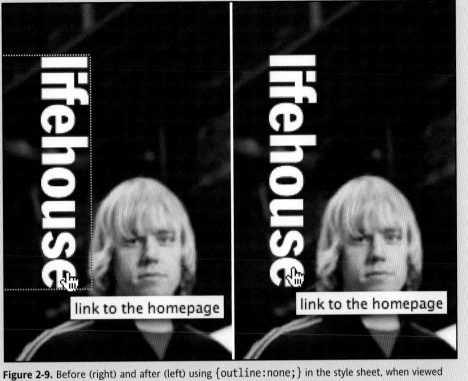

Figure 2-9. Before (right) and after (left) using {outline:none;} in the style sheet, when viewed in Firefox

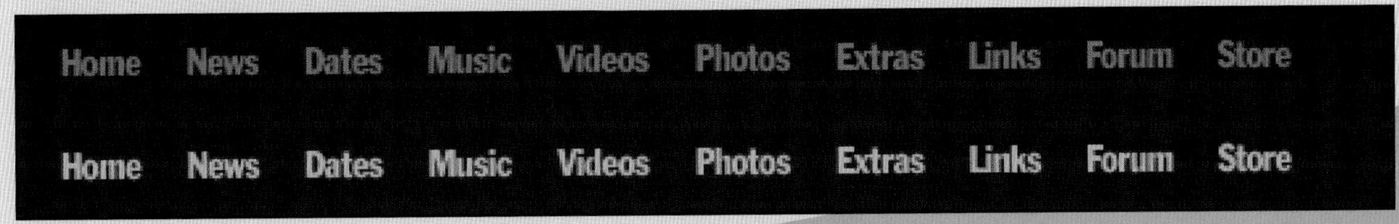
Home News Dates Music Videos Photos Extras Links Forum Store
Home News Dates Music Videos Photos Extras Links Forum Store

Figure 2-10. Navigation bar styled with the Navigation Matrix Reloaded technique

Issues with the design

One of the bigger challenges I faced with implementing the design as I envisioned it involved Internet Explorer/Windows and the transparent background of the #teaser <div>. I had two options:

- Fake the transparency for all browsers by exporting one image with the transparent areas and the photo.

- Use a transparent PNG for the background image along with JavaScript or Internet Explorer conditional comments to "fix" PNG transparency for Internet Explorer versions 6 and earlier (Internet Explorer 7 includes native support for PNG transparency; see Chapter 5 for more transparent PNG goodness).

I chose the second option, to make it easier for the band members to replace the homepage image on their own. More specifically, I decided to use Internet Explorer conditional comments to allow Internet Explorer to process the PNG correctly using its proprietary AlphaImageLoader filter; see http://alistapart.com/articles/pngopacity/ for a few good methods. The necessary code gets dropped in the <head> of your document, and looks like this:

```
<!-- fixes IE 5.5/6 png transparency -->
  <!--[if gte IE 5.5]>
    <![if lt IE 7]>
      <style type="text/css">
        #sidebar-tab { filter:progid:DXImageTransform.Microsoft.➥
        AlphaImageLoader(src='i/bg_sidebartab_events.png');
        background-image:none; }
        #teaser {
        background-image:none;
        z-index:10; }
        #teaser-ie { filter:progid:DXImageTransform.Microsoft.➥
        AlphaImageLoader(src='i/bg_teaser.png',sizingMethod='crop');
        position:absolute;
        left:0;
        bottom:0;
        width:507px;
        height:230px;
        bottom:-1px;
        z-index:0; }
      </style>
    <![endif]>
  <![endif]-->
```

I also use this block to adjust the CSS for each affected <div> so the markup is all in one place. Ideally, this "one place" would be the external style sheet. Unfortunately, Internet Explorer conditional comments work only within an HTML document, though you *could* place the Internet Explorer-specific styles within a separate style sheet and link it within the conditional comment. The only customization needed when preparing a new image, and one that won't "break" the design if the client forgets, is the shadow at the bottom edge of the photo. However, faking transparency is still a viable option if you don't want to use a JavaScript or proprietary workaround to support PNG transparency in Internet Explorer 6 and earlier, and if creating the special images is not a problem in your production environment.

Such a #teaser

After styling the #teaser <div>, I realized I was accounting for only a single-line <h3> heading (with or without sIFR). Since the <div> height and background image were specified, this would definitely cause problems if a longer article title were used. So I decided to remove the assigned height entirely from #teaser, and increase the bottom padding on the <div>. Because the entry footer and read more button are absolutely positioned, they are not affected by this change; only the <h3> heading and <p> will interact with the padding. I adjusted the transparent background image (bg_teaser.png) to make it taller (300px is reasonable), and resaved the band's photo with a drop shadow at the bottom. The photo was originally on the background image for #teaser, but that wouldn't work now that the <div> height is variable. However, I could still keep the left shadow on bg_teaser.png. This gives a solution that works with a multiline headline in the #teaser <div>, as shown in Figure 2-11.

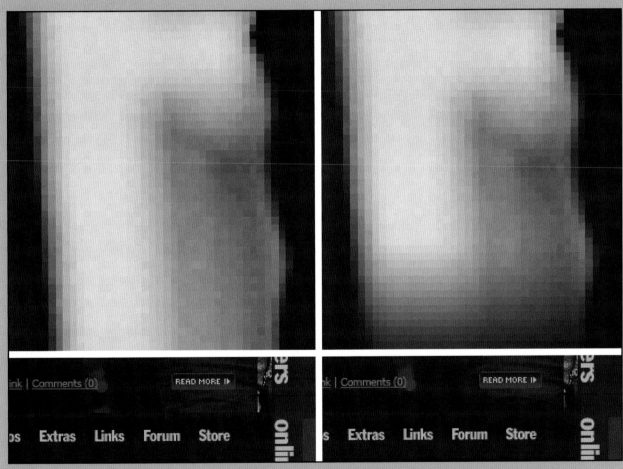

Figure 2-11. It's a subtle difference, but the shadow at the bottom of the main photo allows the base of the image to blend into the background color of the navigation bar below, and works nicely with the transparent background of the #teaser <div>.

Taking care of Internet Explorer

There were a few more oddities visible in Internet Explorer 6 (no surprise), but these were almost all taken care of by using the Star-HTML hack—which is most often used as part of the Holly hack, named after Holly Bergevin—and redeclaring the rules for the problem elements. The Star-HTML hack takes advantage of an extra element recognized by the rendering engines of Internet Explorer versions 6 and earlier. This *universal selector* (*) is outside <html>, and since it is ignored by any non-Internet Explorer browser, it can be used to send specific styles to Internet Explorer.

Take the CSS for the band's logo as displayed on the homepage:

```
h1#logo {
position:absolute;
left:15px;
top:20px;
margin:0;padding:0;
}

body.homepage h1#logo {
z-index:100;
left:29px;
top:39px;
}
```

Internet Explorer version 6 doesn't take too kindly to the absolute positioning and z-index, and thus the logo is rendered invisible—it's still there, but the browser chooses not to display it where we can *see* it. So instead of spending tons of time working out a solution that will work properly across all browsers—the ideal situation, but remember that tight budget and timeline—changing the way the <h1> displays in Internet Explorer is the way to go. The Star-HTML hack allows us to send different styles to *only* Internet Explorer:

```
* html body.homepage h1#logo {
position:relative;
margin-bottom:-170px;
}
```

So I change the positioning from position:absolute to position:relative, and then adjust the bottom margin until the logo is positioned where I want it (in this case, −170 pixels). The hack works thanks to its higher specificity (* html body.homepage h1#logo is more specific than body.homepage h1#logo), so not only is Internet Explorer the only browser that can understand the rule, but it gives it priority over the previous rules.

One more thing: because the flaw that allowed this hack to work has been fixed in Internet Explorer 7, it's best to place this hack, and any others for Internet Explorer, in a separate style sheet, and link it within a conditional comment that will hide it from version 7, like so:

```
<!--[if lte IE 6]>
  <link rel="stylesheet" href="css/iehacks.css" type="text/css" media="screen" />
<![endif]-->
```

When time is of the essence, hacks can protect your sanity, and your project, from the poor standards support in Internet Explorer 6 and earlier. But this may not hold true once the new version takes hold. If you use hacks, you must be prepared for the possibility of having to revisit older projects if the hacks break in the future.

> *While Internet Explorer receives much of the negative attention regarding rendering bugs, the fact is that all browsers have bugs. We just have to find the best ways to work around the ones that cause us the most problems.*

Conclusion

If you examine the source of the live site, you'll notice how much needless markup still exists within the structure of their CMS. Optimizing the output is an ongoing effort, and I will continue to make recommendations to the label's development team. Ultimately, if you are in a position where you must work with a CMS that's not totally under your control for whatever reason, it is important to remember that there are still many tricks and tools at your disposal, to help you avoid falling into a rut of creating boring designs within the cold and cramped confines of the generated markup. As a designer, it's worth taking on the challenge of beating a CMS into submission, rather than simplifying your designs to fit the technical requirements. You'll definitely sleep better when the site launches

3

New York Magazine: My, What a Classy <body>

ethan *marcotte*

www.vertua.com

Ethan Marcotte has been designing and developing online for nearly a decade, and he is still amazed and excited at how much there is to learn. He is the cofounder and design lead of Vertua Studios (www.vertua.com), a standards-savvy design studio that builds elegant, usable websites.

Ethan has emerged as a well-respected voice on the subject of standards-based web design. He has been a featured speaker at Web Design World and the South by Southwest Interactive Conference, and he runs the popular (if infrequently updated) sidesh0w.com blog. His clients have included *New York* Magazine, Harvard University, The Walt Disney Company, and State Street Bank.

When he grows up, Ethan wants to be an unstoppable robot ninja (www.unstoppablerobotninja.com). Beep.

Mo' metro, mo' style

The *New York* Magazine (www.nymag.com) website redesign was, to be honest, something of a departure for me. My little company, Vertua (www.vertua.com), typically bills itself as a full-service web shop—or, at least, as full-service as an "army of one" studio can be. However, this project was a welcome change from the norm, as it was essentially a "code-only" job: the magazine had partnered with another studio to design the new site and was looking for someone to work on building out standards-based templates. (I'd like to make an "Enter the Dragon" joke here, but I think that would just be silly.)

The template list for the redesign was nothing less than impressive: the magazine had years of legacy content on the site, all presented in different layouts and templates. Furthermore, the magazine's content management system (CMS) was powerful, but rather lightweight—much of the pages' content is hand-rolled by a team of skilled but largely nontechnical content producers. How, then, could a standards-based design make the magazine employees' lives easier?

In this chapter, I discuss how assigning multiple class values to an element—in this case, body—can really streamline your code and make your Cascading Style Sheets (CSS) much more modular. By writing CSS code that detects different "toggles" you write into the body element's class, your style sheet can style the same markup in drastically different ways across pages. The result is a drastic reduction in the number of HTML templates required and the ability to make radical changes to a page's design a snap.

For the bulk of this chapter, we'll focus on the generic article template, shown in Figure 3-1.

With the small talk out the way, let's walk through how to put this together, step by step.

Figure 3-1. The finished article template

Getting started

The article template was handed off with the requirement that it be a flexible-width design, with a fixed-width sidebar on the right. Figure 3-2 shows us something of how the page needs to flex.

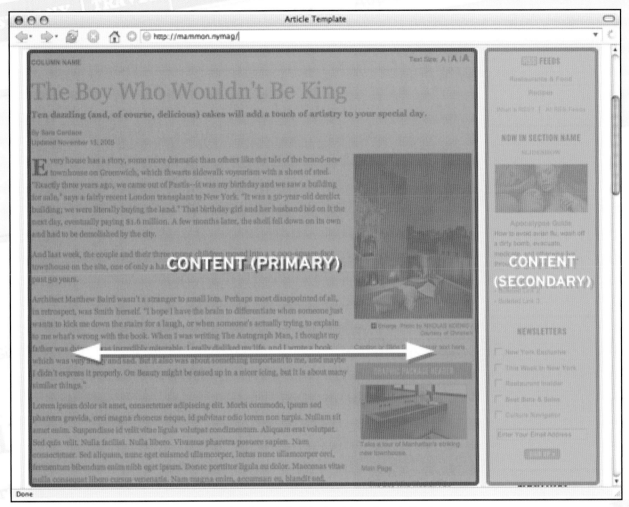

Figure 3-2. The page layout requirements. The left column is flexible; the right column is fixed.

To create a fluid-width content area with a fixed-width sidebar for *New York* Magazine, I used Ryan Brill's negative margins technique, which is written up in detail at http://alistapart.com/articles/negativemargins. After studying that approach, we can create an empty markup shell, ready to receive the content's design:

```
<!DOCTYPE html PUBLIC "-//W3C//DTD XHTML 1.0 Transitional//EN"➡
  "http://www.w3.org/TR/xhtml1/DTD/xhtml1-transitional.dtd">

<html xmlns="http://www.w3.org/1999/xhtml">
<head>

<title>Article Template</title>

<meta http-equiv="Content-Type" content="text/html; charset=utf-8" />

<link type="text/css" rel="style sheet" href="/style/screen.css"➡
  media="screen, projection" />
<!--[if lt IE 7]>
<link type="text/css" rel="style sheet" href="/style/patches-ie.css"➡
  media="screen, projection" />
<![endif]-->

</head>

<body id="www-newyorkmag-com">

<div id="wrap">
  <div id="content">
    <div id="content-layout">
      <div id="content-primary-wrap">
        <div id="content-primary">

        </div><!-- /end #content-primary -->
      </div><!-- /end #content-primary-wrap -->

      <div id="content-secondary">

      </div><!-- /end #content-secondary -->
    </div><!-- /end #content-layout -->
  </div><!-- /end #content -->
</div><!-- /end #wrap -->

</body>
</html>
```

According to the approach outlined in Brill's article, we need not only two divs for our two content areas (the inventively named content-primary and content-secondary), but also a wrapper div around content-primary—let's call that one content-primary-wrap. Stay tuned, true believers: there will be more on this wrapper later.

Structuring the CSS

Looking above the content area, you might notice two link elements in the head of the document: one for screen.css and another for patches-ie.css. Inside our linked style sheet, screen.css, I've placed the following:

```
@import url("core.css");

/*\*//*/
@import url("patches-mac.ie5.css");
/**/
```

On the first line, the @import rule (www.w3.org/TR/CSS21/cascade.html#at-import) references another, external CSS file, core.css. This style sheet contains the bulk of our CSS rules, free of any browser-specific style sheet patches. core.css is seen by all browsers and contains our pure, hack-free style rules.

And speaking of hacks, this is exactly what the second @import statement is wrapped in. That odd-looking series of CSS comments is in fact the IE5/Mac Band Pass Filter (www.stopdesign.com/examples/ie5mac-bpf), which prevents any browser *except* Internet Explorer 5 (IE5) on the Macintosh from seeing the code therein. So now, with our semicloaked patches-mac.ie5.css in place, we can place any style rules required to work around CSS bugs in that browser.

Why bother with this CSS-within-CSS approach? One of the benefits to this approach is ease of maintenance: by separating this code out, we can make it much easier to remove these CSS "patches" if we ever need to stop supporting IE5/Mac. We don't need to sift through a few hundred lines of one style sheet—instead, we can quarantine these fixes in a separate file altogether. Once we do need to discontinue support of that browser, we can simply delete that one @import statement in our screen.css file, and it's bye-bye to IE5.

Returning to our HTML template, we see that patches-ie.css is surrounded by some odd-looking comments:

```
<!--[if lt IE 7]>
  <link type="text/css" rel="style sheet" href="/style/2/ie-width.css"➥
    media="screen, projection" />
<![endif]-->
```

These are known as **conditional comments**, and they're an IE-only HTML extension that allows us to build programmatic logic into our markup. We can serve up chunks of markup to specific versions of Internet Explorer on Windows, specifying version numbers and other conditions within this special comment syntax.

Conditional comments are a proprietary, nonstandard extension to HTML, and as a result, they've been the subject of no small amount of controversy over the years. You can find more information about conditional comments on Microsoft's website (http://msdn.microsoft.com/workshop/author/dhtml/overview/ccomment_ovw.asp), *as well on numerous industry blogs, such as mezzoblue* (www.mezzoblue.com/archives/ 2005/11/03/ie7_conditio).

Here, we're using those conditional comments to hide our second link from versions of IE *prior to* version 7 (<!--[if lt IE 7]>) and then linking to two additional style sheets within patches-ie.css, like so:

```
@import url("patches-win.iex.css");

@media tty {
  i{content:"\";/*" "*/}} @import 'patches-win.ie5.css'; /*";}
}/* */
```

As with our IE5/Mac-specific CSS file, these two @import rules bring in external style sheets that patch bugs in different versions of IE/Windows: the first is for all versions of Internet Explorer on Windows, and the second is seen only by IE5/Windows. Even better, every other non-IE browser on the planet is oblivious to these browser-specific workarounds, since these conditional comments are seen as *regular* HTML comments by standards-compliant browsers. As a result, the link to patches-ie.css is essentially invisible to most browsers and handily parsed by IE/Windows.

At this point, you're likely wondering (read: "screaming furiously at the ceiling") why you should bother to fork your CSS like this. Why link to two separate style sheets, which only exist to @import *other* CSS files, some of which are filled with nothing but workarounds for different browser-specific CSS bugs? (See Figure 3-3.)

As you might be aware, you have any number of ways to insert browser-specific CSS patches alongside your other CSS rules (see http://cssdiscuss.incutio.com/?page=CssHack for a few examples). While keeping your CSS all in one file only leaves you one CSS file to worry about, tracking down and updating fixes for individual browsers can quickly become a nightmare. With the multiple style sheets approach, you can intelligently quarantine CSS patches into browser-specific style sheets, which will make future updates a breeze. And what happens when you stop supporting a browser? Well, instead of searching through more than 2,000 lines of a style sheet for every IE5/Mac hack you wrote into your main CSS file, you can simply delete the @import reference to that browser's CSS patches in one of the linked style sheets. 'Nuff said.

With this hack management framework in place, we can now start in on the interesting stuff: applying some basic style to our document's markup. Yes, I realize that it's about darn time.

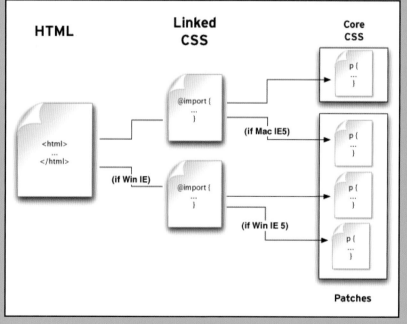

Figure 3-3. Our CSS architecture

The approach outlined here was inspired by Molly Holzschlag's excellent article, "Integrated Web Design: Strategies for Long-Term CSS Hack Management" (www.informit.com/articles/article.asp?p=170511&rl=1). Written nearly two years ago, the article reads as well today as it did when it was first published. Read it, bookmark it, rinse, repeat.

Adding a layer of style

OK, enough about browser bugs and CSS patches. Let's add some basic style to core.css:

```
body {
   background: #FFF;
   color: #000;
   font: 62.5%/1.5 Arial, Helvetica, Verdana, Geneva, sans-serif;
   margin: 0;
   padding: 0;
}

#wrap {
   margin: 0 auto;
   min-width: 770px;
   max-width: 980px;
}

#content {
   background-color: #EBEAE8;
   border-top: 1px solid #D6D5D3;
   padding: 7px 8px 9px;
}

#content-layout {
   background: #FFF;
}
```

With these few lines, we drastically change the appearance of our sparse-looking XHTML. We establish some basic font and color properties on body; give #content a splash of . . . well, gray; and center our design by placing automargins on our "wrapper" div. In Figure 3-4, you can see how far we've come: our two soon-to-be columns are nicely framed, albeit stacked directly on top of one other.

Figure 3-4. The default stacking order for the divs

Furthermore, we apply `min-width` and `max-width` values to `#wrap`, ensuring that our design meets our client's goal. The template's width will expand in size until it reaches 980 pixels, and it will shrink down as far as 770 pixels. Looking sharp, no?

Well, almost. There often is one blue "E"-shaped hiccup: versions 6 and below of Internet Explorer don't support the `max-width` and `min-width` properties. A number of workarounds are available to us for IE on Windows. For *New York* Magazine, however, I settled on the following scrap of CSS:

```
#wrap {
    width:expression(document.body.clientWidth > 980 ? "980px" : ➥
        (document.body.clientWidth < 772 ? "770px": "auto" ));
}
```

`expression()` is a **dynamic property**, which is a proprietary Microsoft invention (`http://msdn.microsoft.com/workshop/ author/dhtml/reference/methods/setexpression.asp`) that works only in Internet Explorer on Windows. It muddies the otherwise clear waters between style sheets and scripting—as you can see, I've written a small snippet of JavaScript directly into the `#wrap` rule. When loaded by Internet Explorer, this JavaScript detects the width of the page (using `document.body.clientWidth`, another IE-only bit of code) and constrains the width of `#wrap` div if the window gets larger or smaller than our target widths.

At this point, the standardistas in the audience might be asking, "But Ethan, why would you resort to nonstandard code in an otherwise standards-compliant template? And where do you live, so that I might throw pointed sticks at your W3C-hating house?"

It's at this point that our numerous CSS "patch" files come in handy. Since this is a fix for IE/Windows only, we can safely place the nonvalid code in our `patches-win.iex.css` file. Tucked away into this separate file, our nonstandard code is hidden from standards-compliant browsers and devices—and yes, that includes the beloved W3C CSS validator.

Negative margins and columns and stuff! Oh my!

With some markup and CSS foundations in place, it's time to finish up our columns. Ryan Brill's negative margins technique (`http://alistapart.com/articles/negativemargins`) is implemented in three simple steps:

1. Set a width on the fixed-width sidebar (here, it's `content-secondary`).
2. Float the `content-primary-wrap` container to the left, and set its width to 100%.
3. Set a negative `margin-right` on that container, the width of which should be equal to the width of the sidebar from step 1.

The required CSS is as straightforward as it sounds. First, we need to float our two columns, like so:

```
#content-primary-wrap {
    float: left;
    width: 100%;
}

#content-primary {
    padding: 0 12px 0 13px;
}

#content-secondary {
    float: right;
}
```

A quick preview of our code at this point shows that not much has changed, except that we've lost part of our gray border (Figure 3-5).

You may be asking, what in the name of Tim Berners-Lee is going on here? Or you might not be. We really don't know.

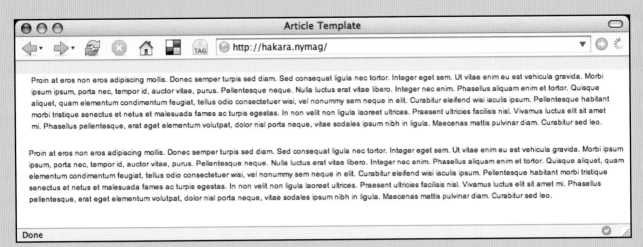

Figure 3-5. The layout is unchanged, but where's our border off to?

Clearing time

Even though our two content divs don't *look* drastically different than before, they are nonetheless floated elements, and as a result, they'll "escape" from their non-floated container, the content-layout div. So the border that we see at the top of our document is actually the *whole* border for content-layout: the two floated divs that it contains have simply flowed out of their parent, effectively completely collapsing our poor container. So content-layout now has no nonfloated elements to give it some height, and our lovely four-sided border just looks like a thick gray line. Naturally, this won't do. But don't start in quite yet with the gnashing of teeth and the pulling of hair. Thankfully, there's a solution.

To make sure that our container . . . well, *contains* the two columns, we'll use the "Easy Clearing Method," which is written up at http://positioniseverything.net/easy-clearing.html. First, we place the following in our core.css file:

```
#content-layout:after {
  content: ".";
  display: block;
  height: 0;
  clear: both;
  visibility: hidden;
}
```

Here we used the :after pseudo-element (www.w3.org/TR/CSS21/generate.html#x5) to generate extra content (namely, a period) at the end of our container, after all other elements. That extra content is then hidden from the user's eye, but turned into a block-level element that will clear all other floats preceding it in the markup. Unfortunately, this rule won't work in any current version of IE. And what's more, to placate the Windows version of IE, we actually need *two* solutions: one for the latest version, 7, which is a public beta at the time of this writing (but should be released properly by the time the book hits the shelves), and one that's a hack for earlier versions currently in use.

To make IE7 play nicely, we simply insert the following after our :after rule:

```
#content-layout {
  display: inline-block;
  display: block;
}
```

To give credit where credit's due, web designer and standards guru Roger Johansson (www.456bereastreet.com) was the one who first published this workaround (www.456bereastreet.com/archive/200603/new_clearing_method_needed_for_ie7). The display: inline-block; triggers the nonstandard hasLayout property in IE7, which forces the container to automatically contain any floated elements within it.

For more information about hasLayout, *read Ingo Chao's excellent article on the topic:* www.satzansatz.de/cssd/onhavinglayout.html. *Of course, doing so is likely to make your eyes cross and/or your hair fall out, so maybe it's best if you take the whole thing on faith.*

To trigger hasLayout in older versions of IE/Windows, let's add the following rule to our patches-win.iex.css file:

```
#content-layout {
  height: 1%;
}
```

And finally, let's crack open our patches-mac.ie5.css file and add this:

```
#content-layout {
  display: inline-table;
}
```

As the French designers say, *le voilà*—Figure 3-6 shows us that our floats have once again been contained, and our borders are standing strong, gray, and proud.

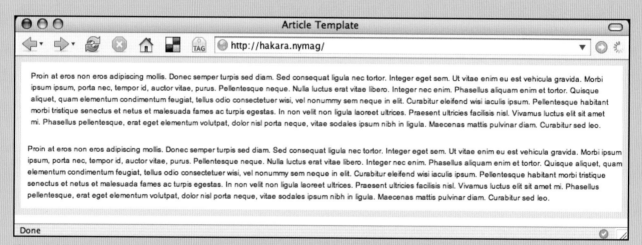

Figure 3-6. With some clearing implemented, our border's back again.

I never said I was good at this whole "metaphor" thing. Moving along.

Getting column-tastic (finally)

Now that our container is back on track, all we need to do to create our two-column effect is to apply the appropriate margins to our divs: a negative right margin to content-primary-wrap and a right margin to content-primary. The values used in these margins should be equal to, or larger than, the width of content-secondary, which we'll now set.

For our narrow, 190-pixel-wide right column, we can use the following code:

```
/*
   Set the column offset on the content divs
*/
#content-primary-wrap {
  margin-right: -200px;
}

#content-primary {
  margin-right: 200px;
}

/*
   Set the right-hand column width
*/
#content-secondary {
  width: 190px;
}
```

And with that, our column effect is complete, as shown in Figure 3-7.

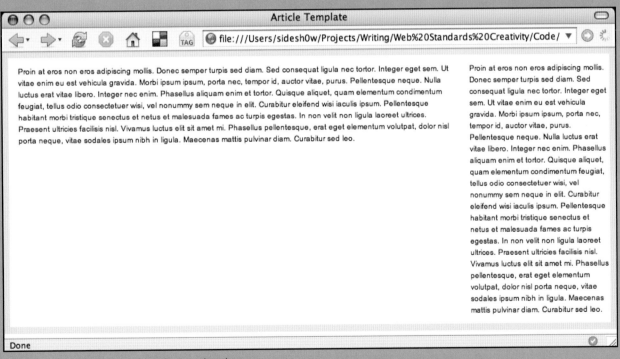

Figure 3-7. Finally, our two-column layout takes shape.

As you can see in Figure 3-8, this flexible-width layout scales down admirably in smaller window widths, which should make our client oh-so-very happy.

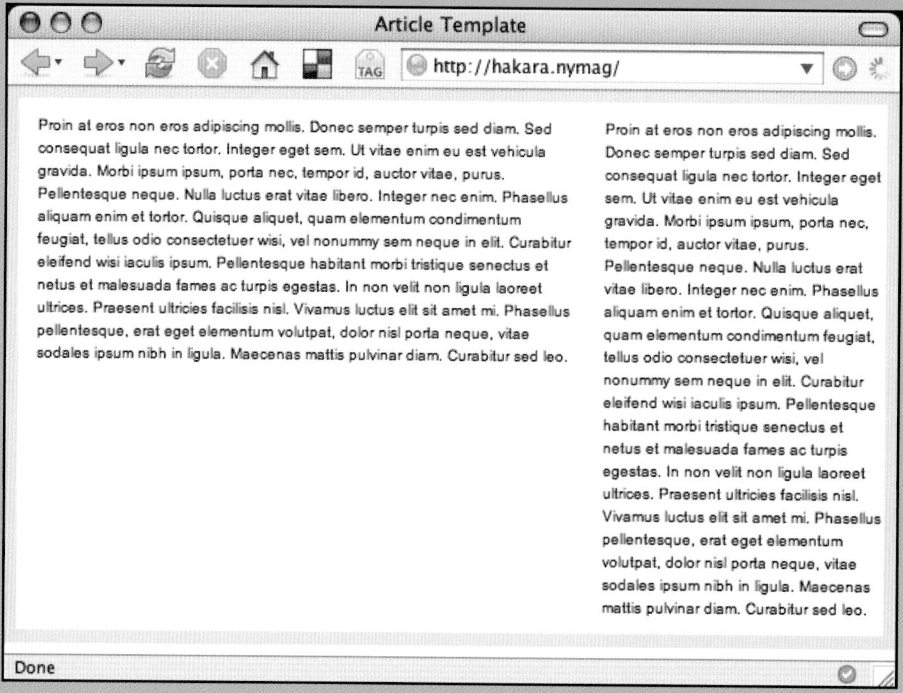

Figure 3-8. Our flexible-width design shrinks down admirably to smaller window widths. Hurrah!

Simple, yes? But remember that we have *two* right column widths to worry about: the narrow one we've just coded, and a 360px column for wider sidebar content. Do we have to build a separate template for this new sidebar width, or can we reuse the work done so far? And don't you just adore leading questions?

My class-fu is unstoppable

Here is where, at long last, we can use the `class` attribute on the body element to our advantage. If we know that we have two separate sidebar column widths, why not assign a `class` that "describes" the document accordingly? So for our narrow advertising column widths, I settled on

```
<body id="www-newyorkmag-com" class="ad-column-180">
```

For the wider one, I used

```
<body id="www-newyorkmag-com" class="ad-column-300">
```

> *Strictly speaking, these class names might not be the most ideal. In general, try to avoid using class or ID val-*
> *ues that represent the way an element will be displayed to the user (such as* red-link, big-headline, *or even*
> ad-column-300). *The main reason for avoiding these "presentational" names is that they're not especially*
> *future-proof: what happens when you redesign your site, and all of those* red-link *elements need to be*
> *green?* ad-layout-1 *or* ad-layout-2 *might have been more abstract, and perhaps a bit better; however, we*
> *decided that the production staff might better manage the more descriptive names, and the rest is history. Or*
> *class names. Or something.*

In effect, this gives our template a kind of toggle that we can exploit with our CSS. If we know that one of these two templates will be applied to our body element, we can modify our style rules accordingly:

```
/*
  Set the column offset on the content DIVs
*/
body.ad-column-180 #content-primary-wrap {
  margin-right: -200px;
}

body.ad-column-180 #content-primary {
  margin-right: 200px;
}

body.ad-column-300 #content-primary-wrap {
  margin-right: -370px;
}

body.ad-column-300 #content-primary {
  margin-right: 370px;
}

/*
  Set the right-hand column width
*/
body.ad-column-180 #content-secondary {
  width: 190px;
}

body.ad-column-300 #content-secondary {
  width: 360px;
}
```

Here, we flesh out our original rules and prepare for the two separate column widths with the appropriate body.ad-column-180
and body.ad-column-300 selectors.

As you've likely noticed, the `ad-column-300` column is actually going to be 360 pixels wide. I never was good at math, but there is a reason for this little naming discrepancy: the wider column will hold advertising banners that are 300 pixels wide. Since nontechnical content producers would ultimately "own" these templates, I settled on a `class` name that would make sense to them.

What's more, we can apply a different horizontally repeating background graphic to content-layout (see Figures 3-9 and 3-10) to give the illusion of a "gray" background behind the right column.

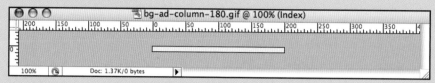

Figure 3-9. The gray background image for our narrow right column

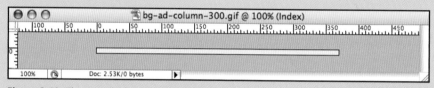

Figure 3-10. The gray tile for our wide right column

All we need to do is replace our `content-layout` rule with the following CSS:

```
#content-layout {
  background-color: #FFF;
  background-position: 100% 0;
  background-repeat: repeat-y;
}

body.ad-column-180 #content-layout {
  background-image: url("bg-ad-column-180.gif");
}

body.ad-column-300 #content-layout {
  background-image: url("bg-ad-column-300.gif");
}
```

Our column's "background" will adjust automatically, as shown in Figures 3-11 and 3-12.

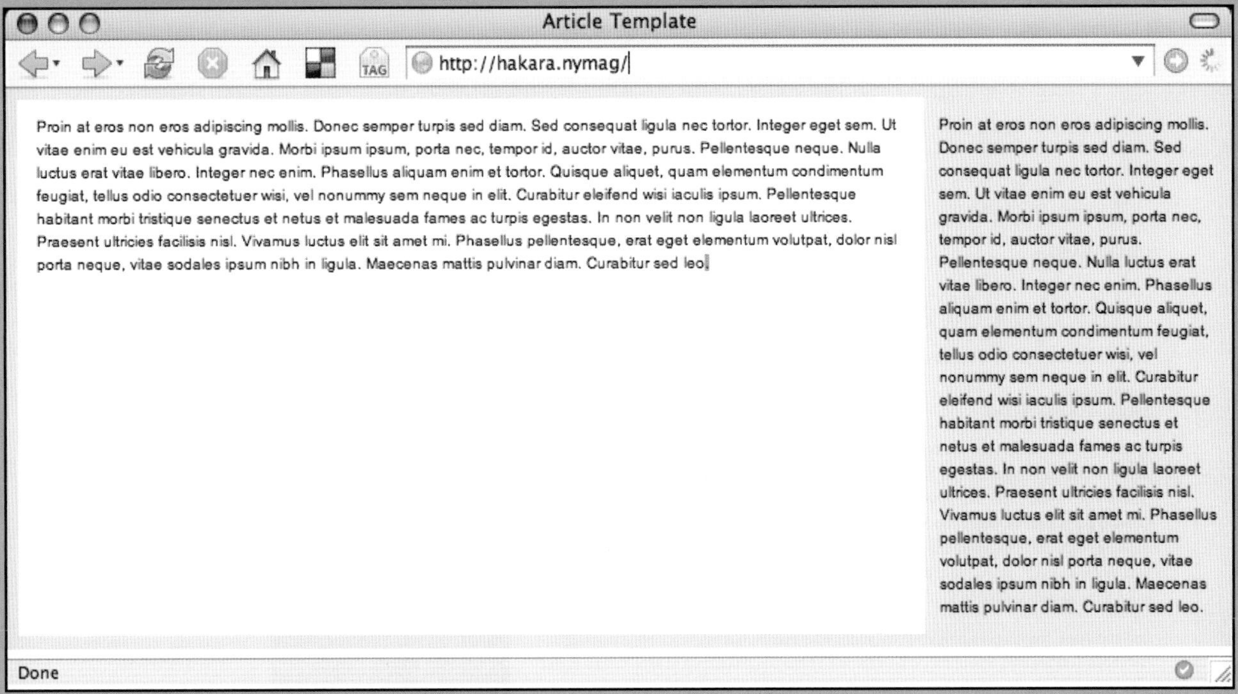

Figure 3-11. The narrow graphic is applied with the `ad-column-180` class on the body element.

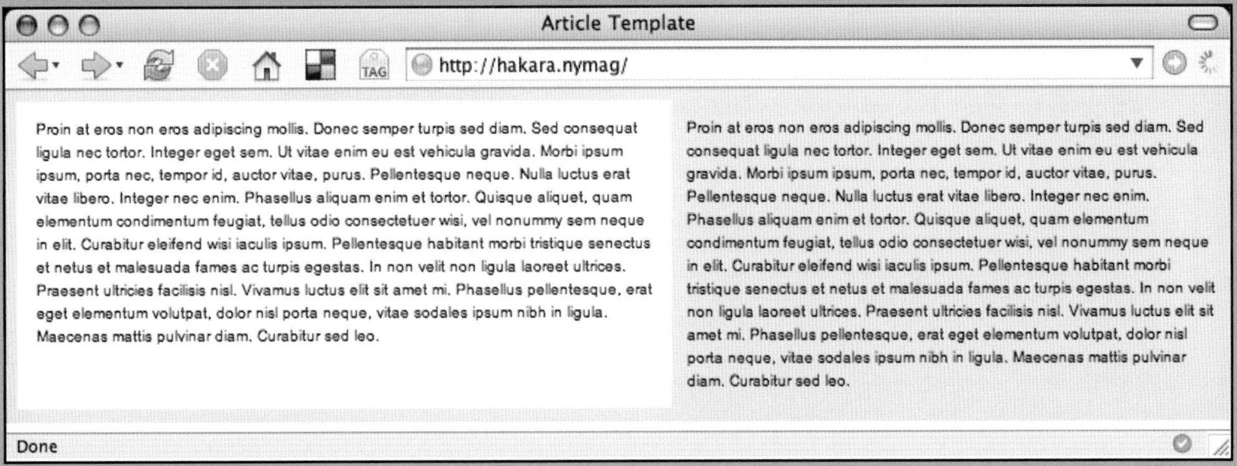

Figure 3-12. By switching the `class` to `ad-column-300`, we've changed to the larger image for our wider column.

What's the benefit to this approach, you may ask? By relying on this `class`-driven toggle, the rest of our markup can be reused for both layout scenarios: simply by changing ad-column-180 to ad-column-300 in our template's body, we can instantly restyle the display of our markup. Figures 3-13 and 3-14 show this in action on two different live, production-ready article templates—and the only thing that's changed between the two are a few characters in the body element's `class` attribute. The rest of the markup on these two pages is *identical*. I don't know about you, but I tend to get geekily excited about stuff like this.

Figure 3-13. Our finished article template, with ad-column-180 in the body element's `class` attribute.

○○○   Article Template

← ▾   → ▾   ⟳   ✕   ⌂   ○   ⓔ http://mammon.nymag/   ▼

COLUMN NAME

Text Size: A | **A** | **A**

The Boy Who Wouldn't Be King

Ten dazzling (and, of course, delicious) cakes will add a touch of artistry to your special day.

By Sara Cardace
Updated November 15, 2005

Every house has a story, some more dramatic than others like the tale of the brand-new townhouse on Greenwich, which thwarts sidewalk voyeurism with a sheet of steel. "Exactly three years ago, we came out of Pastis--it was my birthday and we saw a building for sale," says a fairly recent London transplant to New York. "It was a 50-year-old derelict building; we were literally buying the land." That birthday girl and her husband bid on it the next day, eventually paying $1.6 million. A few months later, the shell fell down on its own and had to be demolished by the city.

And last week, the couple and their three young children moved into a 5,000-square-foot townhouse on the site, one of only a handful built from the ground up in Manhattan in the past 50 years.

Architect Matthew Baird wasn't a stranger to small lots. Perhaps most disappointed of all, in retrospect, was Smith herself. "I hope I have the brain to differentiate when someone just wants to kick me down the stairs for a laugh, or when someone's actually trying to explain to me what's wrong with the book. When I was writing The Autograph Man, I thought my father was dying, I was incredibly miserable, I really disliked my life, and I wrote a book which was very angry and sad. But it also was about something important to me, and maybe I didn't express it properly. On Beauty might be cased up in a nicer icing, but it is about many similar things."

➕ Enlarge   Photo by NIKOLAS KOENIG / Courtesy of Christie's

Caption or Slide Show teaser text here

GRAPHIC PACKAGE HEADER

Take a tour of Manhattan's striking new townhouse.

Main Page

RSS FEEDS

Restaurants & Food   Recipes

What is RSS? | All RSS Feeds

NOW IN SECTION NAME

SLIDESHOW

Apocalypse Guide
How to avoid avian flu, wash off a dirty bomb, evacuate, medicate, and otherwise live through a disaster.

- Bulleted Link 1
- Bulleted Link 2
- Bulleted Link 3

NEWSLETTERS

☐ New York Exclusive   ☐ Best Bets & Sales

☐ This Week In New York   ☐ Culture Navigator

☐ Restaurant Insider

Enter Your Email Address   SIGN UP ▸

NEWSLETTERS

Restaurant Insider: One line description here.

Enter Your Email Address   SIGN UP ▸

MOST EMAILED STORIES

PAST 24 HR | 7 DAYS | 30 DAYS

1. Judith Miller, Right Wing Hero?

Done

Figure 3-14. The exact same template code, but with `ad-column-300` in the `class`. Hot.

Intelligent modules

So with our page-level layout controlled by our new class-driven toggle, let's try to bring the same level of control to the page's finer details. Earlier, I mentioned that other than the body element's class attribute, the pages' markup was identical—including the small army of content blocks, or **modules**, in the right column. Like the two columns we just created, those modules will resize themselves to fit within either sidebar width.

Let's take a quick look at one example, the "Now In . . ." module. In its narrow format (Figure 3-15), the content is stacked in a single column; however, when the content-secondary column is in its wide format, the two content areas are placed side by side (Figure 3-16). (I'd like to state for the record that I didn't select this picture.)

Using what we learned from building the two-column layout, let's try for the same level of markup reuse here. If we can have one HTML template for these two different module layouts, that would be ideal.

To that end, let's take a quick mental inventory of our different content areas in the module. We can see that there are two distinct content areas, capped by a header at the top (Figure 3-17). This is true even in the two-column version (Figure 3-18), but the first content area appears in the right column, with the second content area appearing to its left.

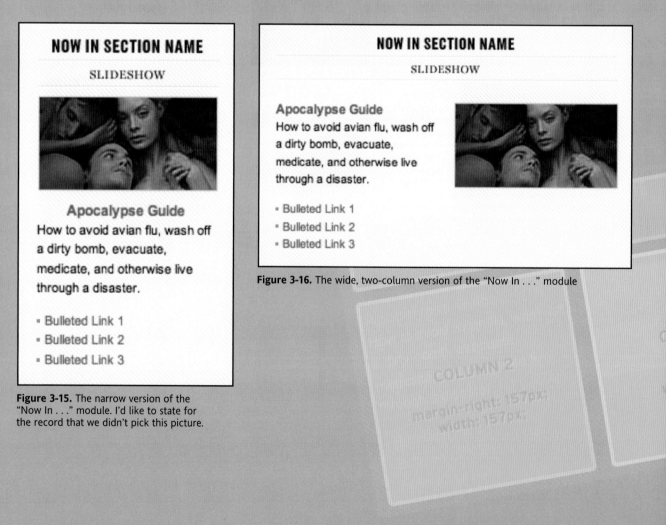

Figure 3-16. The wide, two-column version of the "Now In . . ." module

Figure 3-15. The narrow version of the "Now In . . ." module. I'd like to state for the record that we didn't pick this picture.

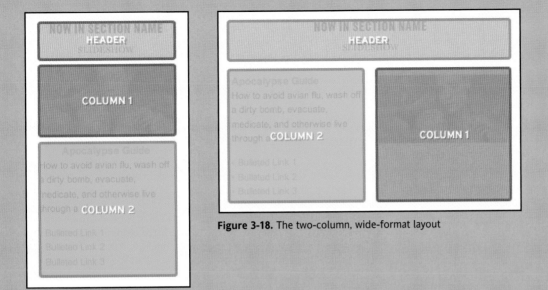

Figure 3-18. The two-column, wide-format layout

Figure 3-17. The anatomy of our narrow module

So with this basic understanding of where the different content areas are in the two layout options (single- and two-column), we can build a basic markup framework.

```
<div class="block module-in-section">
  <div class="head">
    <h5><img src="/images/2/title-in-section.gif"➡
      alt="Now In Section" /></h5>
    <h6><img src="/images/2/title-slideshow.gif" alt="slideshow"➡
      /></h6>
  </div>
  <div class="content">
    <div class="row columns-2">
      <div class="column col-1">
        <img src="/images/photos/156x78-in-section.jpg"➡
          alt="Now In Section" />
      </div>
      <div class="column col-2">
        <h5><a href="#">Apocalypse Guide</a></h5>
        <p>How to avoid avian flu, wash off a dirty bomb, evacuate,➡
          medicate, and otherwise live through a disaster.</p>
        <ul>
          <li><a href="#">Bulleted Link 1</a></li>
          <li><a href="#">Bulleted Link 2</a></li>
          <li><a href="#">Bulleted Link 3</a></li>
        </ul>
      </div>
    </div>
  </div>
</div><!-- /end div.module-in-section -->
```

There are a few items to note here:

- The block value for the module's `class` attribute is a reusable piece of markup I've placed throughout the *New York Magazine* templates. It's simply a hook for the Easy Clearing Method, and it's added to those rules (`.block:after`, etc.) so that it contains any floats inside it.

- The `row` class inside the content area serves a similar function: if any of its child "column" divs are floated, they won't escape their parent "row" div.

- The other value in the module's `class` (`module-in-section`) acts as a kind of unique identifier for this type of module. I couldn't use an actual `id` attribute here, as more than one of these types of modules might appear on a page—and per the HTML specification, an `id` must be unique within the page.

With our markup in place, we can move on to styling it. Given that the wide and narrow versions of the module share the same aesthetic qualities (such as typography, color, and background images), I won't discuss them here; rather, let's focus on building out our two content columns.

In the single-column mode, we can let the markup's source order do the work for us. The first column will simply stack on top of the second, as shown in Figure 3-17. We can, however, apply a little CSS to clean things up a bit:

```
.module-in-section .content {
  padding: 0 14px 13px;
}

body.ad-column-180 .module-in-section .col-1 {
  text-align: center;
  margin: 7px 0 10px;
}
```

The first rule simply applies some padding to our content div, giving our columns some breathing room. The second rule centers the column's content (namely, the img) and adds some top and bottom margins. But as you might have noticed, we preface that second rule with the same `body.ad-column-180` rule we used to create our narrow sidebar (in the "My class-fu is unstoppable" section). One class, two separate effects. Lightweight code is a beautiful thing, isn't it?

From this logic, we can apply the `ad-column-300` class to the body element to create our two-column effect. We'll need to float each column div—the first column floated to the right, and the second column to the left, as shown in Figure 3-19.

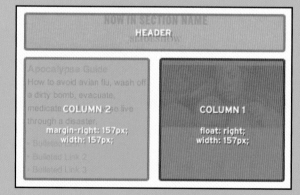

Figure 3-19. The code to get our two-column layout in place

```
body.ad-column-300 .module-in-section .column {
  width: 157px;
}

body.ad-column-300 .module-in-section .col-1 {
  float: right;
}

body.ad-column-300 .module-in-section .col-2 {
  float: left;
}
```

So there we have it: a single class value on our body attribute can act as a kind of traffic cop for each module on our sidebar. We've written some CSS that expects (and exploits) the presence of either ad-column-180 or ad-column-300, leaving our markup completely untouched.

Additional classes, additional control

At this point, we've been using one value in the class attribute. By using ad-column-180 or ad-column-300, we can instantly reformat our right sidebar and its contents. As we've discussed, the class attribute can accept multiple values, but can we use the body element to control other aspects of our page's presentation? There I go with the leading questions again.

Starting small (980 pixels' worth)

When I came on board with the *New York* Magazine website redesign, I was told that the production team wanted to be able to selectively override the flexible-width design on certain pages, effectively fixing the page's width at the full 980 pixels. Presumably, some of the pages would contain wide-format media (e.g., large photographs), and the client wanted to ensure that the rest of the page's layout would remain intact.

Let's take another look at our #wrap rule, which contains our min-width and max-width parameters:

```
#wrap {
    margin: 0 auto;
    min-width: 770px;
    max-width: 980px;
}
```

So if this is the default behavior, let's add a new class value to our body element to override it—say, "fixed"?

```
<body id="www-newyorkmag-com" class="ad-column-180 fixed">
```

We can now drop in the following CSS to turn our flexible design into a static one:

```
body.fixed #wrap {
    width: 980px;
}
```

And there we have it. Since we've now set a width on our wrap block, the min-width and max-width properties are obsolete. Our design's container div is fixed at the requested 980 pixels, which fulfills our client's request.

> *A word of caution about multiple* class *names: The aged IE5/Mac has a whitespace parsing bug (www.macedition.com/cb/ie5macbugs/substringbug.html) that can cause it to become confused when encountering a* class *name that is a substring of another* class. *As a result, try to make the categories of* class *types you're applying as unique as possible, and test thoroughly in that browser.*

Tying in JavaScript

We can invoke a number of other visual effects with the body class, but let's shift away from the design for a moment. After all, this technique is far from a one-trick pony. We can also attach classes to our document that act as flags for JavaScript-driven behavior, adding another layer of standards-based sexiness to the site's design.

For example, there's a set of links on some article pages (Figure 3-20) used to dynamically increase (Figure 3-21) or decrease (Figure 3-22) the size of the article text on the page. Why bother? Well, this is actually a rather handy accessibility feature. If a reader has diminished vision, that person might not know how to change the browser's text size. Placing a few links on the page exposes similar functionality in an immediate and easy-to-use fashion.

Figure 3-20. The text-sizing control that appears on certain pages of the website

Figure 3-21. The text size can be increased . . .

Figure 3-22. . . . or decreased by using the links on the page. You're floored, I can tell.

Inspired by a venerable JavaScript-based style sheet switcher (www.alistapart.com/stories/alternate), the *New York Magazine*'s text-sizing code performs a number of different tasks. When a user clicks one of these links, an additional class is appended to the body element that, when present, will change the size of the text in the article template accordingly. Additionally, a cookie stored on the user's browser remembers the user's selection and automatically applies the appropriate text size upon his or her return. It's a rather convoluted piece of JavaScript, but that might be because we're not exactly the Samuel L. Jackson of JavaScript programmers.

It's important to note that the links you see in Figure 3-20 don't actually exist in the HTML. JavaScript injects the three "A" links into the page once the page loads, ensuring that the controls are available only to users whose browsers can support them. And showing a near-compulsive obsession with the body element's class, we can use that attribute to trigger our function, which will allow our content producers to drop a simple word into class to invoke the function, and thereby drop the links into the page.

As always, let's start with our body element—I know, shocking. But this time, let's use text-sizer as our new class:

```
<body id="www-newyorkmag-com" class="ad-column-180 fixed text-sizer">
```

Inside the scripts.js file we referenced from the head of our document is a function called buildTextSizer:

```
<script type="text/javascript" src="/path/to/scripts.js"></script>
```

There's a fair amount of code to this function, so don't worry if you're not exactly a JavaScript ninja (after all, I'm *certainly* not). Thankfully, the part we're most concerned with occurs right at the top:

```
function buildTextSizer() {
    if (document.getElementsByTagName && document.createElement ➥
        && document.getElementById) {
        var trigger = document.getElementsByTagName("body")[0];
    if (findWord("text-sizer", trigger.className)) {
        if (document.getElementById("article-content")) {
            var container = document.getElementById("article-content");
        } else {
            var container = document.getElementById("content-primary");
        }

        if (container) {
            // Build elements
            var slugs = new Array("small", "medium", "large");
            var controlContainer = document.createElement("div");
            var topList = document.createElement("ul");
            var innerList = document.createElement("ul");
            var listItem = document.createElement("li");
            var span = document.createElement("span");
            var labelText = document.createTextNode("Text Size:")

            // Loop over the text size "slugs", and build a link for
            //each one
            for (var i = 0; i < slugs.length; i++) {
                var text = document.createTextNode("A");
                var anchor = document.createElement("a");
                var item = document.createElement("li");

                anchor.appendChild(text);
```

```
          anchor.setAttribute("href", "javascript:textIt('txt-" +➥
            slugs[i] + "');");
          anchor.setAttribute("title", "Make the story text " +➥
            slugs[i] + ".");
          item.appendChild(anchor);
          item.setAttribute("id", "txt-" + slugs[i]);

          innerList.appendChild(item);
        }

        // Assemble everything, and insert it into the
        //document
        span.className = "label";
        span.appendChild(labelText);
        listItem.appendChild(span);
        listItem.appendChild(innerList);
        topList.appendChild(listItem);
        controlContainer.setAttribute("id", "text-size");
        controlContainer.appendChild(topList);
        container.insertBefore(controlContainer, container.➥
          childNodes[0]);
      }
    }
  }
}


/*
  Find full word (needle) in a string (haystack)
*/
function findWord(needle, haystack) {
  return haystack.match(needle + "\\b");
}
```

What we have here, in essence, are two separate functions: one to build the text sizing controls (buildTextSizer, continuing my streak of award-winning names), and another function, findWord, used by the first function. In the section of code highlighted in bold, buildTextSizer inspects our body element (var trigger = document.getElementsByTagName("body")[0];) and searches its class attribute for the presence of the text-sizer string (findWord("text-sizer", trigger.className)). If that search results in a match, then the rest of the function continues to build the text sizing links; if no match is found (i.e., if text-sizer doesn't appear in the body element's class attribute), then the function stops running and the links are never seen.

Since this function is set to fire on every page of the site, content producers can place the class selectively on pages where they would like the sizing controls to appear, and omit it on others. The function will fail silently if it doesn't find text-sizer in the body element, affording the site's authors flexibility and ease when toggling the function. Which, of course, is a good thing.

Summary

This chapter is by no means an exhaustive list of the ways in which the body element's class attribute is used on the *New York* Magazine site; I'd love to provide you with such a list, but I don't think I could force you to sit through a Tolstoy-length chapter on the body element. Rather, I hope that the information in this chapter sparks some ideas on how this multiple class value technique can be a boon to you, and how an intelligent application of it can decrease your site's template count, reduce markup clutter, and give you ample hooks for both JavaScript and CSS. On the *New York* Magazine site, we've used additional classes to dynamically swap out section-specific logos and automatically highlight the current navigation tab. Additional applications for this are entirely up to you.

Web standards are about improved control over your design, not maintaining bulky code. Embrace your body, and your sites will be easier to maintain, update, and improve. And, of course, your users will love that.

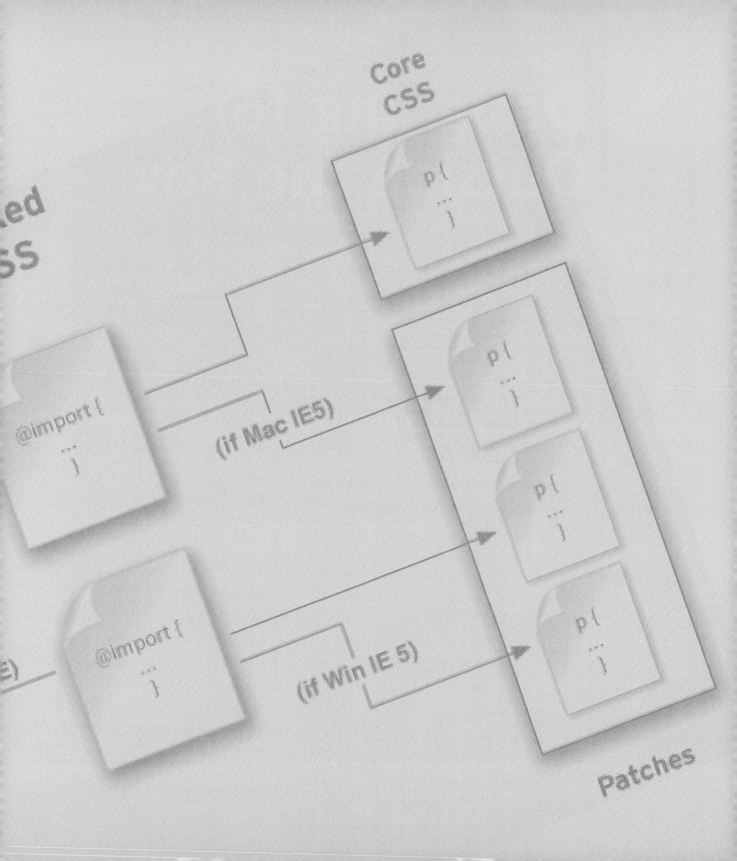

4

Designing for Outside the Box

andy
clarke

www.malarkey.co.uk
www.stuffandnonsense.co.uk

Based in the UK, **Andy Clarke** (Malarkey) has a background in advertising. He started his own design consultancy, Stuff and Nonsense (www.malarkey.co.uk), in 1998. Since then, he has designed sites for Disney Store UK, British Heart Foundation, Save the Children, and the World Wildlife Fund UK.

Andy is passionate about design and about Web Standards; he bridges the gap between design and code. Outside the studio, Andy is a member of the Web Standards Project, where he redesigned the organization's website in 2006 and is an Invited Expert to the W3C's CSS Working Group.

Andy is an internationally known trainer and conference speaker, and he regularly trains designers and developers in the creative applications of Web Standards. He writes about aspects of design and popular culture on his personal website, All That Malarkey (www.stuffandnonsense.co.uk), and is the author of *Transcending CSS: The Fine Art of Web Design*, published by New Riders in 2006 (www.transcendingcss.com).

Worries?

"Oh baby, what's the matter?" she said. "You look so stressed and worried."

"I am," I replied. "I'm worried that our car needs new tires, we have nothing in the fridge for tea except a paper bag of mushrooms and a tube of tomato puree, *and* my mother is having trouble with her feet again."

Worrying—it's no laughing matter, I can tell you. If worrying about your own problems is not bad enough, worrying about someone else's can be maddening. Still, help is on hand in the form of a new, fictitious service called WorrySome.net.

This will not be your common or garden-variety web application, with enough venture capital to mount a small war and a call center in New Delhi. This site is "by real people, for real people"—people who will worry for you, for a fee, of course. The service will leave you free to live your life, free from worry, as long as you keep on paying the subscription.

WorrySome.net needs a new website, and you are the just the person for the job. It's a tricky one, but don't worry; help is on hand to guide you through making this design into a reality. If you feel at any stage that you are starting to get even the tiniest bit concerned, you can always pay one of WorrySome's worriers to take the weight off your shoulders.

In this chapter, you are going to take the WorrySome.net homepage from design visual to a working prototype with XHTML and CSS. You will start with meaningful, content-out markup, which is always the first step in developing a creative, standards-based design. You will learn how to use powerful CSS selectors and layout techniques to bring this design to life.

Worrying about the Web

Personally, I'm very glad that WorrySome.net can worry on my behalf, because in the past two years, I have been worried about web design. The Web is a youthful, dynamic medium, where people should love to interact with sites that they visit. Creating sites that people love to use is one of the main goals of creative web design. But web designers and developers too often focus on the technical aspects of markup, CSS, Ajax, or on the "science" of usability and accessibility, rather than on connecting with visitors' emotions through good design.

We've seen advances in the tools provided by CSS and wider support for these tools in mainstream web browsers. I hope that we can stop worrying about supporting browsers that are past their sell-by date and look forward by creating new and inspirational designs that break out of the boxes of current thinking.

Designing for WorrySome.net

As WorrySome.net is a novel new way of dealing with the worries of the world, the site calls for a design that breaks away from the familiar conventions of many of today's shiny web applications. The brief calls for this design to be open and friendly. It must make the visitor feel as "welcome as a trusted friend, rather than as a customer."

When creating the look for WorrySome.net, the design took on many forms. I made several experimental layouts with many different interface ideas, only a few of which made it into the final design. Figure 4-1 shows the one that you'll be working on in this chapter.

Let's get started making the design for the WorrySome.net homepage into a reality. You'll use meaningful XHTML markup and CSS, but not just any old CSS. This minimal markup will demand that you use techniques and CSS selectors that you may not yet have implemented in your own work. You can download all of the necessary files from www.friendsofed.com.

Figure 4-1. WorrySome.net homepage

Stop worrying, start with markup

One of the aims of a designer working on the Web should be to convey meaning. I'm not just talking about the meaning expressed through a visual design to reinforce brand values, but also the meaning conveyed through the XHTML elements chosen for the content. Choosing elements appropriately for their meaning, rather than their visual presentation, will help you to create designs that are as flexible and accessible as they can possibly be. (Of course, you also need to make sure that your markup is as lean and flexible as possible.) You want to make sure that the elements will convey the full meaning of the content when it is viewed without the visual richness provided by your CSS.

Look back at Figure 4-1 and write down the meaning of each of the visual elements on the page. In this design, you see the following elements:

- A branding area that contains the name of the site and its tagline, a lyric from Bob Marley, a master of the laid-back approach to life
- A list of navigation links
- Three headings that are each followed by paragraphs of text and an inline image of a worrier
- A heading that is followed by a list of topics that people often worry about: from conspiracies to George W. Bush (I can't think of any connection there, no sir)
- Site information, commonly containing legal notes, copyright information, and design credits

With this content outline complete, you are ready to flesh out the markup that will be most appropriate to convey its meaning. At this point, you should be concerned only with describing the meaning of this content and not any division elements or presentational markup hacks.

You should begin at the top of your content outline's order and work downwards, so we'll start with the branding.

Adding the content elements

On the homepage of WorrySome, the name of the site can be a good choice for the top-level heading on the page.

```
<h1>Worrysome.net</h1>
```

Many designers will choose to vary this on internal pages, opting instead for a second-level heading and reserving the top-level heading for the page name. On internal pages, this name will likely also include a link back to the homepage, which would be redundant on the homepage.

Next comes the tagline. Written on the steps of Marley's house in Jamaica, where the smokes kept a rollin', this extract from "Three Little Birds" is perfect for a site about chilling out. Flip through the pages of the XHTML specification and look for a `lyric` element if you want. I'll just wait here, singing "sweet songs of melodies pure and true" until you return.

Back already?

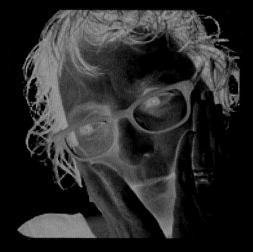

In the absence of a more appropriate element to mark up this poetry from the great man of reggae, a blockquote element will do; after all, he sang those words.

```
<blockquote cite="http://www.bobmarley.com/songs/songs.cgi?threebirds">
<p>Don' worry 'bout a thing, cos every lil thing is gonna be alright.</p>
</blockquote>
```

> *Notice that the URL source of the quotation has been cited. Although this information will not be visible in a visitor's web browser, you should always cite the sources of any quotations that you reference. For an example of a way to display the URL of a quotation using scripting, see Jeremy Keith's book* DOM Scripting: Web Design with JavaScript and the Document Object Model *(friends of ED, ISBN: 1-59059-533-5).*

If you are still in a "Mellow Mood," the list of links to the subscription page, worries list, and shopping cart that form the main navigation are ordered without any importance or weight attached to any particular link. An unordered list is the appropriate choice to mark up these links.

```
<h4>Main navigation</h4>
<ul>
  <li><a href="#" title="Subscribe">Subscribe</a></li>
  <li><a href="#" title="Worrylist">Worrylist</a></li>
  <li><a href="#" title="Worrycart">Worrycart</a></li>
</ul>
```

But what's the heading doing in there? Low-level headings atop lists of navigation links can be a helpful way to inform a visitor who is using a screen reader (or another form of assistive technology) of the purpose of a list. You may choose to make these headings visible or to hide them from view, perhaps by text-indenting them off the screen. This technique has become known as providing an *embedded alternate*.

Now we are really "Jamming," and it is time to move on to the main content of interest on this homepage: the descriptions of the services that this site provides. You will choose a second-level heading for each of the content areas, followed by their related content.

```
<h2>Worriers</h2>
<p>Introduction text</p>
<img src="images/worryone-i.png" alt="Lynda" />
<p>Name and role of worrier</p>
<p>Further descriptive text</p>

<h2>Worries</h2>
<p>Introduction text</p>
<img src="images/worrytwo-i.png" alt="Andy" />
<p>Name and role of worrier</p>
<p>Further descriptive text</p>

<h2>Worry done</h2>
<p>Introduction text</p>
<img src="images/worrythree-i.png" alt="Brain" />
<p>Name and role of worrier</p>
<p>Further descriptive text</p>
```

A third-level heading proudly announces the list of topics that the site's team of expert worriers can take off your shoulders. As this list has been written in alphabetical order, it is debatable whether it would be most appropriate to choose an ordered list, rather than an unordered list. For this example, I have chosen unordered, as no one item is more important than its siblings.

```
<h3>Recently worried about</h3>
<ul>
  <li><a href="#">Worry item</a></li>
  <li><a href="#">Worry item</a></li>
  <li><a href="#">Worry item</a></li>
</ul>
```

You are now almost at the bottom of the page, at the site information and a handy link back to the top to save the visitor's scrolling finger.

```
<p><a href="http://www.stuffandnonsense.co.uk">&copy; Stuff and➥
  Nonsense Ltd.</a> A demonstration site by Andy Clarke</p>
<ul>
  <li><a href="#worrysome-net" title="Top of this page">Top</a></li>
</ul>
```

With your meaningful markup neatly written, now is your opportunity to preview your page in your development browser (see Figure 4-2) and to validate your code to ensure that no errors have crept in along the way.

> If, like me, your choice of development browser is Firefox, you can find a host of developer extensions that will keep your markup valid as you work, not least of which is Chris Pederick's essential Web Developer Toolbar. You can download the Web Developer Toolbar from http://chrispederick.com/work/webdeveloper/.

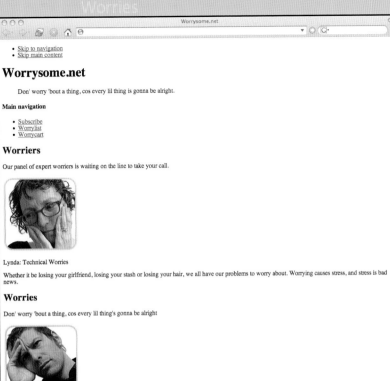

Figure 4-2. Previewing the page in a browser to ensure that the content is well ordered when read without syles is your first step in developing visually expressive but accessible designs.

Adding divisions from the content out

In general, web designers' understanding of markup and CSS has developed over recent years, but often our thinking about the ways to accomplish a visual design using CSS has changed little since we worked with tables for layout. Strip away the visual skin of many standards-based sites, their W3C "valid XHTML and CSS" badges glinting in the sunshine, and you will find a mass of nonsemantic and unnecessary <div> and <span> elements.

Working from the content out means starting with only the structural elements such as headings, paragraphs, and lists. This is an ideal method for keeping your markup free from presentational elements.

Next, you will group only those related elements that you have previously chosen into divisions, giving each an identity that describes the content that it contains.

> Much has been written on the subject on semantic element naming. Former CSS Samurai John Allsopp has created WebPatterns (www.webpatterns.org), a site dedicated to element-naming conventions. My original article on the subject of naming conventions can be found at All That Malarkey (www.stuffandnonsense.co.uk/archives/whats_in_a_name_pt2.html).

To avoid repetition of code, the next example shows only the content areas, rather than reproducing every nuance of markup.

```
<div id="branding">
  <h1>Worrysome.net</h1>
  <blockquote cite="http://www.bobmarley.com/songs/songs.cgi?threebirds ">
    <p>Don' worry 'bout a thing, cos every lil thing is gonna be alright.</p>
  </blockquote>
</div>

<div id="nav_main">
  <h4>Main navigation</h4>
  <ul>
    <li><a href="#" title="Subscribe">Subscribe</a></li>
    <li><a href="#" title="Worrylist">Worrylist</a></li>
    <li><a href="#" title="Worrycart">Worrycart</a></li>
  </ul>
</div>

<div id="content">
  <div id="content_main">
    <div id="worriers">
      <h2>Worriers</h2>
      <p>Introduction text</p>
      <img src="images/worryone-i.png" alt="Lynda" />
      <p>Name and role of worrier</p>
      <p>Further descriptive text</p>
    </div>
```

```
    <div id="worries">
       <h2>Worries</h2>
       <p>Introduction text</p>
       <img src="images/worrytwo-i.png" alt="Andy" />
       <p>Name and role of worrier</p>
       <p>Further descriptive text</p>
    </div>

    <div id="worrydone">
       <h2>Worrydone</h2>
       <p>Introduction text</p>
        <img src="images/worrythree-i.png" alt="Brain" />
       <p>Name and role of worrier</p>
       <p>Further descriptive text</p>
    </div>
  </div>

  <div id="content_sub">
     <h3>Recently worried about</h3>
     <ul>
        <li><a href="#">Worry item</a></li>
        <li><a href="#">Worry item</a></li>
        <li><a href="#">Worry item</a></li>
     </ul>
  </div>
</div>

<div id="siteinfo">
   <p><a href="http://www.stuffandnonsense.co.uk">&copy; Stuff and Nonsense Ltd. </a>
   A demonstration site by Andy Clarke</p>
   <ul>
      <li><a href="#worrysome-net" title="Top of this page">Top</a></li>
   </ul>
</div>
```

These appropriately identified divisions not only add the structure that will enable you to develop the visual layout with greater ease, but their identifiers also serve to enhance the meaning of the content that they contain. This minimal use of divisions should always be your approach in a content-based workflow. This places the content, rather than the visual layout, at the center of your thinking when writing your markup.

If additional divisions are required to accomplish any specific design, these should be added one at a time until your design can be achieved. For this design, only one additional container division, wrapped around all of your elements, is required. This container is a common approach for allowing you further styling options in addition to the html and body elements.

```
<div id="container">
All document content
</div>
```

You may have noticed that, in this markup example, no additional identifier or class attributes have been added, despite the complexity of the design. Such presentational attributes should rarely be required, as your markup already contains all the elements and attributes (href, title, alt, and so on) that you should ever need when you take a mature approach to your standards-based design.

With the elements and appropriate divisions in your markup complete, but before you start working with CSS, you should take a moment to consider adding one further element. This will help those visitors browsing the site using a screen reader or a small-screen browser that has no support for style sheets.

While it is an impossible dream to expect that this site, or any other, can be fully accessible to *every* visitor, a few unobtrusive additions to your document will help some people enormously. For this example, you will add a short list of skip links, to allow a screen reader user to skip to either the main navigation or the main content.

```
<ul id="nav_access">
<li><a href="#nav_main">Skip to navigation</a></li>
<li><a href="#content_main">Skip main content</a></li>
</ul>
```

You should insert this list directly beneath the opening <body> tag and outside the container division.

Satisfying your soul (with CSS)

If markup was your "Punky Reggae Party," transforming this into the visual design layout should be your "Satisfy My Soul" time. (OK, that's the last of the Bob Marley song title malarkey, I promise.)

Implementing design layouts using CSS has come a long way since the early days of the Noodle Incident (www.thenoodleincident.com) and The Blue Robot (www.bluerobot.com). In those days of practical CSS use, positioning was the method of choice for achieving columns and other layout features. Before long, as designers became more ambitious in their attempts to make complex designs using CSS, positioning gave way to the use of floats. Unfortunately, positioning and its associated z-index stacking have since somewhat fallen from favor.

Although positioning is, on a first glance, more difficult to understand, it remains possibly the most powerful of CSS design tools. Implementing the WorrySome.net layout will make heavy use of both positioning and the z-index, in combination with floats.

You will also be working with image replacement and a whole host of CSS selectors. Many of these will be familiar to you if you have been working with CSS for some time; others might seem strange. You are about to use selectors that have until recently been the stuff of dreams for web designers. Don't worry "Buffalo Soldier" (sorry, I couldn't resist that), I will explain each new selector and technique as we progress.

Train to Styleville

Until recently, your choice of CSS selectors and techniques that could be used reliably across different browsers was limited to the few simple selectors supported by the world's most used browser, Microsoft's Internet Explorer 6 for Windows. That situation has now changed, thanks to the hard work and passion for standards of Internet Explorer 7's developers, and to the dedication of people like Molly E. Holzschlag of the Web Standards Project (www.webstandards.org), who built the bridges between the web developer community and Microsoft. We should all be grateful for their work.

Internet Explorer 7 is far from a perfect browser (what browser is?), but it does level the browser playing field. It has good support for so-called "advanced" CSS selectors, and it fixes the rendering issues and bugs of previous versions that have made the lives of web designers difficult over recent years.

I'm in the mood for style

Despite their broadly consistent rendering of CSS, most browsers will have a different default rendering of a page—the look of the page before author or user styles are applied—using what are known as *user agent* or *browser styles*, also conventionally known as *default* styles. Therefore, you should start by adding a few simple rules to your style sheet to guarantee that the styling of any element is as you, rather than the browser, intends. This example contains a broader range of elements than you will be using to implement WorrySome.net, to enable you to work with any elements that you may require in the future.

```
/* =reset.css */

body, div, dl, dt, dd, ul, ol, li, h1, h2, h3, h4, h5, h6, pre, form,➡
   fieldset, input, p, blockquote, address, th, td {
margin : 0; padding :0; }

h2, h3, h4, h5, h6 {
font-size : 100%;
font-weight : normal; }

ol, ul {
list-style-type : none; }

table {
border-collapse : collapse;
border-spacing : 0; }

caption, th {
text-align : left; }
fieldset, img { border : 0; }

dt, address, caption, cite, code, dfn, em, i, strong, b, th, var {
font-style : normal;
font-weight : normal; }

q:before, q:after { content :''; }
```

In addition to this reset CSS, I also recommend that you specify margin and padding on commonly used text elements.

```
/* =blocktext */
h2, h3, h4, h5, p, ul {
margin : 0 20px;
padding : .5em 0; }
```

Styling WorrySome.net

Whereas many web designers take a granular approach to implementing their designs using CSS, you are going to take an outside-in approach, concentrating first on the outer elements of your design before working on the fine details. You'll begin by applying styles that set up the structure of your layout, starting with html, body, and the container division that encompasses all your content.

A background-color, background-image, and font color applied to the root element html will get the ball rolling. A slim background-image will repeat horizontally (repeat-x) to create the site's striped background.

```
html {
background : #f7d8e8 url(../images/html.png) repeat-x;
color : #333; }
```

> *Many of the image filenames that I have chosen relate precisely to the elements that they are styling. This approach helps to save time and reduce confusion when returning to a site after several months, or when a number of designers or developers are working together.*

Next, you should apply styles to the body element. This design will be fixed-width and centered in the browser window.

```
body {
position : relative;
width : 740px;
margin : 20px auto 0 auto;
padding-top : 10px;
background : url(../images/body.png) repeat-y;
font : 88%/1.5 Calibri, Trebuchet, "Trebuchet MS", Helvetica, Arial, sans-serif; }
```

You may be wondering why position : relative; should be applied to the body element. After all, body is unlikely to be positioned or offset from its natural position. Many of the visual elements in this design are absolutely positioned on the page. Applying position : relative; to the body element will establish it as the positioning context for any of its positioned descendents.

Next, it's the outer container division's turn. Once again, this element has been established as a positioning context for its descendents and is centered within body to allow that element's background-image to create the subtle drop shadow for the depth of the page.

```
div[id="container"] {
width : 700px;
margin : 0 auto; }
```

If the selector in the example is unfamiliar to you, don't worry. This is an attribute selector, *a type that has largely been avoided by web designers and developers because of a lack of support for it in Internet Explorer 6. An attribute selector is made of three parts:*

- The element that you are selecting (div in this example)
- The attribute that you are using to select a specific element (id in this example)
- The value of the attribute (container in this example)

You could select the same element by using either div#container *or even* #container, *but that wouldn't be as much fun, would it?*

Styling basic page divisions

With the outer regions in place, you can turn your attention to defining the branding, navigation, and content areas of this design. For each, you will apply basic styling, including box and background properties. Start at the top with the branding area.

```
div[id="branding"] {
height : 200px;
margin-bottom : 10px;
background : #f0a4c7 url(../images/branding.png) repeat-x; }
```

This can be followed by the main navigation's outer division.

```
div[id="nav_main"] {
background : #fedaeb url(../images/nav_main.png) repeat-y; }
```

And finish by applying styling to the remaining main divisions:

```
div[id="content"] {
margin-bottom : 80px; }

div[id="content_main"] , div[id="content_sub"] {
width: 100%;  }

div[id="siteinfo"] {
clear : both;
min-height : 120px;
padding: .5em 0;
background : url(../images/siteinfo.png) repeat-x;  }
```

Take a peek at how your design is coming together by loading the page in your development browser (see Figure 4-3). Not too shabby a performance for such little effort, but you're still only a new entry at number 40, and you have a way to go to hit the top of the charts. Don't worry; it won't be as hard as you might think.

Figure 4-3. Styling the basic page divs, html, and body to create the canvas on which to create the WorrySome.net design

Making columns

I think it was Steve Krug who, in his book *Don't Make Me Think*, suggested that Leonardo da Vinci invented tabs. I'm not sure who invented columns. Maybe it was Lord Nelson, but I digress.

The homepage of WorrySome.net divides its three main content areas into columns, each containing a different explanation of the service, topped by a different-colored rounded image. Your next task is to create the three columns using floats.

The following rule will apply to all three columns. It floats each to the left and gives them a minimum height, width, and margin; a small amount of bottom padding; and a background-image that will be positioned at the bottom of the division.

```
div[id="worriers"], div[id="worries"], div[id="worrydone"] {
float : left;
min-height : 42em;
width : 220px;
margin-right : 20px;
padding-bottom : 1em;
background : url(../images/worryone-b.png) no-repeat 0 100%; }
```

Now you can select the worrydone division that will appear on the far right and remove its right margin, to place it at the outermost edge of its container.

```
div[id="worrydone"] {
margin-right : 0; }
```

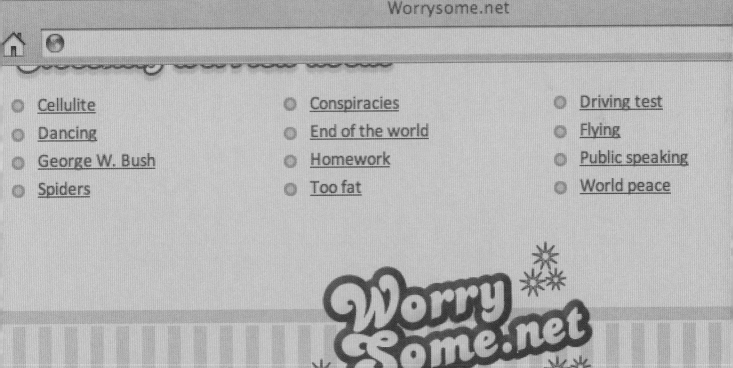

Worrysome.net

- Cellulite
- Dancing
- George W. Bush
- Spiders

- Conspiracies
- End of the world
- Homework
- Too fat

- Driving test
- Flying
- Public speaking
- World peace

© STUFF AND NONSENSE LTD.
A DEMONSTRATION SITE BY ANDY CLARKE

The final result of your column-making expedition is shown in Figure 4-4.

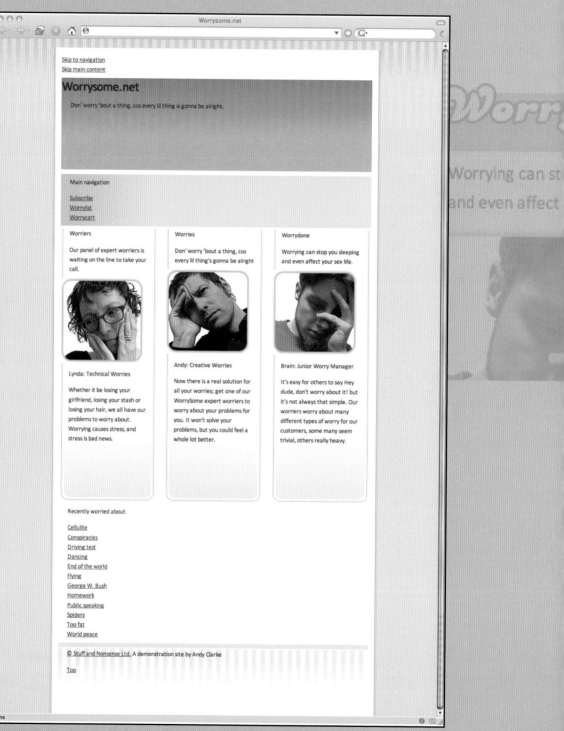

Figure 4-4. Floating the divisions to make three columns worthy of Trafalgar Square

Next, you will add the individual styling to each of the three columns, starting with the headings and working down. You will use the popular Phark negative text-indent technique (as in Chapter 2, "Taming a Wild CMS with CSS, Flash, and JavaScript"; see http://phark.net). This method applies a background-image to each heading and moves the text off the left side of the browser window by indenting it by a large amount of pixels.

The first rule applies to all three headings.

```
div[id="worriers"] h2,
div[id="worries"] h2,
div[id="worrydone"] h2 {
min-height : 50px;
margin : 0;
text-indent : -9999px; }
```

This should be followed by rules that will add a unique background-image to each of the headings, as shown in Figure 4-5.

```
div[id="worriers"] h2 {
background : url(../images/worryone-t.png) no-repeat 0 0; }

div[id="worries"] h2 {
background : url(../images/worrytwo-t.png) no-repeat 0 0; }

div[id="worrydone"] h2 {
background : url(../images/worrythree-t.png) no-repeat 0 0; }
```

Figure 4-5. Using image replacement to style the headings

Each of the paragraphs of introductory text will be styled with a different-colored background image and a larger type size, as shown in Figure 4-6. Once again, the first rule is common to all three paragraphs.

```
div[id="worriers"] h2 + p,
div[id="worries"] h2 + p,
div[id="worrydone"] h2 + p {
min-height : 4em;
margin : 0;
padding : 5px 20px 40px 20px;
font-size : 120%;
line-height : 1;
color : #fff; }

div[id="worriers"] h2 + p {
background : #cc6195 url(../images/worryone-m.png) no-repeat 0 100%; }

div[id="worries"] h2 + p {
background : #dd82ae url(../images/worrytwo-m.png) no-repeat 0 100%; }

div[id="worrydone"] h2 + p {
background : #f0a4c7 url(../images/worrythree-m.png) no-repeat 0➥
   100%; }
```

Figure 4-6. Distinctly different syling for the three introductory paragraphs

Wait, what is that + symbol doing in these selectors? This symbol is known as a sibling combinator and forms an adjacent sibling selector. This type of selector selects one element based on the element that precedes it; in this case, a p element that immediately follows an h2. Web designers and developers have largely avoided this type of selector because of a lack of support for it in Internet Explorer prior to version 7.

your columns are taking shape. Lastly, you can tidy up the space around the portraits and the names of the worriers, centering the text and reducing the type size, as shown in Figure 4-7.

```
div[id="worriers"] img,
div[id="worries"] img,
div[id="worrydone"] img {
margin-left : 15px; }

img + p {
padding-top : 0;
font-size : 92%;
text-align : center; }
```

Our panel of expert worriers is waiting on the line to take your call.

Don' worry 'bout a thing, cos every lil thing's gonna be alright

While floats and image replacement are still fresh in your mind, let's give the list of worry topics and its heading some stylish treatment. Once again, use the Phark method to replace the heading text.

```
div[id="content_sub"] h4 {
height : 35px;
width : 300px;
padding : 0;
background : url(../images/h4.png) no-repeat;
text-indent : -9999px; }
```

The list of topics that the site's team of experts can worry about on your behalf will be transformed into a three-column design. You can achieve this by floating each of the list items and by using a background-image to provide a decorative bullet to complete the effect.

```
div[id="content_sub"] ul {
float : left;
padding-bottom : 80px; }

div[id="content_sub"] li {
display : block;
float : left;
width : 190px;
padding-left : 20px;
background : url(../images/li.png) no-repeat 0 50%; }
```

The result is shown in Figure 4-8.

Figure 4-8. Floating list items: an effective way of creating column designs with simple lists

Styling the footer

Footers can sometimes be neglected parts of a design. Often, their minimal treatment can make your eyes simply wander off the bottom of the page.

The WorrySome.net footer features a smaller version of the main logo and one of those ever so useful top links, so that the site's visitors won't need to worry about getting out of breath by scrolling all that distance up to the top of the page.

First, start by styling the short paragraph of text inside the footer. Transform its content into uppercase letters, and reduce its type size and contrast to de-emphasize it.

```
div[id="siteinfo"] p {
padding-top : 40px;
font-size : 82%;
text-transform : uppercase;
color : #999;  }

div[id="siteinfo"] p a {
display : block; }
```

Wouldn't it be fantastic if you could be more specific about the anchors that you target, perhaps by styling external links differently from those links to other pages on your site? Now, in many circumstances you can. With the exception of Internet Explorer 7, all the major standards-aware browsers support selectors such as this:

```
div[id="siteinfo"] a[href^="http"] {
display : block; }
```

The selector with the ^ is a type of substring matching attribute selector, *a mouthful to say, but one of the most interesting selector types in CSS. From now on, I'll refer to it as a* substring selector, *to save ink and trees.*

There are different varieties of this type of selector, many of which could make accomplishing this design much easier. The example here targets all links contained within the siteinfo *division, where the* href *begins with* http. *You will see more substring selectors as you progress through this chapter.*

Now it is time to turn your attention to adding the small WorrySome.net logo. A peek into the markup for this page reveals that there is no in-line logo image present. There is just the link to the top of the page, inside an unordered list. Start by removing any margins from this list.

```
div[id="siteinfo"] ul {
margin : 0; }
```

Now you can use a combination of positioning and image replacement to transform this humble link into a shiny logo. First, set its proportions and position it absolutely: 240px from the left and 50px above its positioned ancestor.

```
div[id="siteinfo"] ul a {
position : absolute;
display : block;
top : -50px;
left: 240px;
height : 120px;
width : 230px; }
```

Apply a background image and slide its text off screen, and you are good to go.

```
div[id="siteinfo"] ul a {
background : url(../images/a-t.png) no-repeat;
text-indent : -9999px; }
```

Well, maybe you're not quite finished yet. Preview the result in your browser, and you will see that the logo has not fallen into the position just above the footer, as you might have expected. Instead, it has been positioned 50px above the body element, as this is its closest positioned ancestor, as seen at the top of Figure 4-9.

You can easily remedy this. Make the site information division itself a positioning context by applying position : relative; but no offsets.

```
div[id="siteinfo"] {
position : relative; }
```

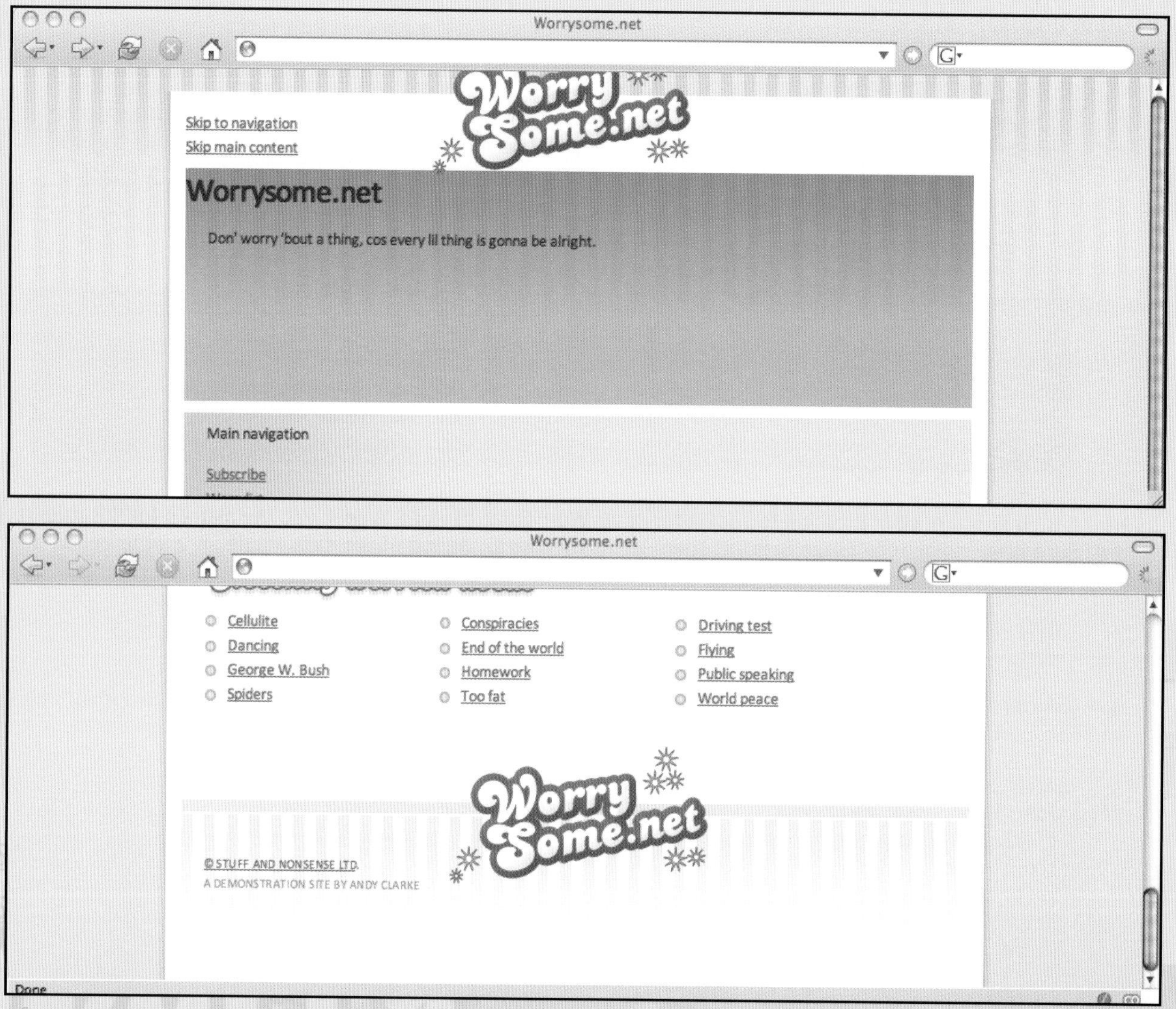

Figure 4-9. Correcting the position of the footer logo. Call me old-fashioned, but I think it looks better at the bottom.

Styling the main navigation

Understanding the power and flexibility of substring selectors is important, as you are about to put them to even greater use in styling the main navigation for this page. Once again, you will use a range of different techniques, including positioning and image replacement. The main navigation will look as shown in Figure 4-10.

Figure 4-10. The finished look of the main navigation

But how do you achieve this? Your first, simple task is to remove the heading from view, this time by positioning it off the top edge of the browser window.

```
div[id="nav_main"] h4 {
position : absolute; top : -9999px; }
```

With the heading now banished, except for people browsing the page without styles, you can set the proportions of the unordered navigation list and add a background image that contains all three of the button graphics.

```
div[id="nav_main"] ul {
width : 310px;
height : 38px;
margin-left : 200px;
padding : 0;
background : url(../images/li_nav_main.png) no-repeat; }
```

The navigation links in this list will be accomplished by positioning the three anchors. Next, establish this unordered list as a positioning context and set all list items to display as inline, rather than block-level elements.

```
div[id="nav_main"] ul {
position : relative; }

div[id="nav_main"] li {
display : inline; }
```

With position : relative; applied to the list to establish a positioning context, now set a general rule for all three anchors.

```
div[id="nav_main"] a {
position : absolute;
top : 0;
display : block;
height : 38px;
width : 104px;
text-indent : -9999px; }
```

This will be followed by a specific rule for the individual anchors, according to their `title` attributes. These `title` attributes add a visual tooltip for each link and also allow you to target their anchors.

```
a[title="Subscribe"] {
left : 0; }

a[title="Worrylist"] {
left : 104px; }

a[title="Worrycart"] {
left : 208px; }
```

> *You have already encountered the ^ symbol in previous selector examples and learned that this targets an attribute that begins with a particular value. In contrast, the $ symbol targets an attribute that ends with a particular value.*
>
> ```
> <a href="#" title="Worries in your Worrycart">Worrycart</a>
>
> a[title$="worrycart"] {
> left : 208px; }
> ```

Preview the finished result in your browser. To illustrate the anchors in position, I have added a red border to each of the anchors in Figure 4-11 (using the outline feature of the Web Developer Toolbar for Firefox).

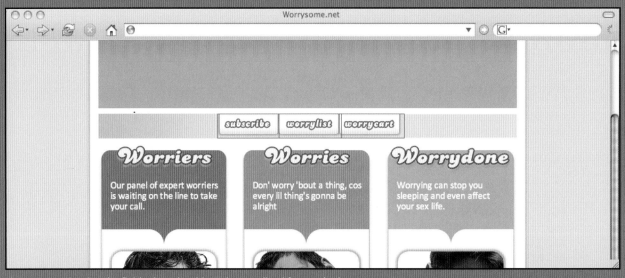

Figure 4-11. Showing the finished result, with anchors outlined for emphasis

Styling the branding

I hope that despite all the new techniques and selectors, your mind is free from worries. There is one more area of the page for you to work on, and that's my favorite part of any site design: the branding.

At this point, you have already worked with all of the techniques and types of selectors that will transform the branding area's top-level heading and the extract from Marley's "Three Little Birds" into attractive and meaningful visual elements.

As these elements will be positioned to create the visual effect of the logo "breaking out of the box," start by turning the branding division into a positioning context for these elements.

```
div[id="branding"] {
position : relative; }
```

Now you are all set to position the top-level heading and blockquote. Use the Phark image replacement method to replace the text with a background-image.

```
h1 {
z-index : 1;
position : absolute;
left : -50px;
top : -30px;
height : 178px;
width : 379px;
background : url(../images/h1.png) no-repeat;
text-indent : -9999px; }

div[id="branding"] blockquote {
z-index : 2;
position : absolute;
left : 225px;
top : 85px;
height : 103px;
width : 198px;
background : url(../images/blockquote.png) no-repeat;
text-indent : -9999px; }
```

> To ensure that the catchy blockquote *always stays in front of its neighboring heading, the* blockquote *has been given a higher* z-index. *For a more detailed explanation of the creative flexibilities of* z-index, *read my 24ways article at* http://24ways.org/advent/zs-not-dead-baby-zs-not-dead.

Recently worried about

- Cellulite
- Dancing
- George W. Bush
- Spiders
- Conspiracies
- End of the world
- Homework
- Too fat
- Driving test
- Flying
- Public speaking
- World peace

The result of this is that your catchy site slogan is transformed into something more attractive, as seen in Figure 4-12.

Figure 4-12. Positioning and z-index combine to create the branding of the site with few worries.

Smile for the accessibility guy

Your work is almost complete, but one important aspect of the WorrySome.net brand is still missing: the yellow smiley face. If you flick backwards a few pages to look at the markup for this page, you will see that every element and attribute has been used; nothing has gone to waste. Nothing that is, except the unordered list that holds the handy skip links.

Don't worry; this element will soon become useful to you. Many web designers and developers choose to hide these embedded accessibility helpers, often pushing them off-screen and out of view. You are going to use this element to bring the branding area to life, by attaching the smiley face background-image.

```
ul[id="nav_access"] {
position : absolute;
top : -33px;
right : -50px;
height : 291px;
width : 340px;
margin : 0;
padding : 0;
background : url(../images/a-access.png) no-repeat;
text-indent : -9999px; }
```

Preview the branding area in all its smiley glory in your browser, and you will see that the face is not smiling out at you. There is one important line of CSS missing, along with an important lesson to learn. Unless you specify a z-index value for any positioned element, those that follow it in the order of the document will always sit on top. The closer to the closing </body> tag they are, the higher in the stacking order they will be.

The accessibility list comes at the very start of the document, and so it sits behind all other positioned elements in the stacking order. You can rectify this and restore the smiley face to happiness by giving it an explicit z-index that will ensure that it takes its rightful place in the design, as shown in Figure 4-13.

```
ul[id="nav_access"] {
z-index   : 2; }
```

Figure 4-13. Smile, hidden tools to help visitors with special needs can also be used as hooks for visual design elements.

We'll give you another look at the final design (Figure 4-1), in all its glory:

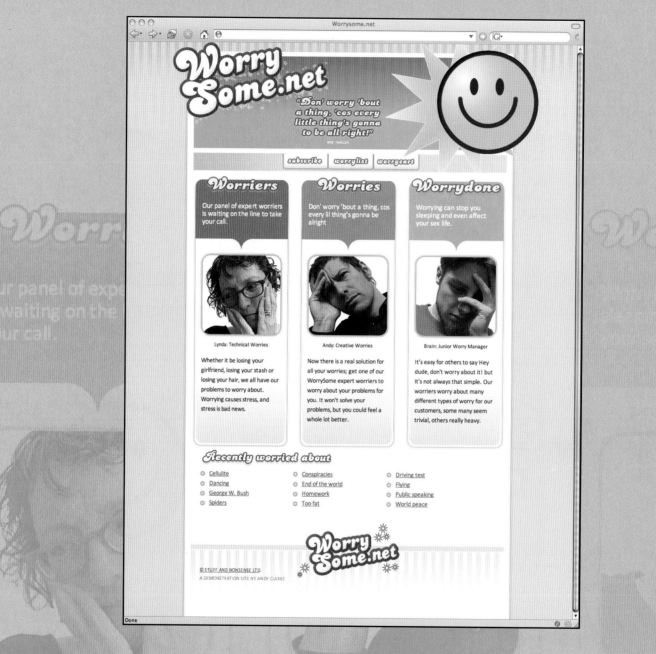

Dealing with legacy browsers

Whereas many books have been written about CSS, few of them cover the practical use of what have been viewed as advanced selectors. One reason is that the Web's most used browser, Internet Explorer for Windows, has not supported these selectors. Web designers and developers have avoided using these selectors, or they have concentrated instead on limiting their designs so that the pages will appear the same across browsers of different ages or capabilities.

If design for the Web is to progress, new methods must be found. Not all of the techniques that you have used in this chapter will work or look the same across all browsers. Don't worry; this is intentional.

In many working environments, web designers and developers must deal with the capabilities of browsers that are still in everyday use but are also well beyond their best-used-before date. Unfortunately, this ragtag band of older browsers includes Internet Explorer 6 for Windows. Fortunately, there is a solution—one that makes it possible for you to fully adopt the techniques and selectors that you have been working with while developing WorrySome.net.

Dean Edwards's IE7 scripts (`http://dean.edwards.name/IE7/`) use JavaScript to parse style sheets into a form that can be understood by Internet Explorer 6 and older versions. They enable you to use CSS2 and even some CSS3 selectors in your style sheets and transform legacy versions of Internet Explorer into a worry-free new browser that is capable of understanding the following:

- Child selectors
- Adjacent sibling selectors
- Attribute value selectors
- `:first-child`, `:last-child`, `:only-child`, and `:nth-child` structural pseudo-classes
- `:before` and `:after` generated content

> Dean Edwards's IE7 scripts may not be appropriate for use in every situation. This is not an enterprise-level solution or suitable for high-traffic sites.

As more people upgrade their browser to Internet Explorer 7, with its increased support for CSS2.1, the number of Internet Explorer 6 users will reduce. This makes Edwards's solution a useful choice for designers and developers of sites with low to medium traffic, whose aim is to use so-called advanced techniques safely across a wider range of browsers.

Microsoft has suggested that designers and developers stop using CSS hacks and switch instead to using Microsoft's proprietary conditional comments. These comments are supported only by Internet Explorer for Windows, and they make it simple to target versions of Internet Explorer by placing comments in the <head> portion of a document.

The most common use for conditional comments is to serve a specific style sheet to work around bugs and rendering errors in legacy versions of Internet Explorer. They can just as easily be used to serve Dean Edwards's IE7 scripts to browsers that need them. For example, this comment will serve the script only to versions of Internet Explorer before version 7.

```
<!--[if lte IE 7]>
<script src="js/ie7-standard-p.js" type="text/javascript"></script>
<![endif]-->
</head>
```

No worries!

In this chapter, you have learned that there is nothing to worry about when using what has been previously thought of as advanced CSS to create a design layout that breaks out of the box. Modern, CSS2.1 selectors, floats, and positioning are the perfect tools for creating engaging website designs with the most minimal, nonpresentational markup.

You have seen how these tools and techniques can be put into action in CSS-savvy web browsers and how to use clever scripting to plug the holes in older, sadder browsers. I look forward to seeing what you will make with the lessons that you have learned.

My suit is pressed, my shoes are shined, and the Mods are marching on Brighton. It's time for you to meet the "ace faces" in the remaining chapters.

5

Creative Use of PNG Transparency in Web Design

jeff
croft

www2.jeffcroft.com

Jeff Croft is a web and graphic designer focused on standards-based development who lives and works in Lawrence, Kansas. As the senior designer at World Online, Jeff works on such award-winning news sites as www.lawrence.com and www.ljworld.com. Jeff also runs a popular blog and personal site at www.jeffcroft.com, where he writes about many topics, including modern web and graphic design.

Jeff has been making the Web about as long as there has been a Web to be made. He created his first web pages in 1994 using SimpleText and Netscape Navigator 1.1N on a Macintosh Performa 600. He started working on the Web full time in 1996 and has been at it ever since.

Although Jeff enjoys technology and gadgets, what truly inspires him about the Web is its ability to communicate and connect people. Jeff is a constant consumer of design, finding inspiration nearly everywhere.

When he's not hunched over a computer, Jeff enjoys photography, music, film, television, and a good night out on the town.

PNG, GIF, and JPEG

The PNG image has been widely overlooked by the web design community—and mostly for good reason. Until recently, it hasn't been possible to take full advantage of the format and have it work reliably in all browsers. But, with proper PNG support in Internet Explorer 7, and some handy JavaScript and CSS tricks to account for older browsers, we can use PNG images to greatly enhance our design vocabulary.

What is PNG?

PNG, usually pronounced "ping," stands for Portable Network Graphics. It is a losslessly compressed bitmap image format. In plain English, it's a way of saving graphic images that reduces file size without reducing image quality. It was originally created as a replacement for the ubiquitous GIF format, which used to require a patent license for producers of imaging software to use it legally (the GIF/LZW patent has since expired, so this is no longer a factor). PNG is also an International Standard (ISO/IEC 15948:2003) and an official W3C recommendation (www.w3.org/TR/PNG/).

Besides being a freely available format, PNG offers several practical advantages over GIF for the web designer:

- **Greater compression:** For most images, PNG achieves a smaller file size than GIF.

- **Greater color depths:** PNG offers truecolor up to 48 bits, whereas GIF allows only 256-color palettes.

- **Alpha-channel transparency:** Whereas GIF offers only binary transparency, PNG allows for virtually unlimited transparency effects by enabling an alpha channel for transparency.

It's worth mentioning that PNG does not allow for animation, as GIF does. There is a related standard called Multiple-image Network Graphics (MNG, www.libpng.org/pub/mng/) that does allow both, but it is not widely supported by web browsers or imaging software.

So why is GIF still so popular?

You're probably wondering why PNG isn't the most commonly used image format on the Web, if it's as good as advertised. The answer, for the most part, lies in misconceptions about the format and the browser support for it.

Because Internet Explorer 6 and lower do not support the full spectrum of PNG's features (including alpha-channel transparency), people seem to believe (albeit erroneously) that Internet Explorer doesn't support PNGs at all, or at least doesn't support transparency. In reality, Internet Explorer 5 and 6 both support enough of the PNG spec to make PNG images functionally equivalent to (or better than) nonanimated GIF images. All other notable browsers—including Firefox, Netscape 6 and higher, Mozilla, Opera 6 and higher, Safari, and Camino—offer full support for PNG transparency.

Besides the misconceptions about browser support, GIF's built-in support for animation was (and continues to be) a key reason for its success. In recent years, however, this use of GIF has become less popular as other technologies (notably Flash) have become more common for animation.

Transparency is a key feature of both GIF and PNG that is often the reason either one gets chosen as a web designer's format of choice for a particular image element. Although PNG offers far more extensive support for transparency, web designers are often required to create GIF versions of the images as well to accommodate older browsers. Using CSS, it's possible (and somewhat commonplace) to send GIF images to older browsers and higher-quality PNGs to browsers that understand them. But the creation of two images is extra work for the web designer, and this has often resulted in people settling on the lowest common denominator, which continues to be GIF images.

In the end, there are several reasons why GIF is still so popular, but most of them are based on misconceptions or use case scenarios that are becoming less and less common. Armed with some new knowledge of how PNG works and how it can be used reliably across browsers, you should be able to take advantage of all that the format offers without having to rely on GIF.

What about JPEG?

JPEG, the Web's other ubiquitous file format, is almost always a better choice than either PNG or GIF for photographic (or photo-like) images. PNG was not intended to compete with JPEG. JPEG's lossy compression (which results in some reduction in quality each time the image is saved) will produce considerably smaller files than PNG when dealing with photos. PNG, on the other hand, will produce smaller files when the images within are text, line art, logos, flat colors, and so on.

Some great uses for the humble PNG

Now let's look at some great uses for the PNG in web design. I've included all the files for each example in a separate folder inside the code download for this chapter, available at www.friendsofed.com.

The gradient

In the past few years, the gradient—a smooth transition between two or more colors—has become the web designer's best friend. Especially popular is the subtle, barely noticeable gradient fill, which adds a feeling of depth and texture without being overt and cheesy.

GIF is sometimes a good choice for gradients. If the gradient is a simple two-color fade, GIF usually works just fine. However, the GIF 256-color limit often causes noticeable and unsightly banding across more complex gradient transitions. JPEG, on the other hand, can render quite pleasing gradients, but often at the cost of a higher-than-desired file size. And while JPEG gradients are usually "good enough," keep in mind that JPEG does use lossy compression, which means the reproduced image is never as high fidelity as the original, uncompressed image.

Consider the typical background gradient style often used for buttons, boxes, and just about anything else. It may look something like Figure 5-1. Clockwise from the top left, we have the original (uncompressed) image, a GIF version, a PNG version, and a JPEG version. You can see that PNG results in the smallest file size (515 bytes). It's about four times smaller than the GIF image. The JPEG is slightly larger than the PNG at 637 bytes, and it is also of lower quality due to the lossy compression (admittedly, the ability for the human eye to detect the difference in quality in this simple example is questionable at best).

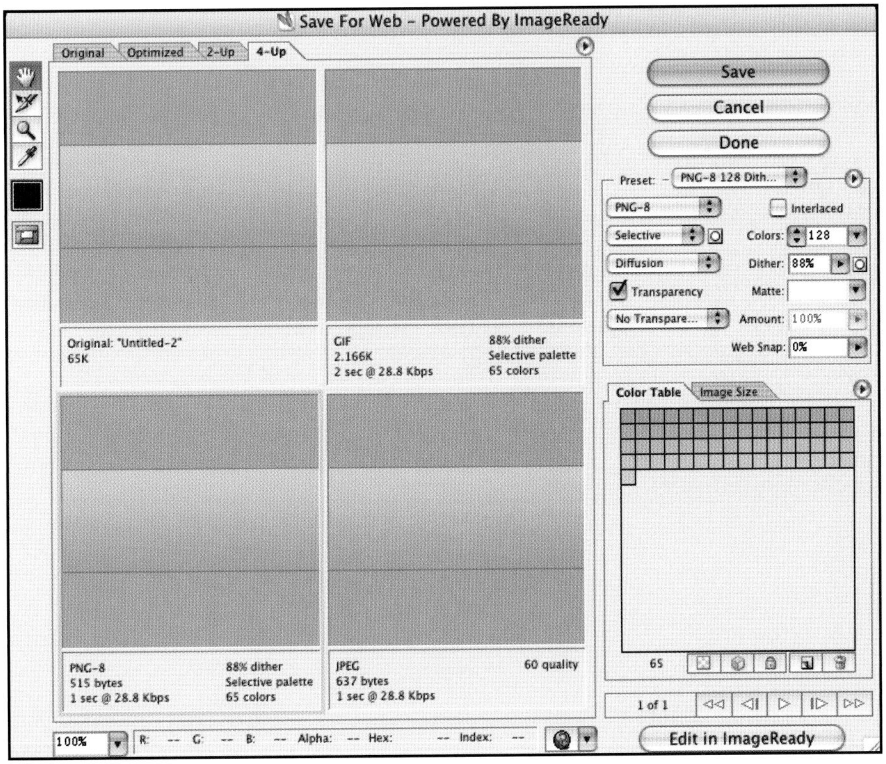

Figure 5-1. Photoshop's Save For Web panel displaying file size differences for the same image in various formats

The image that needs to work on any background

Sometimes it's necessary to create an image that works equally well on a variety of backgrounds. Some common examples are logos and icons. These situations have traditionally been the domain of the GIF file, but there are several reasons why PNG may be a better choice. PNG is almost always the winner in a file-size shootout on logos and other simple artwork. In addition, PNG's native transparency makes it simple to create a single file that works on top of any background you can throw under it. PNG does offer binary transparency—the same as GIF—but also provides the much more exciting alpha-channel variety, in which pixels can be *partially* transparent, rather than simply on or off. Using the latter does increase the file size—sometimes beyond that of a (binary) transparent GIF—but also allows for antialiasing the edges of your artwork, which makes for a much more elegant placement atop your background.

For the website of KTKA Channel 49 News in Topeka, Kansas (www.49abcnews.com), World Online staff crafted beautiful weather iconography to indicate the current conditions in the site's header. But, thanks to a clever bit of programming that causes the header to change from a daytime color scheme to a nighttime version precisely at sunset, the weather images needed to work equally well on different backgrounds. Take a look at Figures 5-2 and 5-3.

Figure 5-2. www.49abcnews.com header, daytime

Figure 5-3. www.49abcnews.com header, nighttime

By using PNG, I was able to do the designer's work justice whether it appeared on the day or night background. And, should we choose to change the backgrounds at some point, I won't have to remake any weather icons, because the alpha-transparent PNG files will look great on anything.

If I had chosen to use GIF instead, I would have been limited to GIF's binary transparency. The result would have looked like Figure 5-4. I think we can all agree that's not good enough.

Figure 5-4. www.49abcnews.com header, nightime, with GIF image instead of PNG

The translucent HTML overlay

A very common graphic design technique is to overlay a photo or other image with a partially transparent region, usually containing text. This allows for readable text without completely obscuring the view of the image below. Designer Wilson Miner (www.wilsonminer.com) uses this to great effect on the Gingeroot jewelry site (www.simplygingeroot.com), as you can see Figure 5-5.

Figure 5-5. www.simplygingeroot.com, designed by the talented Wilson Miner (www.wilsonminer.com)

Wilson includes his transparent region and text in the JPEG image. He created them beforehand in Photoshop. This works fine, and it is totally appropriate for the site's needs. But what if the text in the translucent area needed to change very frequently—perhaps even be different for every visitor? In this case, it wouldn't be practical to put the text in the image. The text would need to be crafted in HTML and CSS. Using PNG's transparency alpha channel, we can emulate Wilson's style without putting the text in the image itself.

I'll start with a photograph of my daughter, Haley Madysan, and put it into a simple XHTML page with some basic CSS styling (this is haley_example/index.html in the code download). Note that I'm using an embedded CSS style sheet for demonstration purposes only. In real-world situations, using a linked external style sheet typically provides more flexibility, less code repetition, and more practical file management.

```
<!DOCTYPE html PUBLIC "-//W3C//DTD XHTML 1.0 Strict//EN"➡
  "http://www.w3.org/TR/xhtml1/DTD/xhtml1-strict.dtd">
<html xmlns="http://www.w3.org/1999/xhtml" xml:lang="en" lang="en">
<head>
  <meta http-equiv="Content-Type" content="text/html; charset=utf-8"/>
  <title>Haley's web site</title>
  <style>
    body {
      font-family: "Lucida Grande", Helvetica, Arial, sans-serif;
      background-color: #304251;
      color: #304251;
      margin: 20px auto;
      width: 720px;
    }
    #feature {
      position: relative;
      width: 720px;
      height: 439px;
    }
    #feature-content {
      position: absolute;
      bottom: 0;
      left: 0;
      height: 125px;
      width: 720px;
      background-color: #dfdfdf;
    }
    #feature-content h1 {
      margin: 0;
      padding: 0;
      line-height: 125px;
      padding: 0 30px;
      font-weight: normal;
      font-size: 2.3em;
    }
    #feature-content a {
      float: right;
      font-size: .6em;
      color: #fff;
      text-decoration: none;
      text-transform: uppercase;
```

```
      }
    </style>
  </head>
  <body>
    <div id="feature">
      <img src="haley.jpg" alt="Haley Madysan Croft" />
      <div id="feature-content">
        <h1>Sweet. Smart. Beautiful. <a href="/haley" ➥
title="Haley Madysan Croft">Learn more &raquo;</a></h1>
      </div>
    </div>
  </body>
</html>
```

With that, I've more or less duplicated what you saw in Wilson's Gingeroot site, except without any transparency (yet), as shown in Figure 5-6.

Figure 5-6. Emulating the www.simplygingeroot.com style with HTML and CSS, but no transparency (yet)

Now I'll create a 1-by-1-pixel image in Photoshop. I fill the image with a shade of light blue and set the layer to 70% opacity. Finally, I save the image using Photoshop's PNG-24 setting, enabling transparency. Then I simply use this image as the background for the overlay, instead of the solid gray you see in Figure 5-6.

```
#feature-content {
    position: absolute;
    bottom: 0;
    left: 0;
    height: 125px;
    width: 720px;
    background-image: url('transparent.png');
}
```

The result is quite similar to the original, but with the HTML and CSS text, it becomes more flexible, as shown in Figure 5-7.

Figure 5-7. Adding transparency via the PNG image format nearly duplicates the www.simplygingeroot.com style.

Wilson Miner actually used the same concept in a different area of the www.simplygingeroot.com site. On pages that show available products, a transparent PNG image is used to display an On Sale flag in the upper-left corner of sale item product photos, as shown in Figure 5-8. By creating the On Sale image once, and saving it with a transparent background as a PNG image, Wilson avoided the need to create separate versions of every product image with the flag embedded.

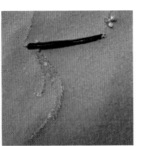

Figure 5-8. www.simplygingeroot.com's Necklaces section uses a PNG image with a transparent background overlaid on top of the product image to display an On Sale flag in the upper-left corner.

I also used this technique on Explore Steamboat (www.exploresteamboat.com), a site dedicated to events, entertainment, and activities in Steamboat Springs, Colorado, as shown in Figure 5-9.

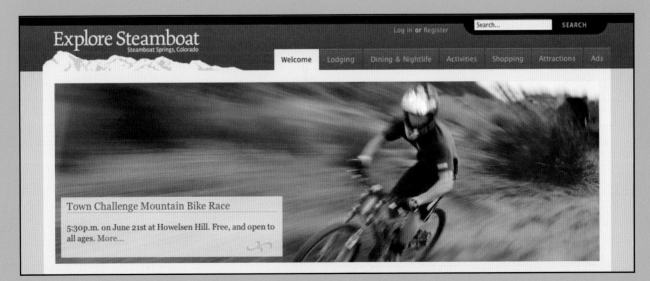

Figure 5-9. www.exploresteamboat.com has a translucent box sitting atop an image by way of transparent PNG.

In another creative example, designer Bryan Veloso (www.avalonstar.com) used a transparent PNG image anchored to the bottom of the page to create a "fade-in" effect, in which the text seems to appear out of thin air as you scroll down the page. The effect, found at www.revyver.com (see Figures 5-10 and 5-11) is better seen than described, so be sure to check it out for yourself. Additionally, the tree graphic sits in front of the text content of the page, producing an unexpected visual. It has quite a "wow" factor when you first see it.

Figure 5-10. At www.revyver.com, designer Bryan Veloso has used a transparent PNG to create a "fade-in" effect as you scroll down the page, and to place his artwork in front of the text content of the page.

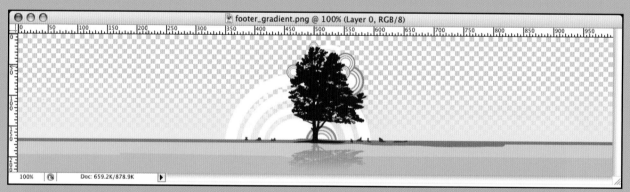

Figure 5-11. By viewing Bryan's footer PNG image in Photoshop, we get an idea of how the transparent alpha channel was constructed to achieve the designed effect.

The watermark

Another common graphic design technique is the subtle watermark overlaid on top of an image. This may be done purely for visual style, but it may also be done as a way of indicating the copyright holder or origin of the image.

On my personal website (www.jeffcroft.com, see Figure 5-12), I display a large gallery of photos I've taken (currently over 2000 photos). These photos are actually uploaded to Flickr (www.flickr.com), the popular online photo sharing site, and then displayed locally on my site by way of Flickr's open API.

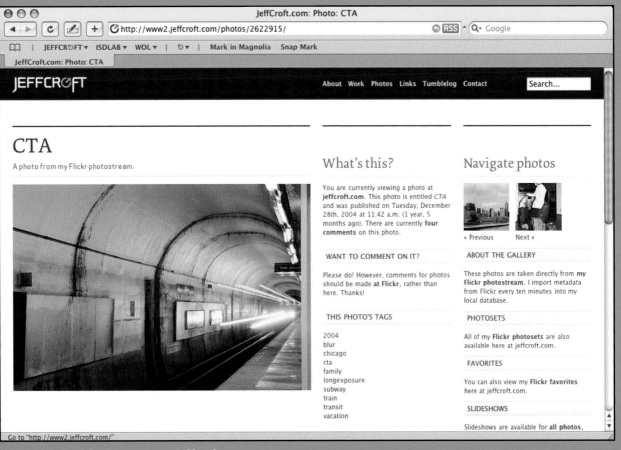

Figure 5-12. Photo detail page on www.jeffcroft.com

What if I wanted to place my personal logo on all of my photographs? Yes, it's possible to open each image in Photoshop, apply the logo, and resave the image. However, this becomes terribly impractical when dealing with thousands of images that are frequently updated—and sometimes updated when I'm nowhere near a computer (for example, when I send photos to Flickr via my cell phone). Wouldn't it be nice if the logo were added automatically? PNG can help do just that.

The HTML used to display the photo in the page looks like this:

```
<a class="photo-container" href="http://www.flickr.com/photos/jcroft/2622915/">
  <img class="full-size-photo" src=http://static.flickr.com/2/2622915_8b78c1207d.jpg➡
alt="CTA, a photo by Jeff Croft" />
</a>
```

I created an 80-by-80-pixel version of my logo in white and then set the opacity to 15% in Photoshop. Saved using Photoshop's standard PNG-24 optimization setting, the 15% translucency is preserved in the resulting PNG image. Then I simply added that image into my HTML as well:

```
<a class="photo-container" href="http://www.flickr.com/photos/jcroft/2622915/">
  <img class="full-size-photo" src="http://static.flickr.com/2/2622915_8b78c1207d.jpg"➥
alt="CTA, a photo by Jeff Croft " />
  <img class="watermark" src="http://media.jeffcroft.com/img/core/jeffcroft_logo_watermark.png"➥
alt="Watermark" />
</a>
```

A bit of CSS is then used to position it in the right spot:

```
a.photo-container {
  position: relative;
  display: block;
}

img.watermark {
  position: absolute;
  top: 2em;
  left: 1em;
}
```

The result is a watermark that appears to be embedded in the photo itself, but is actually a separate PNG image sitting on top of it, as shown in Figure 5-13. By putting this into my templates for my content management system, I get the watermark on every image without having to do it all 2000 plus times.

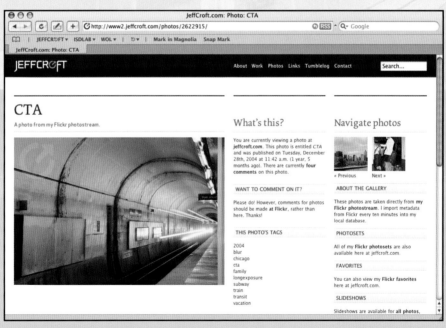

Figure 5-13. Subtle www.jeffcroft.com logo mark appears via transparent PNG in the upper-left corner of the photo.

If you wanted to be extra-clever, you could even use DOM scripting to insert the additional (X)HTML markup for the watermark on the fly.

The mask

Another handy use for the PNG image and its alpha-channel transparency is to mask an image below it. Technically, this is very similar to what you just saw with the watermark, but it achieves a different visual effect.

This time, I'll make a larger version of my logo in Photoshop. Instead of making the logo white, I'll make it transparent and the rest of the image white, because white is the background color of the page, as shown in Figure 5-14.

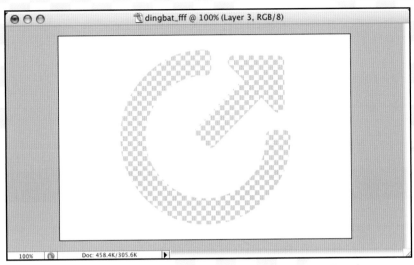

Figure 5-14. Creating an image in Photoshop for use as a transparent PNG mask

As I said, the technical aspects of this are nearly identical to the watermark in the preceding section, starting with the HTML:

```
<a class="photo-container" href="http://www.flickr.com/photos/jcroft/2622915/">
  <img class="full-size-photo" src="http://static.flickr.com/2/2622915_8b78c1207d.jpg"➥
    alt="CTA, a photo by Jeff Croft" />
  <img class="mask" src="http://media.jeffcroft.com/img/core/jeffcroft_logo_mask.png"➥
    alt="Mask" />
</a>
```

And then the CSS:

```css
a.photo-container {
  position: relative;
  display: block;
}

img.mask {
  position: absolute;
  top: 0;
  left: 0;
}
```

See Figure 5-15 for the finished result.

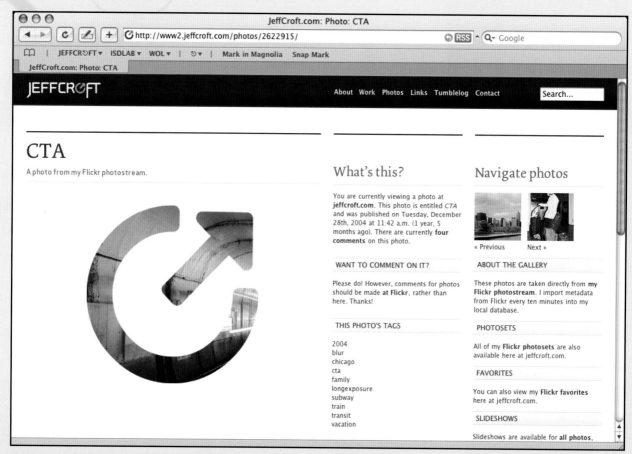

Figure 5-15. The PNG mask is layed on top of the photo to created a "punched-out" effect.

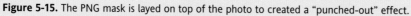

The color-changing icon

By using the mask concept you saw in the previous example, some people have created icons that can change color, using only CSS. The idea is both simple and ingenious: place a transparent image with the icon symbol "punched-out" over a square, rectangle, or other shape with a flat-color CSS background, and you've got yourself an icon. By simply changing the CSS color of the background, you give the impression of the icon changing color.

Perhaps we need a set of icons indicating common sports, as shown in Figure 5-16.

Figure 5-16. Some common sports iconography

I've created white images with a transparent punch-out in the shape of the icon symbol, just as I did with the logo in the mask example in the previous section, as shown in Figure 5-17.

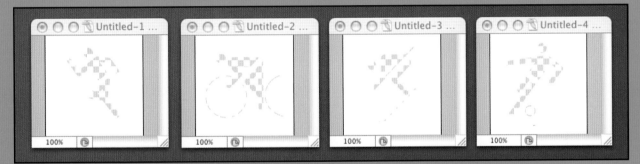

Figure 5-17. Creating "knocked-out" PNG masks for each icon

After scaling the images down to the appropriate size (I chose 48 by 48 pixels), I saved them using Photoshop's PNG-24 default with transparency enabled. Then I created a simple XHTML file that references each image (sports_icons_example/index.html in the code sample download package):

```
<!DOCTYPE html PUBLIC "-//W3C//DTD XHTML 1.0 Strict//EN"➥
  "http://www.w3.org/TR/xhtml1/DTD/xhtml1-strict.dtd">

<html xmlns="http://www.w3.org/1999/xhtml" xml:lang="en" lang="en">
<head>
  <meta http-equiv="Content-Type" content="text/html; charset=utf-8"/>
  <title>OMG Sports Icons!</title>
  <style>
    img {
      background-color: #cc0000;
    }
  </style>
</head>
```

```
<body>
  <img src="running.png" alt="Running" />
  <img src="biking.png" alt="Biking" />
  <img src="skiing.png" alt="Skiing" />
  <img src="soccer.png" alt="Soccer" />
</body>
</html>
```

I've specified #cc0000 (a strong red) as the background color for images in this file. The result is the red shining through the punched-out shapes, as shown in Figure 5-18. Note the beautifully smooth edges thanks to the antialiasing allowed by PNG's support for partially transparent pixels.

Figure 5-18. Transparent PNG images in place as web icons. Notice the CSS background color (red) showing through the image.

As you can see in Figure 5-19, I can change the color of the icon images simply by changing the color value in my CSS:

```
img {
  background-color: #000066;
}
```

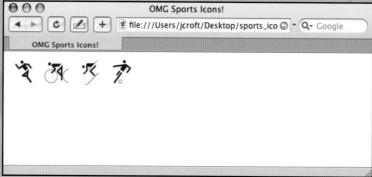

Figure 5-19. Changing the background color in CSS changes the apparent color of the icon.

This kind of simple color changing can be very handy when you need to rework the design of your site. Instead of remaking all of your icon images, you simply change the color one time in CSS. It's also a great way to achieve a simple mouseover effect for linked images. For example, you could use the red for the standard color and the blue for the hover style (sports_icons_example/index_links.html in the code sample download package):

```
<!DOCTYPE html PUBLIC "-//W3C//DTD XHTML 1.0 Strict//EN"➡
  "http://www.w3.org/TR/xhtml1/DTD/xhtml1-strict.dtd">

<html xmlns="http://www.w3.org/1999/xhtml" xml:lang="en" lang="en">
<head>
  <meta http-equiv="Content-Type" content="text/html; charset=utf-8"/>
  <title>OMG Sports Icons!</title>
  <style>
    a:link img,
    a:visited img,
    a:active img {
      background-color: #cc0000;
    }
    a:hover img {
      background-color: #000066;
    }
  </style>
</head>

<body>
  <a href="/running/"><img src="running.png" alt="Running" /></a>
  <a href="/biking/"><img src="biking.png" alt="Biking" /></a>
  <a href="/skiing/"><img src="skiing.png" alt="Skiing" /></a>
  <a href="/soccer/"><img src="soccer.png" alt="Soccer" /></a>
</body>
</html>
```

You can use additional CSS to do even more creative things with your masked icons, such as adding a border (see Figure 5-20):

```
img {
  background-color: #000066;
  padding: 2px;
}
```

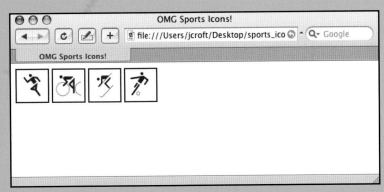

Figure 5-20. Using CSS to further enhance the appearance of the icons by adding a border

Dan Cederholm (www.simplebits.com) wrote about a very similar technique in his blog way back in 2003 (www.simplebits.com/notebook/2003/07/24/magic_icons_for_lazy_people_like_me.html), and PJ Onori (www.somerandomdude.net) gives away a great set of icons (called Sanscons) based on it at his website (www.somerandomdude.net/srd-projects/sanscons/).

However, I've reversed their concept by using a white image with a punched-out symbol. They used a white symbol on a transparent background, which can be very effective as well. In this case, your CSS background color shines through as the square or rectangle surrounding the symbol, rather than as the symbol itself.

Both Dan and PJ used transparent GIFs instead of PNGs. This is completely appropriate for their needs, as the style of the icons they created are bitmap, pixely looking little guys. By using PNGs, you can apply the same technique, but take advantage of antialiased edges and partial transparency for use in more detailed icons.

OK, but what browsers does it work in?

I know what you're thinking: all of this PNG transparency business seems really nice, but is it practical?

The good news is that almost all modern browsers fully support PNG images, including the alpha-channel transparency I've taken great advantage of in the examples. Safari (all versions), Firefox (all versions), Opera (version 6 and higher), Netscape (version 6 and higher), and Mozilla (all versions) will happily do everything I've asked it to. The bad news is that the one browser I haven't mentioned is the one your users are most likely to have: Internet Explorer.

Internet Explorer 6 and lower do not support the alpha-channel transparency built into the PNG format. Since this has been the browser of choice (or non-choice) for the vast majority of web surfers for several years now, this glaring hole has kept many web designers away from PNG. But, with the release of Internet Explorer 7, we finally have full support of PNG alpha transparency in all of the major browsers. What's more, there are ways to make alpha-transparent PNGs work in Internet Explorer 6 and lower. So, if you want to use these effects, nothing is stopping you. Internet Explorer 6 and its older siblings make it a little more work than it should be, but it's certainly possible.

The Internet Explorer workaround: AlphaImageLoader

Internet Explorer includes several proprietary filters. They're used in CSS, but they're not part of any official CSS specification. In other words, they're *not* a web standard. It's unfortunate that Internet Explorer 6 and lower do not fully support the PNG image format (which is recommended by the W3C), but Microsoft does include a filter that overcomes this weakness: AlphaImageLoader.

According to Microsoft's official web page on the topic (http://msdn.microsoft.com/workshop/author/filter/reference/filters/alphaimageloader.asp), AlphaImageLoader "displays an image within the boundaries of the object and between the object background and content." In other words, AlphaImageLoader does load a PNG image with its full transparency in tact, but it loads it as a layer of its own, underneath the content of the object to which it is applied. PNG images loaded this way act similarly to background images, rather than foreground images (although they actually sit on top of the object's background).

In short, you can simply apply the AlphaImageLoader CSS to an `img` element and have it produce the desired results. Doing so will load the image, transparency intact, but will also load the image again—as the foreground content of the object—with no transparency (thus obscuring your transparent version).

You can't use a transparent PNG as a CSS background image for an (X)HTML element (say, a <div>) and expect the AlphaImageLoader filter to make it work as expected in Internet Explorer. Remember that AlphaImageLoader inserts your image in between the background and foreground of the object. So, while it will load your image in all its transparent glory, it will still load it as the CSS background image as well, and without your beautiful translucent pixels.

A real-world use of AlphaImageLoader

Let's go back to one of the earlier examples and try to make Internet Explorer load the image properly. Remember Channel 49, the TV station in Topeka? Sure you do. Figure 5-21 shows how the site looks in Internet Explorer 6.

Figure 5-21. www.49abcnews.com header, displayed in Internet Explorer 6 for Windows, with PNG transparency intact

The HTML for the weather part of the header looks as you might expect:

```
<div id="weather">
  <a href="/weather/"><img id="weatherImage"➥
src="http://media.49abcnews.com/img/weather/overcast-night.png"➥
alt="Overcast" /></a>
  <p><a href="/weather/">Currently in Topeka, KS:<br />➥
<strong>82&deg; Overcast</strong><br /><span>Get the forecast➥
and more...</span></a></p>
</div>
```

You can see the image in question is a PNG, and yet Internet Explorer loads it flawlessly. The secret ingredient here is JavaScript. I've actually used a bit of DOM scripting to remove the img element on the fly and replace it with a div element that—you guessed it—has the AlphaImageLoader CSS applied to it. The JavaScript is referenced within *conditional comments*, another handy but completely nonstandard idiom Microsoft has built into Internet Explorer. Conditional comments let you target code at particular versions of Internet Explorer. The code is then ignored by all other browsers, so it doesn't affect them. In the <head> element of www.49abcnews.com, you'll find:

```
<!--[if lte IE 6]>
  <script src="http://media.49abcnews.com/js/fixWeatherPng.js" type="text/javascript"></script>
<![endif]-->
```

Thanks to the first line, if lte IE6, this script element will be included in the rendered document only if it is being displayed by a version of Internet Explorer less than or equal to (that's what lte stands for) 6. All other browsers, including the forthcoming Internet Explorer 7, will ignore it completely.

So what's in the JavaScript file fixWeatherPng.js, anyway? Take a look:

```
window.attachEvent("onload", fixWeatherPng);

function fixWeatherPng() {
    var img = document.getElementById("weatherImage");
    var src = img.src;
    img.style.visibility = "hidden";
```

```
        var div = document.createElement("DIV");
        div.style.filter = "progid:DXImageTransform.Microsoft.➥
    AlphaImageLoader(src='" + src + "', sizing='scale')";

        // Some 49abcnews.com-specific CSS styling omitted for brevity.

        img.replaceNode(div);
    }
```

Let's analyze what this script is doing step by step. First, we tell the browser that we want to run the `fixWeatherPng` function when the page loads. The rest of the script is the function itself.

To start off with, we find the image we're dealing with by its `id` attribute and store it in a variable called `img`. We save the `src` attribute (the URL to the image file) in a variable called `src`. Then we hide the `img` element by setting its `visibility` CSS property to `hidden`.

Next, we create a new `div` element and store it in a variable we'll call `div`. We'll apply the AlphaImageLoader filter to it, using the URL from the `src` variable we saved before.

Finally, we replace the original `img` element (which is hidden) with the newly created `div` element, which has the AlphaImage-Loader goodness attached.

Using DOM scripting to insert your AlphaImageLoader-filtered bits on the fly has the side benefit of keeping the unpretty-but-necessary invalid CSS out of your CSS files. Likewise, it keeps the nonsemantic `div` elements out of your (X)HTML markup. And since all of this is referenced only within conditional comments, there's no chance of other browsers choking on Microsoft's proprietary code.

If you must do something invalid, at least you can abstract it and keep it quarantined from everything that doesn't need it.

Conclusion

PNG, as an image file format, offers many technical advantages over the much more widely used GIF. In fact, the advantages are so great that PNG should have taken over as the file format of choice for just about all nonphotographic images long ago. But Internet Explorer's lack of proper support for some of PNG's more exciting features, such as alpha-channel transparency, has resulted in many web developers shying away from it. But there are two very good reasons why you shouldn't be scared of PNG.

First, even Internet Explorer 6 and earlier versions' less-than-perfect support for PNG still offers everything you can get with GIF (save for animation, of course). And PNG almost always results in smaller files for faster transfer and less bandwidth usage.

Second, Internet Explorer 7 offers full support for PNG's alpha-channel transparency. The effects that can be achieved with the complete gamut of opacity options are virtually endless. I suspect designers who find interesting ways to use transparent PNGs, such as those outlined in this chapter, will open the doors to a whole new level of style not widely seen online to date. I've given you a handful of ideas on how you can get creative with PNGs and transparency, but don't stop there. Find your own, as well!

Effective Print Techniques Applied to CSS Design

part 2

In the next part of your journey, you'll be looking at how effective print design techniques can be carried over into the web design world. No matter what your background, you have to agree that a lot of parallels can be drawn between the two mediums, and some of the age-old lessons learned by print designers can be very valuable to their digital brethren.

First, Mark focuses on a fairly experimental area—grid design for the Web. He demonstrates how powerful grids can be when used on websites.

Then Rob gives a fascinating look into typographic principles. He shows how even a simple site can be transformed by putting a bit of thought into typography.

Both designers have a background in print design, and it shows. I wish more of their kind would take a trip over into the land of web.

6

Grid Design
for the Web

mark
boulton

www.markboulton.co.uk

Mark Boulton is a typographic designer from Cardiff, UK. He has worked as an art director for design agencies in Sydney, London, and Manchester, serving clients such as the BBC, T-Mobile, and British Airways. For four years, Mark worked as a senior designer for the BBC, designing websites and web applications, before leaving to set up his own design consultancy, Mark Boulton Design.

He is an active member of the International Society of Typographic Designers and writes a design journal at www.markboulton.co.uk.

What is a grid system?

A grid system is a framework. It's a system used to create compositions. Everywhere you look, you see grid systems: city blocks, magazines, newspapers, building elevations. It's because we humans like to organize things, and, in many western cultures, we understand them when they are organized into straight lines. We know what to look at next, what to push or click next, and what to do next because of grid systems. Grid systems aren't just functional though; they can be beautiful.

A grid system can be designed using the Golden Section, a ratio that has been linked to aesthetic beauty for centuries. If something is perceived as beautiful, then according to the Aesthetic Usability Effect, it is more usable as well.

> *For more on the Golden Section, check out* http://en.wikipedia.org/wiki/Golden_section.

Grid systems are incredibly important in the design process. Along with typography, they determine the visual organization of information.

In this chapter, I'm going to show you how I designed a simple grid system for a recent project. Before I launch into that though, I feel it's important to give a brief overview of grid system design—how and where grid systems came into being, and the changes they've gone through over the decades.

Through the ages

No one really knows where grid systems originated. Some would argue they've been around ever since man started producing art. Others would say they started when man developed written language. However, I think they started when designers consciously began developing them to solve compositional problems. This, I believe, began with Villard's diagram, which was in use since at least medieval times.

Prior to World War II, grid systems were very formulaic, straightforward affairs—rectangular structures built around the proportions of devices such as Villard's diagram. They were often limited by the technology that produced them, and involved columns of text occasionally punctuated by an image. Grid systems of that era rarely used whitespace as a design device, let alone more than one typeface. That was until a few notable designers came along, including Josef Müller-Brockmann, who challenged the design conventions of the time. They proposed a new system: a more flexible grid with more tools at the designer's disposal, called the *modular grid*.

The importance of these designers' thinking shouldn't be underestimated. Much of what we understand as modern typography and grid system design came from them. Evidence of their work can be seen permeating graphic design of everything from magazine design (see Figure 6-1) to websites (see Figure 6-2).

Tue 19 Sep 2006

AIGA Here and There

11:36 PM

REMARKS (6)

Just a reminder for those in the Baltimore/D.C. area: I' giving a talk on Thursday night at Villa Julie College f Baltimore chapter of AIGA. I'm going to cover a wide

Figure 6-1. Magazine layouts, even one as complex as this, use grid systems to help the designers lay out the pages.

Figure 6-2. Khoi Vinh's Subtraction.com is one of a few websites that use a grid system to great effect.

Ratios and the canvas

Ratios are at the core of any well-designed grid system. Sometimes those ratios are rational, such as 1:2 or 2:3, and sometimes they are irrational, such as 1:1.618 (the ratio of the Golden Section). The challenge in designing grid systems is using those ratios to create harmonious compositions.

Ratios are applied to a grid system using the measurement of our choice. One thing we cannot control on the Web, however, is the canvas on which the grid sits—the browser window.

The canvas size for print design is determined by the media size, whether it's paper, signage, envelope, or whatever. The canvas size for grid design on the Web is normally determined by the browser window size, which can, in turn, be determined by the user's screen resolution. These are not fixed. To take into account this flexibility, a designer should design to the minimum requirement, which is normally the average screen resolution for the majority of users.

I'm not going to quote figures here, because I'll probably be wrong, but for quite a few years now, the screen resolution to design has been 800 × 600 pixels.

With the relaunch of sites like A List Apart (see Figure 6-3) and Stylegala, there has been a renewed discussion about fixed-width grids for 1024 pixels. In terms of the actual grid design, it really doesn't matter what size the canvas is. What should be determining the decision to go with 1024 pixels is research into users' screen resolutions. If the user base of a certain site is shown to be using resolutions of that size and above, then a decision to use that size to design to is a valid one.

Figure 6-3. A List Apart, designed by Jason Santa Maria, uses a wider than standard width. This allows more flexibility with the layouts you can produce with a grid.

However, as some people have noted, even if you do run at a higher resolution than 800 × 600, does that mean your browser window occupies the entire screen? We don't know. I personally think that not only is it platform-specific, but it also depends on the individuals and their experience level. Maybe more experienced users on a PC don't use their browsers at full screen. From my experience running user tests with a wide range of people, I've seen that many novice users on a PC run a browser at full screen because that is the default; on a Mac, the default isn't full screen.

Now that you have some background on grid systems, let's look at a practical example.

Putting grid systems into practice

In the spring of 2005, the International Baccalaureate Organization (IBO) approached me to design an intranet application and a new web-based application they had developed in-house. The exciting reason for choosing me as their designer was partly due to the requirement for this project to be built using Web Standards.

The IBO is a recognized leader in the field of international education. The IBO currently works with 1,785 schools in 122 countries to develop and offer curriculum programs to more than 200,000 students, aged 3 to 19 years. In order to teach a lot of students, there has to be a lot of teachers, and all of those teachers need access to document materials.

A few years ago, the IBO developed a teacher intranet called the Online Curriculum Centre (OCC), where IBO teachers could access and share documents. During the following years, the OCC grew, both in terms of users and functionality, until it became obvious a redesign was needed. Right from the start, the IBO wanted something new for the design—something fresh, modern, and usable.

In addition to the OCC, I was asked to help design a new online application for IBO staff called the Workshop Resource Centre (WRC). This is a complex application whereby workshop leaders (the IBO has development workshops with teachers) could select documents from a library, and then have them converted to PDFs for printing. It works kind of like an e-commerce system, with documents added to a user "cart" and then checked out for conversion and storing.

As I said, both projects had to be built using Web Standards, to a selection of standards-compliant browsers, which thankfully, didn't include Internet Explorer 5!

> Internet Explorer 5 can be a challenge to support, as you'll see in other areas of this book, including Ethan Marcotte's Chapter 3. There is also a good discussion of browser support issues in CSS Mastery, by Andy Budd et al (friends of ED, ISBN: 1-59059-614-5).

After reviewing the brief, it became clear that the majority of the content for this project was typographical. A wide variety of content types needed to be incorporated, many of which were still to be created. Therefore, the typographic structure needed to be clear and concise. In addition, the information needed to be presented in four languages: English, French, Spanish, and Chinese.

With all of this type on a screen, not only did there need to be a strong typographic hierarchy, but there also needed to be a strong grid.

Before I even put pen to paper or code to browser, I focused on user requirements and functionality. Once the IBO agreed with those, and everyone was happy, we progressed to the visual design from previously produced wireframes.

Beginning with the pen

I like to start every design with a pen and paper. This approach has a few advantages. Drawing is quick, cheap, and easy. If something doesn't work, you can throw away the piece of paper and start again. You can scribble until something does work. Additionally, working with pen and ink is a much more organic process that allows ideas to flow quicker than if you were sitting in front of a computer screen. In short, it saves time and money, and it also gets you away from your computer!

Producing thumbnail sketches is vital for tackling the scope of the design. The content, functionality, and technical requirements can all be worked out on paper first, before you spend any time on a computer. See Figure 6-4 for examples of my preliminary sketches.

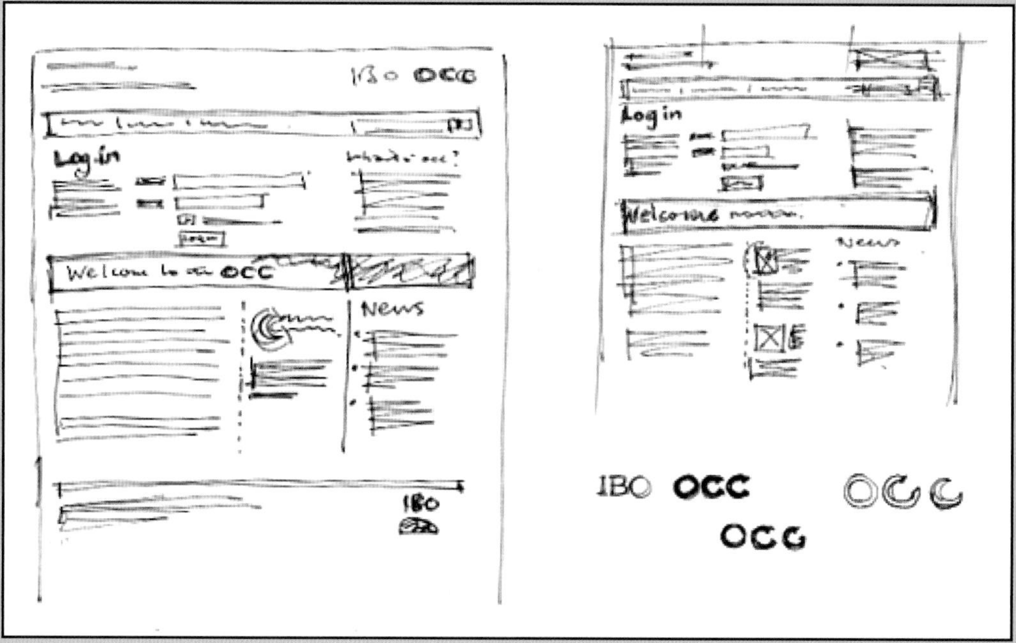

Figure 6-4. Designing before you get anywhere near a computer screen not only saves money, but also your eyes!

Breaking down the elements

After working with the IBO over a period of time, and studying the existing websites and applications the organization offered, we decided on a framework approach to the design, which could be applied to a wide variety of templates. It wouldn't be reasonable to design a project of this size on a page-by-page basis.

The process we undertook was similar to the traditional web design process: brief, discovery, wireframes, design, production, code. However, I adopted more of a partnership role with the IBO. This helped me gain a thorough understanding of the organization's business goals and the users' goals. And so when it came to designing, it was a lot easier.

One vital task was breaking down the content objects of the sites. Now this may seem like a technical, information architecture, or even a project manager's task. I actually see content analysis as part of a designer's task. As this framework was going to be predominantly typography and grid structure, breaking down the content to the micro levels is very important in understanding their relationships. I started this process by identifying the elements in the design. These can be broken down into macro elements and micro elements.

Macro elements

Macro elements are the big things in the design—the structure in which everything fits. The grid is perhaps above a macro element, as the other elements fit into it. Here's my list of macro elements for this project (see Figure 6-5).

- Columns
- Masthead
- Main navigation
- Footer

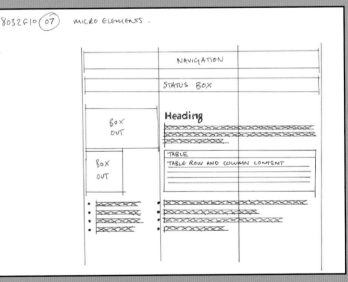

Figure 6-5. Macro elements, such as columns, can be sketched out first.

Micro elements

The micro elements are the bits that make up the rest of the content. They're visual elements that need individual consideration, but they also need to be considered in the context of a wider design system. Here are the micro elements for the IBO project (see Figure 6-6):

- Box outs (sidebar elements)
- Status boxes
- Headings
- Lists (ordered, unordered, and definition)
- Tables
- Links
- Paragraphs
- Images

You can probably see where this is going. This is beginning to look like the structure of a CSS file.

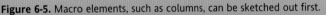

Figure 6-6. Micro elements, which fit in and around the macro elements, make up the content of a page.

Designing the columns

The wireframes that were developed were pretty complex. There was a lot of information that needed to be understood quickly by the user, and most of that information would be typography. The screens would include a lot of words. So, the grid to display this type needed careful consideration.

Following some of the basic guidelines I discussed earlier in this chapter, I began by sketching out the larger grid elements, namely the columns. The three-column layout is a popular grid configuration on the Web, perhaps with good reason.

The Rule of Thirds is a compositional rule. In fact, it's more like a guideline, which is used mainly by photographers but can be applied to graphic design. The Rule of Thirds states that dividing a space into thirds horizontally (or vertically if you're using an image), and aligning your design to these lines, creates more energy and tension. It helps designers by taking some of the guesswork out of creating interesting compositions.

With the Rule of Thirds in mind, I created a six-column grid. Figure 6-7 shows my pen-and-ink rendition, and Figure 6-8 shows the version I created in Photoshop.

You may notice at this point that I haven't mentioned anything specific about screen resolution or browser window width. I like to keep these out of the initial grid design, as I'm dealing with ratios and proportions at this point in the process. I don't like to concern myself with absolute measurements until I get into the nitty-gritty of production.

The columns can then be divided into a number of layout configurations, as shown in Figure 6-9. As you can see, the options for layout here are varied enough for most websites and applications.

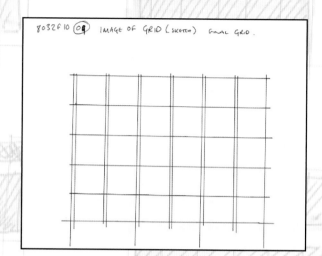
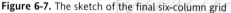

Figure 6-7. The sketch of the final six-column grid

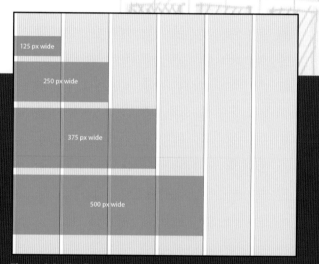

Figure 6-8. The final grid showing column configurations and measurements

Figure 6-9. Many compositional configurations can be obtained from a six-column grid. The examples shown here not only illustrate different column configurations, but also show relative visual emphasis of those columns.

Adding gutters, margins, and padding

You may have noticed there are no gutters in my initial grid design.

Gutters are the gaps in between columns. They are there so text or images from different columns don't run into each other. In grid system design, sometimes (depending on what theory you read), gutters are separate from the columns. This creates practical problems for us when designing grid systems on the Web because of the way we build the columns.

Generally, but not always, the columns we create, using Web Standards, are divs, which are given widths and positioned and styled using CSS. So, ideally, we don't want to be creating separate columns for the gutters. We therefore deal with gutters as *part* of columns (see Figure 6-10), and they are implemented using padding, or by creating margins, for the elements positioned within the columns or sometimes the column divs themselves.

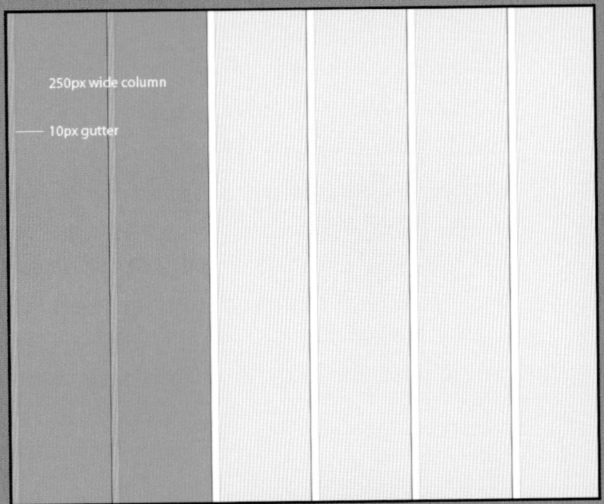

Figure 6-10. The gutters in this example are part of the columns, rather than sitting in between them.

I always choose to add padding to the elements within the columns. This may mean I end up creating more work for myself when I write the style sheets. I could simply add a margin. But doing it this way ensures that when I want to butt elements up against each other, I can. This also avoids box model problems with Internet Explorer, but as that was not a supported browser in this design, I didn't have to worry about that too much.

So, I have my columns—all six of them. Now I can start to add horizontal elements, such as the footer and masthead. But before I do that, I need to address an important typography measurement.

For the build of this project, there was a requirement for the user to be able to choose either a fixed or flexible layout. In the fixed layout, the columns would be determined by pixel measurements and therefore fixed. In the flexible layout, percentages would be used for the columns and ems would be used for the typography.

An em is a typographic measurement equal to the width of the size of the typeface. So, if a typeface is set at 12px, then 1em (width) is 12px. The problem we have when using em as a unit of measurement is that most browsers' internal style sheets render 1em as approximately 16px. This in itself is fine, but it makes using multiples and divisions a little more difficult than it needs to be (unless, of course, you're great at your 16 times table). To get around this, I reduce the default of 16px to 10px (see Figure 6-11). I do this by adding a declaration to the body tag in the CSS file:

```
body {
font-size: 62.5%;
}
```

> Richard Rutter wrote a great article called "How to size text in ems" in 2004, detailing this technique (http://clagnut.com/blog/348/).

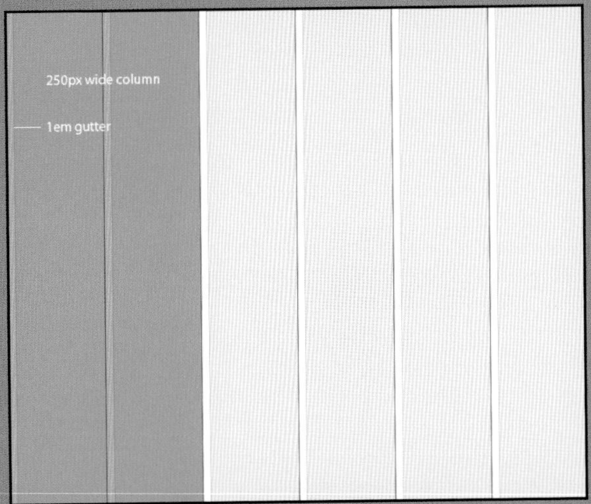

Figure 6-11. The 10px gutter now becomes 1em, as I've defined the font size of the body to be 62.5%.

This makes 1em roughly 10px (16 divided by 100 multiplied by 62.5 equals 10)—a unit of measurement that's easy to handle. Now we can equate pixel size to ems. For example, type that is set to 14px could be expressed as 1.4em, 9px text could be expressed at 0.9em, and so on.

While I'm adding this to the body tag, I also add the Global White Space Reset, which removes all the browser default margins and padding.

```
{ margin: 0; padding: 0;}
```

> The Global White Space Reset was first developed by Andrew Krespanis at www.leftjustified.net in October 2004 (http://leftjustified.net/journal/2004/10/19/global-ws-reset/).

By using the CSS universal selector, *, I'm able to select all elements within the HTML document and then remove all the default padding and margins.

If you want something more rigorous for this, you could use Yahoo's global reset style sheet, which removes pretty much every single default style in a browser. This gives you a completely blank canvas to begin your work. See http://developer.yahoo.com/yui/reset/ for more on this style sheet.

What about colors and other visual elements?

All of the colors and graphical elements for this project are controlled by yet another separate style sheet. This is because the grid, typography, and a lot of base styling for elements (such as unordered lists, definition lists, and images) needed to remain constant throughout the entire site, which had two different color schemes. It was straightforward to design in gray and simply overlay the colors based on the site.

Adding a class to the container div controlled the various layout options. This three-column layout has a class of c1-c2-c3, but layout options were created for a wide variety of layouts, such as c1, c1-c2, c1-c2-c3-c4-c5, and so on. This naming convention told me two things: the number of columns used in the six-column grid and also the document order. For example, c1-c2-c3 could look the same as c2-c1-c3, but the document order would be different: the <div> with the id of c2 would appear before c1 and c3.

All in all, there were six different style sheets for the OCC:

- A global style sheet
- An IBO style sheet, controlling all top-level colors
- A layout style sheet, user configurable
- A typography style sheet, elements of which were user configurable
- A color style sheet, controlling the overall color
- An alternative zoom layout, for accessibility purposes

This proved to be one of the most challenging aspects of this design.

Building the XHTML

Once I had an idea for the grid, I began to think about how to build it using Web Standards. First, I built a rough XHTML template with which to begin development of the CSS.

> *An important consideration in any multicolumn layout is document order. At this stage of the process, you should try to put the look of the grid out of your mind and focus on the content flow in the document. Get the content in first; add the CSS later.*

So, I began to add the various elements stipulated in the wireframes. First, the utilities menu:

```
<!-- BEGIN #utilities -->
<div id="utilities">
  <ul id="accessibility">
    <li><a href="#">High contrast layout</a></li>
  </ul>
  <ul id="services">
    <li><a href="#">IBO</a></li>
    <li><a href="#">OCC</a></li>
    <li><a href="#">IBIS</a></li>
    <li><a href="#">WRC</a></li>
    <li><a href="#">Log out</a></li>
  </ul>
  <!-- END #utilities -->
</div>
```

Then the masthead:

```
<!-- BEGIN #masthead -->
<div id="masthead">
  <!-- branding -->
  <div id="branding">
    <h1><a href="#">International Baccalaureate Organization</a></h1>
    <h2><a href="#" title="The IBO's Online Curriculum Centre→
      Homepage" accesskey="1">online curriculum centre</a></h2>
  </div>
  <ul id="language">
    <li><a href="#">English</a></li>
    <li><a href="#">Francais</a></li>
    <li><a href="#">Espanol</a></li>
    <li><a href="#">Chinese</a></li>
  </ul>
  <!-- END # masthead -->
</div>
```

141

The masthead includes several important elements: the organization's name, the service (or site) you are in, and the language toggles (the two sites were produced in four languages).

I try to avoid id and classnames that are presentational in their meaning. For example, I could have named the masthead topbar, topnavigation, or something like that, but that implies a presentational position, so, masthead it is.

Once I have those two elements, I need to wrap them in a container div that I will use to define the width of the grid, both in fixed and flexible modes.

```
<div id="container">
```

I can then add the columns after the masthead. I'm adding dummy content in there for the purposes of this demonstration.

```
<!-- BEGIN #c1 -->
<div id="c1">
  <p>Some content goes here</p>
  <!-- END #c1 -->
</div>

<!-- BEGIN #c2 -->
<div id="c2">
  <p>Some content goes here</p>
  <!-- END #c2 -->
</div>

<!-- BEGIN #c3 -->
<div id="c3">
  <p>Some content goes here</p>
  <!-- END #c3 -->
</div>
```

I have three columns here, with ids of c1 to c3. Perhaps, semantically, these are not the best names for columns, but without getting quite abstract in the naming convention, I think this is the best option to illustrate the point. Also, for development purposes, they are easy to remember, which is essential when there are hundreds of layout possibilities with a six-column grid.

Now I have the bare bones of the HTML structure. I have a masthead and three columns.

```
<!DOCTYPE html PUBLIC "-//W3C//DTD XHTML 1.0 Strict//EN"➥
"http://www.w3.org/TR/xhtml1/DTD/xhtml1-strict.dtd">
<html xmlns="http://www.w3.org/1999/xhtml">
<head>
  <title>IBO: OCC logged in home page</title>
</head>
<body>

  <!-- BEGIN #utilities -->
  <div id="utilities">
    <ul id="accessibility">
      <li><a href="#">High contrast layout</a></li>
    </ul>
    <ul id="services">
      <li><a href="#">IBO</a></li>
      <li><a href="#">OCC</a></li>
      <li><a href="#">IBIS</a></li>
```

```
    <li><a href="#">WRC</a></li>
    <li><a href="#">Log out</a></li>
  </ul>
  <!-- END #utilities -->
</div>

<!-- BEGIN #masthead -->
<div id="masthead">
<!-- branding -->
  <div id="branding">
    <h1><a href="#">International Baccalaureate Organization</a></h1>
    <h2><a href="#" title="The IBO's Online Curriculum Centre➡
      Homepage" accesskey="1">online curriculum centre</a></h2>
  </div>
  <ul id="language">
    <li><a href="#">English</a></li>
    <li><a href="#">Francais</a></li>
    <li><a href="#">Espanol</a></li>
    <li><a href="#">Chinese</a></li>
  </ul>
  <!-- END # masthead -->
</div>

</body>
</html>
```

Figure 6-12 shows the XHTML at this point. Now let's move on to styling and laying it out using CSS.

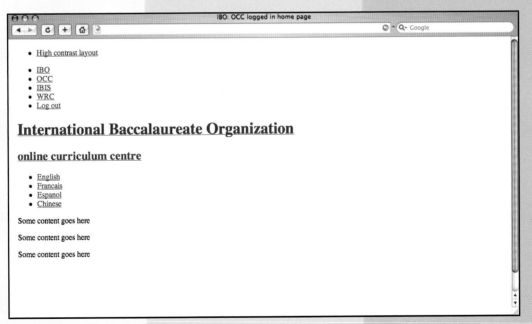

Figure 6-12. The XHTML. No CSS applied just yet, but this stage is very important in showing the document order.

Building the CSS

I'm at the stage in the development of the grid now where I need to move stuff around. I always find it easier to develop a fixed-pixel-based grid first, to make sure I have all my ratios correct and the composition is working. A nice little trick I use for this was first described by Khoi Vinh on his superb site, www.subtraction.com. Remember the grid drawing I did in Photoshop (Figure 6-8)? I export that grid and add it as a background to the container div throughout the development of the grid.

```
#container {
background: url(images/grid_background.gif);
}
```

I now have a visual representation of the grid (see Figure 6-13) to start aligning elements to it. Grids can be complex beasts, so having a visual reference that can be added and removed from the template so easily is really good news for us designers.

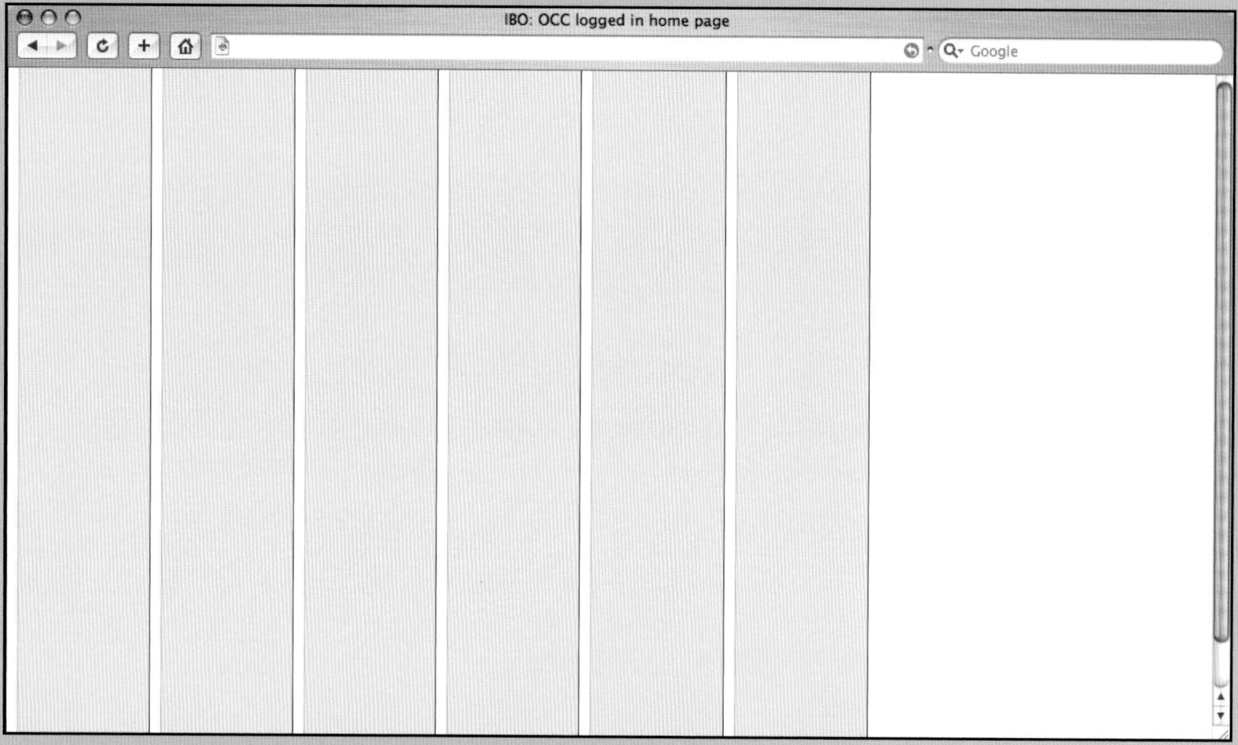

Figure 6-13. Using the grid as a background image allows me to align all elements to it.

Setting the width of the container

I generally start the CSS build working from the outside elements inwards. I begin by setting the width of the container div.

```
#container {
    float: left;
    width:750px;
    margin:0 auto;
    text-align: left;
    background: #fff url(grid_background.gif) repeat-y;
}
```

The declarations are pretty straightforward. I'm defining an overall global width of 750px; this is because my column width is 125px multiplied by 6. The top and bottom margins are effectively removed, and the left and right margins are set to auto to center the div in the browser window (see Figure 6-14).

Figure 6-14. Centering the grid

Setting the width of the columns

Next, I position the columns using floats. First, I float #c1 and #c2 left, and #c3 right.

```
#c1 {
    float: left;
    width: 250px;
}

#c2 {
    float: left;
    width: 250px;
}

#c3 {
    float: right;
    width: 250px;
}
```

This positions the columns over the grid marks of the background image. To make sure, I add different shades of gray as a background color to each div (see Figure 6-15).

```
#c1 {
    float: left;
    width: 250px;
    background: #eee;
}

#c2 {
    float: left;
    width: 250px;
    background: #ccc;
}

#c3 {
    float: right;
    width: 250px;
    background: #999;
}
```

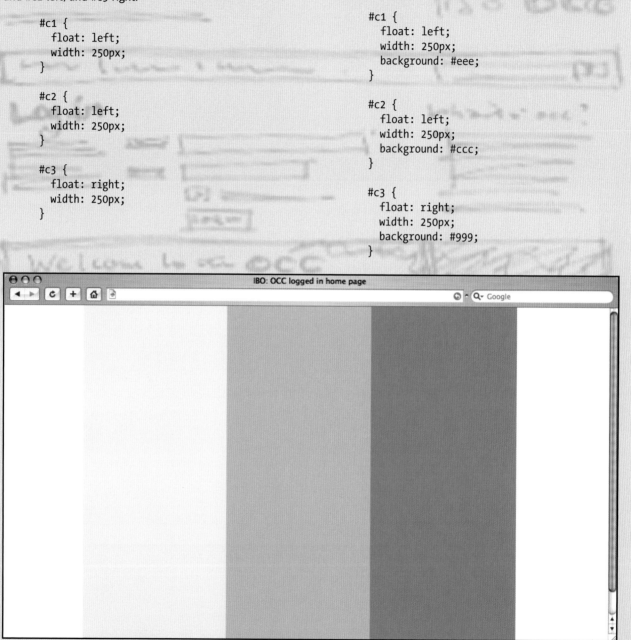

Figure 6-15. The three columns

The columns should now line up exactly with the vertical grid lines. But what about the masthead and all those lists? Well, with a little CSS, I can remove the bullets, display them in a line, and make sure the height of the masthead is related to the typography within it.

Once I have the alignment correct, I remove the gray from the columns and, for the purposes of this example, I add a height to the columns to show how the grid would extend when there is content in the divs.

Styling the masthead and the language menu

The masthead is simply floated left and given a width of 100%, to make sure the div stretches all the way across.

```
#masthead {
    float:left;
    width:100%;
    background: #000;
    margin: 1em 0 0 0;
}
```

The languages menu, as you can see from the HTML, is just a <ul> with an id of language. First, I give it a little padding above so the type doesn't touch the top of the browser window. This is set in pixels, unlike all my other typography measurements, which are set in ems, because I don't want this value to change when the text is resized. I want it to be over on the right, so I float the whole list right and give it a list-style of none, to get rid of the bullets.

```
#language {
    padding: 2px 0 0 0;
    float: right;
    list-style:none;
}
```

Next, I float each <li> left, and add some padding to both sides. Note this padding is declared in ems rather than pixels. This is because when the text is resized, I want this space to be proportionally retained. If this measurement were given in pixels, the space would resize in Internet Explorer, but the text would not. Finally, I add a border to the right to visually separate the elements.

```
#language li {
    float: left;
    padding: 0 1em 0 1em;
    border-right: 1px solid #fff;
}
```

Then I make the links white to stand out against the black. I will be overriding this default color with a separate color style sheet, but I always find it easier to begin developing in black and white.

```
#language li a {
    color: #fff;
}
```

I find that designing in black and white first helps clarify the design decisions I'm making. If color isn't part of the problem, remove it and think about it another time.

Figure 6-16 shows the masthead in the layout.

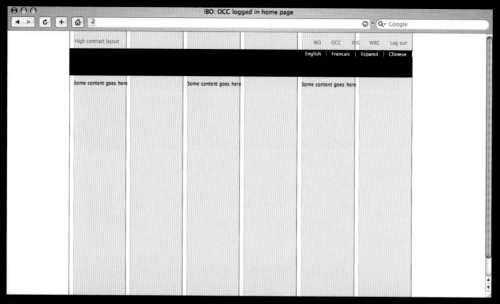

Figure 6-16. Adding the masthead. The layout is really taking shape now.

Styling the accessibility and services menus

I treat the lists in the accessibility and services menus in the same way as with the languages menu. I float the `<li>` elements left, and give them padding and a `list-style` of none:

```
#accessibility {
  float: left;
  list-style:none;
  padding-top: 15px;
}
#accessibility li {
  float: left;
  padding: 0 1em 0 1em;
  border-right: 1px solid #ccc;
}

#services {
  float: right;
  list-style:none;
  padding-top: 15px;
}
#services li {
  float: left;
  padding: 0 1em 0 1em;
  border-right: 1px solid #ccc;
}
```

I've also added some padding to the top of these lists. Again, note that this is fixed padding given in pixels. I don't want this value to change when the text is resized.

Styling the branding

The branding of any site is incredibly important. Here, the branding acts not only as a sign of where you are—what service you are in—but it also serves as a navigational device. Both of the headers will be links to the relevant sites. The h1 and h2 in the branding part of the site are grouped together as a division of like items, a div, with the id of branding. I float that left, give it some margin and padding, and add the IBO logo as a background image.

```
#branding {
    float: left;
    text-align: left;
    margin: 1em 0 0 1em;
    padding: 0 0 1em 6em;
    background: url(ibo_logo.gif) no-repeat 0 0;
}
```

The reason the padding is so large over on the right side is to accommodate the IBO logo, which I'll add in minute when I start to add color and rounded corners.

The headers are sized using ems. The h1 is given a value equivalent to 14px, and the h2 gets a value equivalent to18px.

```
#branding h1 {
    font-size: 1.4em;
}
#branding h2 {
    font-size: 1.8em;
    font-weight: bold;
}
```

Then I color the links white.

```
#branding h1 a,
#branding h2 a {
    color: #fff;
}
```

Figure 6-17 shows how these additions look.

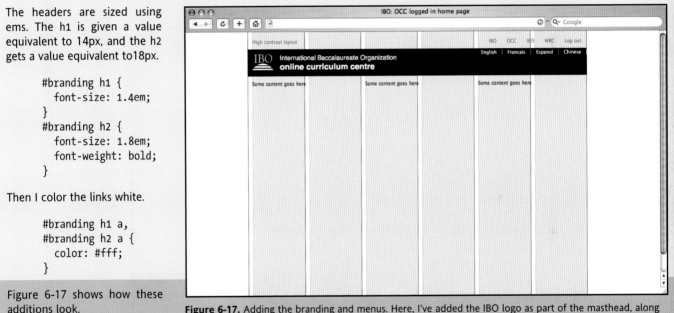

Figure 6-17. Adding the branding and menus. Here, I've added the IBO logo as part of the masthead, along with the other menus.

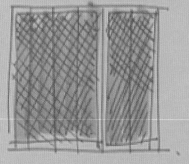
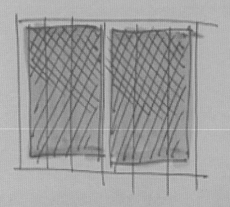
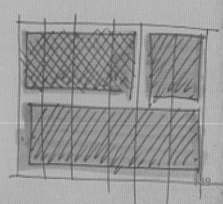

It's starting to look like a website

Things are starting to look more like a website now. I'm adhering to the grid I've built, and the design is beginning to feel right.

Now that I have the basic column structure and masthead, I add some sample content: headings, links, paragraphs, and unordered lists. I'm still working in black and white, so I can stay focused on aligning to the grid and making sure the typography is in good working order.

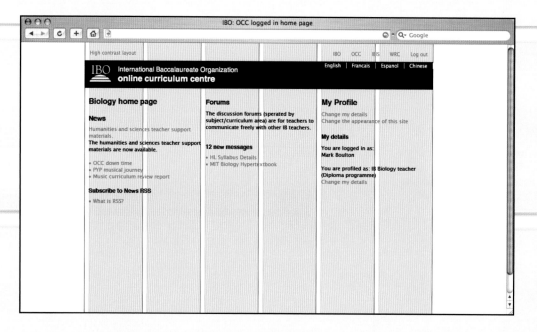

Next, I start adding color (via a separate color CSS style sheet) to the masthead.

And now to the typography. At this stage, I remove the grid image from my background declaration on the body tag. I don't need it now that I know everything aligns correctly.

Finally, I add some margins to the elements in the columns to create some horizontal alignment.

Issues with the design

The project presented many challenges. It was a redesign, so there was legacy content, a history in terms of brand, and a certain level of user expectation that comes with all redesigns. These all had to be considered.

The CSS was a particular challenge. Not for the reason you may expect, though. You thought I was going to say Internet Explorer browser problems, right? Aha! Well, no, that wasn't the problem.

I was lucky, as a designer, to be working for a dream client who basically said, "Oh, ignore browsers that aren't standards-compliant." Of course, I asked if they were sure. At first, I couldn't quite understand why, but I quickly realized it was because we were dealing with a pretty much locked-down audience in terms of recommended and supported software. Within the IBO, Firefox is actually the recommended browser. Of course, Internet Explorer is still a majority browser for the IBO's audience, but I developed the design with Firefox as the primary browser to ensure the code was as standards-compliant as possible. I turned my attention to Internet Explorer 6 afterwards, adding workarounds to ensure it worked in that browser, too. It was nice that the target browsers allowed me to keep hacks to a minimum.

> *I didn't deal with CSS hacks in this chapter. Why? Well, I think they are out of scope here, and could confuse the explanation of constructing the grid. You can add hacks in if your design requires it. There is further hack coverage throughout this book, and CSS Mastery (friends of ED, ISBN: 1-59059-614-5) contains comprehensive information on hacks.*

As I was saying, the challenging thing with this project was how to manage the CSS.

The customization options for this site were plentiful. All of these options would be saved into a user profile, which meant the system had to remember what font size, layout, and so on the user had saved. The brief stipulated the user had to be able to change the layout (fixed or flexible) and the type size. Also, there was a zoom layout for the visually impaired. In addition to that, the two sites, the OCC and the WRC, both had to share common elements such as grid and typography; the only difference was color. It was a complex problem if all this was to be addressed using different style sheets.

Overcoming these issues wasn't particularly easy, but was helped enormously by the project process that was undertaken by the IBO and myself. There were specs, wireframes, use cases, and concepts—all the sort of documentation you would expect in a project of this size. However, the process was small and intimate with the client. There was iteration after iteration. Solving problems together, I'd say, was the real success of this project.

Conclusion

What I have created here is a simple grid system, not just columns.

To the casual observer, this is nothing more than a three-column layout using standard 250px wide columns. However, I carefully constructed the grid, considering all of the compositional options available to me using this six-column grid system. This allowed for a wide variety of layout options that, importantly, relate to each other.

For posterity's sake, and to give you an idea of how radically different the new design is, I've included a few screenshots to show the before and after states. Figures 6-18 and 6-19 show the OCC site, and Figure 6-20 shows the WRC site. I'm sure you'll agree, the new site stands head and shoulders above the old.

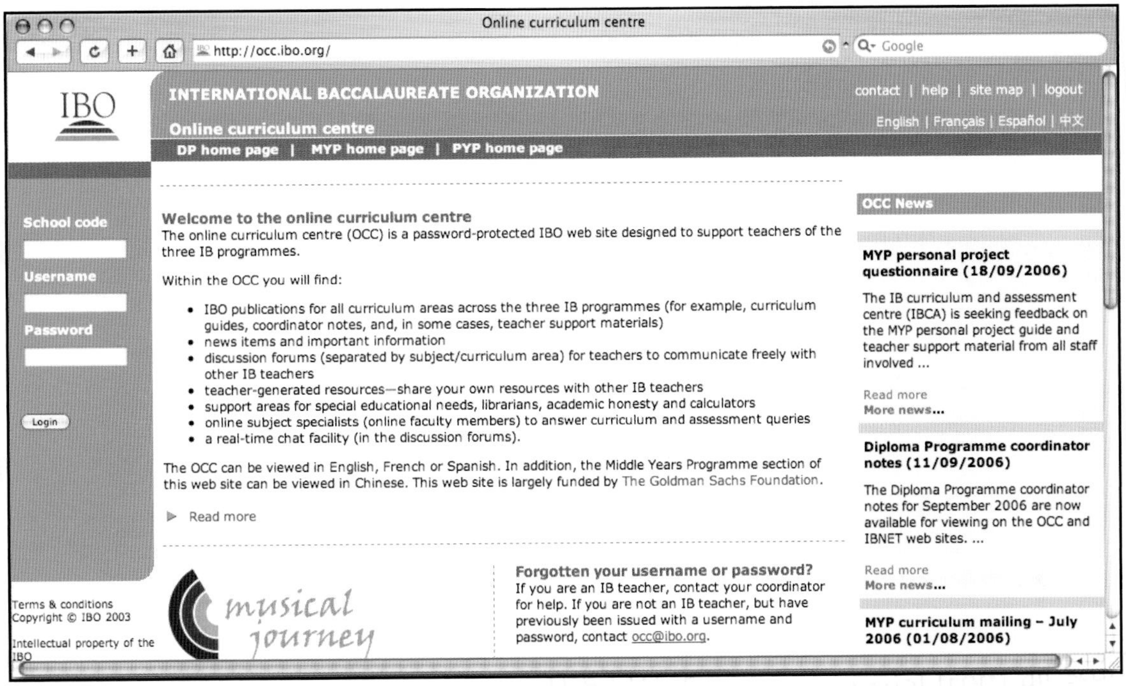

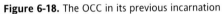

Figure 6-18. The OCC in its previous incarnation

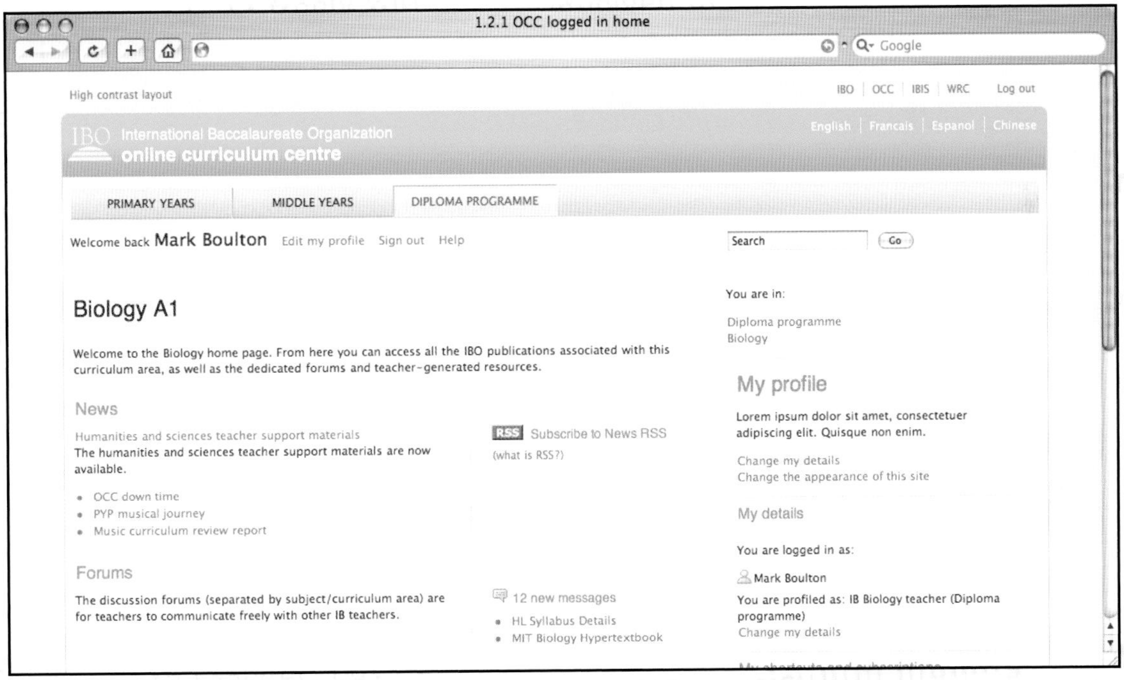

Figure 6-19. The new OCC design uses CSS for layout throughout and has options for the user to change the typeface and size, and a high-contrast layout for visually impaired users—all using CSS!

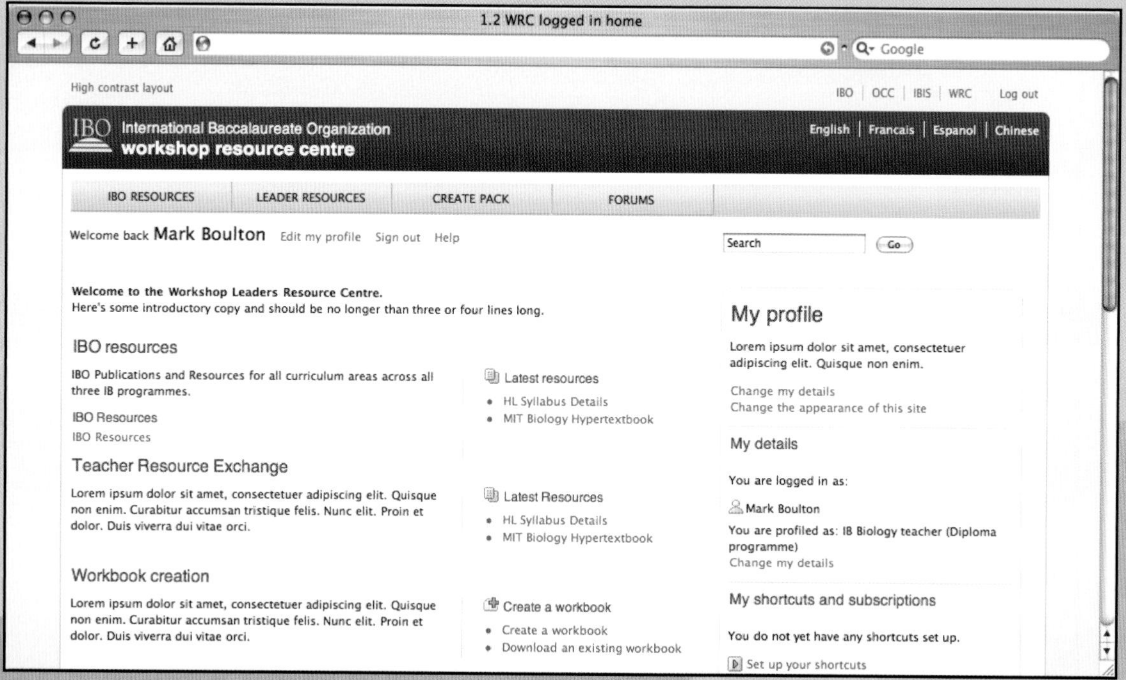

Figure 6-20. The new WRC shares many base style sheets with the OCC. The only difference is a different colour.css, which overides the base colour.css.

EEK SPIRITS

New policies curtail dangerous drinking
and improve campus representation.

son ■ Daily News Editor

n October 15 1998,
Courtney Cantor
went out to party
with friends at the Phi
Delta Theta fraternity
house. Late that night,
he took a cab home

Courtney's death is a horrifying example of what can go wrong at any college
party — and it does not stand alone in the
University's recent history. In the fall of
200, Engineering sophomore Byung-Soo
Kim died after trying to consume 21 shots
on his 21st birthday. In the fall of 2003,
Kinesiology junior Evan Loomis suffered
kidney failure, after being hazed at the
Sigma Chi fraternity. That same year, 25
percent of University students reported
that they binge drunk on a frequent basis.

In light of these incidents, the Inter-
fraternity Council and the University's
Office of Student Activities and Leader-
ship have led a two-pronged movement
to improve the safety of life on campus
for students. The IFC recently passed a
controversial revision to its social policy
and SAL has recently reorganized its student groups to better protect the health
and safety of students, and the hability
of the University. The two movements,
while independently prompted, executed
and motivated, strive to remedy similar
concerns.

Formalizing the University's group recognition process.

controversial proposals the University discussed implementing were
postponing rush until the winter
term and having live-in guardians
within fraternity houses.

"We thought that students might
have time to find themselves a bit
more, and maybe would be able to
withstand the social pressure behind
hazing," Eklund said.

Both proposals were wildly
unpopular among students.

Deferred rush had been discussed
at the University even before Loomis's incident. After the death of
Courtney Cantor, her father, George
Cantor, told the Michigan Daily that
he hoped fraternities and sororities
would delay rush until the winter
term to give students time to adjust
to life at a big University.

The idea of deferred rush was
highly unpopular on campus, and as
a result of the way in which the University recognizes student groups,
deferred rush is not an option at
this point in time, because fraternities and sororities are recognized
the same way as any student group.
If the University were to impose a
deferred rush policy for the Greek
system, they would have to restrict
every group from recruiting new
until the winter semester.

freshman fraternity rush,
also delayed. While uppe
at Emory can rush frat
the fall, the big push o
winter break, at the star
semester. About a third
at Emory participate in
compared with about
Michigan. The bigge
the smaller the perce
pus that participates
because fraternities
can only accommo
number of people. A
of Texas-Austin ab
52,000 students par
life — about 11 per

Emory IFC Pres
said that the defe
several advantage

"A pretty larg
freshman class
rush," he said.
large number of
for rush event

He added tha
compromise
organizations
istration.

"I think tha
you have a fi
identity and
ferent grou
he said. T
because
the alcoho

7

Bridging the Type Divide: Classic Typography with CSS

rob *weychert*

www.robweychert.com

Rob Weychert is a graphic designer, artist, writer, and thinker known for his neurotically meticulous attention to detail. Since the late 1990s, Rob has provided print and interactive graphic design solutions to clients in such disparate industries as entertainment, travel, healthcare, education, publishing, and e-commerce.

When he is not absorbed in design, Rob spends most of his time scrutinizing music and film, writing haiku, screen printing, taking photos, and cruising the streets of his hometown Philadelphia on his BMX. He also writes about these topics and all things design on his personal website, www.robweychert.com.

A brief history of type

Like all the arts, it [typography] is basically immune to progress, though it is not immune to change.

Robert Bringhurst,
The Elements of Typographic Style

The art of typography has a rich and storied tradition, and like most art forms, its production processes have moved at a snail's pace.

After Gutenberg's landmark invention of movable type (a printing method consisting of individual letters carved out of metal) in the fifteenth century, the technology of typography saw no significant change until the Industrial Revolution. The subsequent Linotype and Monotype machines and (the relatively short-lived) phototypesetting process were essentially faster, more efficient models of the same old printing method. However, the Macintosh's introduction of type and design to the digital age in 1984 was the cultivation of a radical new method. Then, less than ten years later, just as graphic designers were becoming accustomed to digital production tools for print, a whole new medium was thrust upon them.

The World Wide Web was a revolutionary means to access information, and as such, it demanded a different way of thinking about design. However, with centuries of printed tradition behind them and a relatively recent adoption of the computer, most designers had a hard time thinking in terms of anything but print, and it didn't help that HTML was never intended to accommodate graphic design. The other half of the Web was being designed by computer enthusiasts, professional and amateur alike. They had a better understanding of the exciting potential of the Web, but little or no knowledge of visual design principles.

So went the early, dark days of web design. Semantic, flexible documents looked anything but good, and good-looking documents were anything but semantic or flexible. Straddling the turn of the century, a greater emphasis on standardized web technologies aimed to solve this problem.

CSS gave designers the tools they needed to craft beautiful web pages without disrupting the underlying semantic structure of HTML. Previously unheard-of typographic control was now possible. But by this time, many designers had come of age online and were oblivious to the time-tested traditions and conventions of nuanced typographic design.

Today, in the increasingly sophisticated infancy of the Web, much of its typography remains limp.

This chapter aims to help put a stop to this trend, by reconciling printed typography's rich visual tradition with web typography's exciting dynamic capabilities. I'll demonstrate where they may converge, where they should agree to disagree, and how just a few simple and subtle typographic techniques can breathe new life into a page.

Know your text face

The number one complaint designers seem to have about setting type on the Web is the small number of typefaces reliably available across platforms. While this can be frustrating, it is important to remember that selecting a typeface is only one aspect of typographic design. Some of the best typographers in the print world limit their arsenal to only a few text faces that they come to know intimately through repeated study and usage. Even if the limited choice of typefaces appropriate for the Web does offer less variety, it forces that same good practice of restraint upon us. And luckily, a number of the faces available are among the very best examples of type designed for the screen. A keen understanding of these typefaces—including their creators and historical contexts—can be a great benefit to the way we use them.

Introducing Georgia

If you're skeptical that a beautiful design can be achieved using one common typeface, it is my hope that this chapter will change your mind. The vast majority of what I'll cover will use Georgia, a serif text face commissioned from renowned type designer Matthew Carter by Microsoft in 1993. According to recent results of an ongoing code style website survey (www.codestyle.org/css/font-family/sampler-CombinedResultsFull.shtml), Georgia is present on about 91% of Macs, 84% of PCs, and 53% of Unix systems, making it one of the most ubiquitous serif typefaces in the world. Thankfully, it is also a stellar design.

Georgia is very similar to Times New Roman (Figure 7-1), one of the only serif faces with a wider distribution. Like Times New Roman, Georgia is a timeless design, embodying aesthetic and practical characteristics from a few different historical periods. However, for our purposes, Georgia trumps Times New Roman on the screen, since that's where it was designed to be displayed.

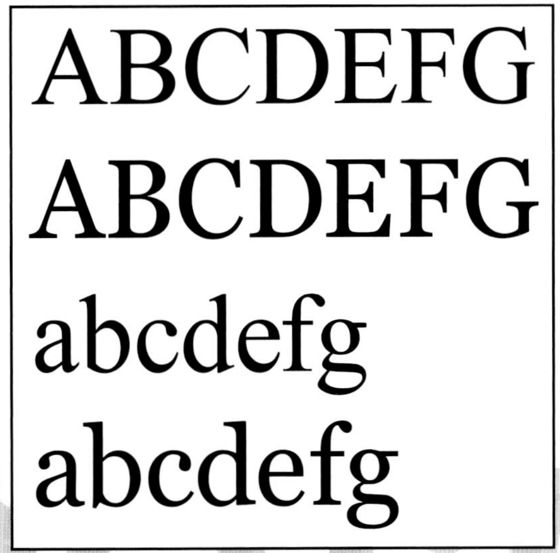

ABCDEFG
ABCDEFG
abcdefg
abcdefg

Figure 7-1. Times New Roman (top) vs. Georgia (bottom)

The process

Typically, when a digital typeface is created, its printed form takes priority. Outlines of the type's shapes are drawn first, and bitmap versions of small text sizes (for clarity on the screen, in case it should wind up there) are drawn based on those outlines. In other words, a resolution-independent design is retrofitted into an extremely low resolution. Results vary, but in many cases, small text sizes are all but illegible on the screen. With Georgia, Carter decided to reverse the process. Since this typeface was intended *primarily* for the screen, the bitmaps were drawn first (at 8- to 12-point sizes), and then the outlines were drawn to accommodate them (Figure 7-2). This resulted in an unprecedented elegant clarity for a screen-based serif face, a classification notorious for its illegibility.

Figure 7-2. Georgia outlines vs. Georgia bitmap

The right man for the job

It was no fluke that Matthew Carter was chosen for the task. The son of an acclaimed type designer and printing historian, he began cutting original designs and revivals of classic typefaces in metal in the late 1950s, before going on to cofound the well-known Bitstream and Carter & Cone digital type foundries. Based on his decades of experience, impressive list of esteemed clients (including *Time Magazine*, *The New York Times*, and *The Washington Post*), and body of work (most notably Bell Centennial, and, later, the screen-based Verdana), few—if any—people could claim to be more qualified to design a timeless, legible typeface, intended for the screen but still rooted in tradition.

OK, now that you've got a handle on how, why, and when Georgia came about, you're ready to put it to use, with a practical example. Let's build something!

A page for Poe

In order to demonstrate some possibilities, I've put together a little homepage for the original master of the macabre, Edgar Allan Poe (Figure 7-3). The basic layout is made up of four columns of approximately equal width. The two center columns compose the main content area, which is flanked by a navigation column on the left and a sidebar column on the right. The header and footer span the full width of the four columns.

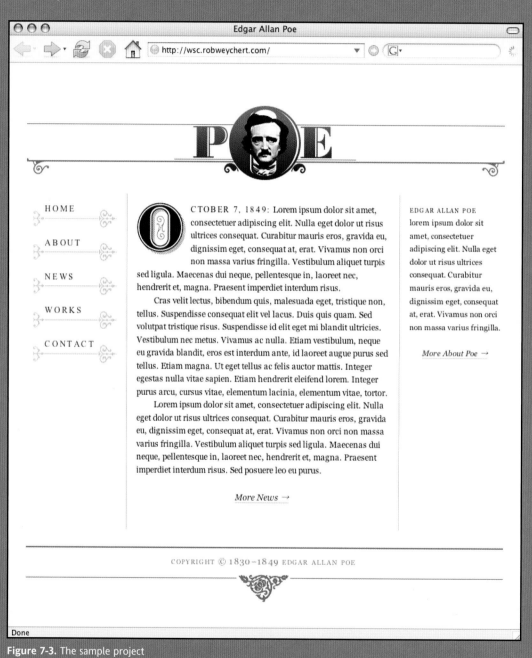

Figure 7-3. The sample project

Here is a simplified version of the markup:

```
<body>
<!-- FULL PAGE WRAP -->
  <div id="wrap">
<!-- NAV -->
    <ul id="nav">
      <li>Home</li>
      <li>About</li>
      <li>News</li>
      <li>Works</li>
      <li>Contact</li>
    </ul>
<!-- MAIN CONTENT -->
    <div id="main">
      <p>Main content copy.</p>
    </div>
<!-- ABOUT -->
    <div id="about">
      <p>About copy.</p>
    </div>
<!-- FOOTER -->
    <h6 id="footer">Copyright information.</h6>
  </div>
</body>
```

This case study is available online for you to view at http://wsc.robweychert.com/, and the source files are available to download from www.friendsofed.com/. The page has been tested in the following browsers:

- Internet Explorer 6 and 7 for Windows
- Firefox 1.5 for Windows and Macintosh
- Opera 9 for Windows and Macintosh
- Safari 1.3 and 2.0 for Macintosh

Because of this chapter's explicit focus on typography, some aspects of the case study's construction won't be covered here, but have been documented in detail elsewhere. These include Roger Johansson's approach to elastic design for the general page layout ("Fixed or fluid width? Elastic!" www.456bereastreet.com/ archive/200504/fixed_or_fluid_width_elastic/) and Douglas Bowman's sliding doors technique for the expanding header and navigation ("Sliding Doors of CSS," www.alistapart.com/articles/slidingdoors/).

A readable line length

The bulk of the techniques I'll be discussing focus on the case study's main content area (#main). This section will demonstrate how its proportions were devised and the effect those proportions have on the rest of the layout.

66: The number of the . . .

Since #main is the most important element in the hierarchy of the page, I want to be sure it carries the weight of a proper focal point and its readability is maximized. The first step is to determine the width of the line length. The standard range for a readable line of text set in a single column is between 45 and 75 characters (including spaces). This range allows lines to break in reasonable increments and prevents them from getting too long or too short for comfortable reading. Many typesetters revere an approximately 66-character line as ideal, and I am among them, so this example will use that width. This is a key proportion, and I want to make sure it is maintained as well as possible, which will be an important factor in how the page is put together.

> Okay, we admit it: This book breaks the line-length convention outlined here on many an occasion, but we have our reasons. It is mainly due to the fact that we are dealing with not only text, but code sections as well; code lines become a lot less readable if you have to break them up into several fragments to fit them on the page.

If I use a liquid layout, the line length will increase or decrease based on the width of the user's browser window (Figure 7-4). On the other hand, if I use a fixed-width layout, the line length will increase or decrease if the user resizes the browser text, and the potential also exists for horizontal scrolling if the browser window is skinnier than my page's specified width (Figure 7-5). Dissatisfied with both of these options, I've chosen instead to use an elastic layout, which gives me the best of both worlds (Figure 7-6).

The layout will expand and contract as the text is resized or as the browser is resized, but it will not expand beyond a specified width. The compromise here is that my line will get shorter as the browser window contracts, but a too-short line is easier to read than one that is too long, and is also a pleasant alternative to horizontal scrolling.

Figure 7-4. Liquid layout: When the browser window is expanded, many find the line too long for comfortable reading.

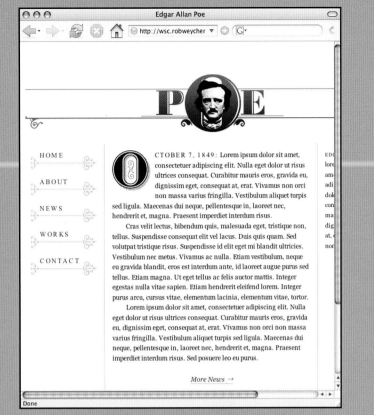

Figure 7-5. Fixed-width layout: Horizontal scrolling is necessary if the browser window gets too small.

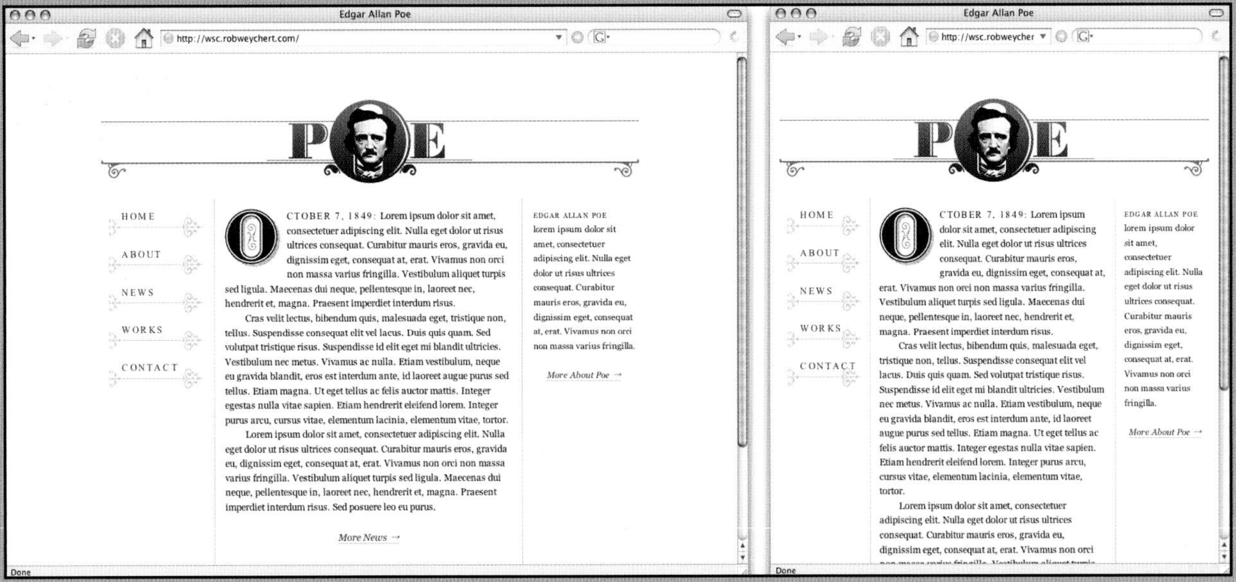

Figure 7-6. Elastic layout, expanded and contracted: The line length maintains the desired proportions when the browser window is expanded (left), but also contracts with the window to avoid horizontal scrolling (right).

The almighty em

An elastic layout's secret weapon is the em. In both the print and web worlds, an em is a square of a typeface size, based on either the width of its widest character or the distance from the bottom of its lowest descender (such as the stem of a lowercase *p*) to the top of its highest ascender (such as the stem of a lowercase *b*) or diacritical mark (Figure 7-7). In CSS, an em is based on the `font-size` of the parent element. Thus, if I specify the width of my layout in ems, it will expand and contract as the text is resized, maintaining the proportion between the text size and the length of the line, thereby keeping my 66-character line intact.

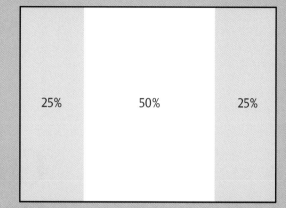

Figure 7-8. Approximate layout proportions

My main content area (`#main`) needs to have a 66-character width, which also needs to be about 50% of the layout's full width (`#wrap`). If I set a block of Georgia text with a width specified in ems, count the characters (including spaces) in a few lines, and divide the average of those lines by the width of the text block, I'll discover that Georgia averages about 2.2 characters to an em. Therefore, a 66-character measure would be 30em, which would make `#wrap` 60em. If I divide 740px by 60, I get 12.3px, and *voila!* I have a `font-size`.

But there's a problem. Internet Explorer will not resize text with a `font-size` specified in pixels. Luckily, modern browsers render `font-size` keywords pretty consistently, and I know that `font-size: small` resolves to about 13px. With this figure and a little more math, I can achieve proportions well within the range of my desired results.

First, I'll need to recalculate `#wrap`'s width, since it is based on my `font-size`, which is now a bit larger. If I divide 740px by 13px, `#wrap`'s new width (rounded up) is 57em. To maintain my 66-character line, `#main`'s width will remain 30em, which is 53% (again, rounded up) of `#wrap`'s width. Finally, accounting for 2% margins for each column will yield the proportions shown in Figure 7-9.

Figure 7-7. A Georgia em

The elasticity of my layout will be suitable for most desktop browser resolutions, but I still want its intended proportions (Figure 7-8) to sit comfortably in an 800×600 browser window, so a native page width of 740px is prudent. In order to specify that width in ems, I'll have to do some math.

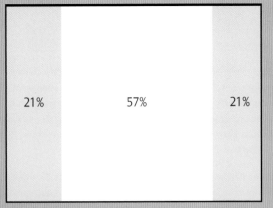

Figure 7-9. Final layout proportions

Translation

With smug simplicity, CSS concisely displays the proportions I worked so hard and verbosely to determine:

```
body {
    font-family: Georgia,"Times New Roman",Times,serif;
    font-size: small;
    }

#wrap {
    max-width: 57em;
    }

#nav {
    width: 19%;
    margin-right: 2%;
    }

#main {
    width: 53%;
    margin-left: 2%;
    margin-right: 2%;
    }

#about {
    width: 19%;
    margin-left: 2%;
    }
```

Figure 7-10 demonstrates the results: a very readable text block whose proportions will remain as consistent as can reasonably be expected. For another approach to using ems in CSS, see Chapter 6, "Grid Design for the Web."

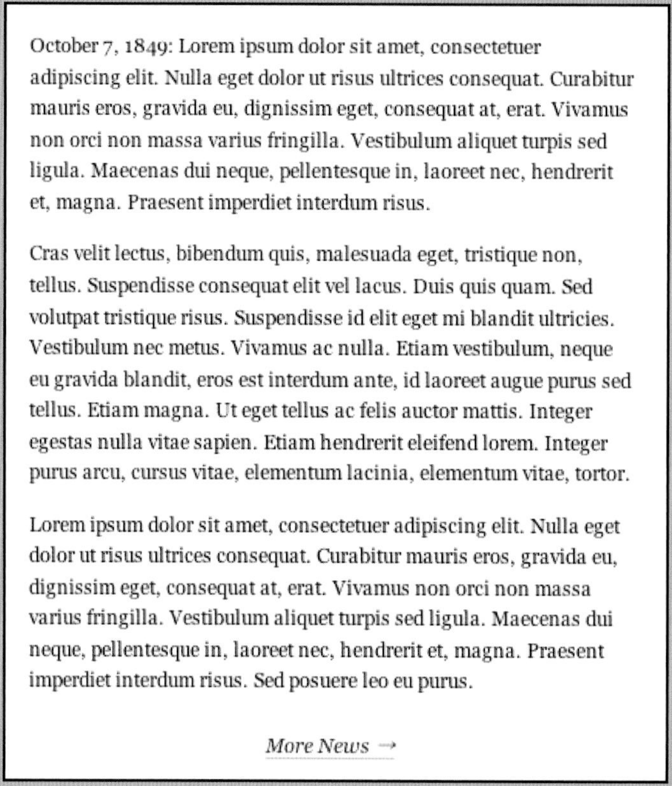

October 7, 1849: Lorem ipsum dolor sit amet, consectetuer adipiscing elit. Nulla eget dolor ut risus ultrices consequat. Curabitur mauris eros, gravida eu, dignissim eget, consequat at, erat. Vivamus non orci non massa varius fringilla. Vestibulum aliquet turpis sed ligula. Maecenas dui neque, pellentesque in, laoreet nec, hendrerit et, magna. Praesent imperdiet interdum risus.

Cras velit lectus, bibendum quis, malesuada eget, tristique non, tellus. Suspendisse consequat elit vel lacus. Duis quis quam. Sed volutpat tristique risus. Suspendisse id elit eget mi blandit ultricies. Vestibulum nec metus. Vivamus ac nulla. Etiam vestibulum, neque eu gravida blandit, eros est interdum ante, id laoreet augue purus sed tellus. Etiam magna. Ut eget tellus ac felis auctor mattis. Integer egestas nulla vitae sapien. Etiam hendrerit eleifend lorem. Integer purus arcu, cursus vitae, elementum lacinia, elementum vitae, tortor.

Lorem ipsum dolor sit amet, consectetuer adipiscing elit. Nulla eget dolor ut risus ultrices consequat. Curabitur mauris eros, gravida eu, dignissim eget, consequat at, erat. Vivamus non orci non massa varius fringilla. Vestibulum aliquet turpis sed ligula. Maecenas dui neque, pellentesque in, laoreet nec, hendrerit et, magna. Praesent imperdiet interdum risus. Sed posuere leo eu purus.

More News →

Figure 7-10. A readable line length for `#main`

Paragraph indents

Now that `#main` has a nice, comfortable width, I'm going to turn my attention to the paragraphs within it. For as long as they have existed, web browsers have typically rendered paragraph elements with a default bottom margin, usually somewhere between 1em and 2em. This has the effect of a blank line between paragraphs, a custom that is certainly not unheard of in print. Just as likely to be seen in print, however, is a convention of delineation that is relatively rare on the Web: paragraph indents.

Where a blank line can sometimes be disruptive to continuous text, an indent on the first line of a paragraph can mark a new passage while maintaining the text's cohesion. Still, it should be used with caution on the Web. Paragraph indents as an alternative to blank lines work well in print because of the other ways the text is physically broken up, such as multiple columns and pagination. Lengthy writing on the Web should likewise occasionally give the reader's eyes the sort of relief a blank line can provide, and thus, paragraph indents on the Web are happiest in the company of brevity.

With just three short paragraphs to its name, #main is a perfect candidate for paragraph indents. There are just two things I need to do:

- Indent the first lines of all but the first paragraph.
- Get rid of those blank lines.

Simple indents

One extremely simple way to both indent my paragraphs and lose the blank lines without modifying my markup would be to do this:

```
p {
    text-indent: 2.1em;
    margin: 0;
    }
```

An indent of 2.1em carves a square out of my text block (Figure 7-11), which looks great. Unfortunately, though the results are otherwise perfect, this CSS rule indents my first paragraph. Just as using blank lines between paragraphs in addition to indents is a redundancy, so is indenting the first paragraph in the text. Two forms of delineation in tandem just belabor the point, like adding some big red text that says, "Behold, the birth of a new paragraph!" OK, maybe it's not that bad, but I'd still prefer not to do it.

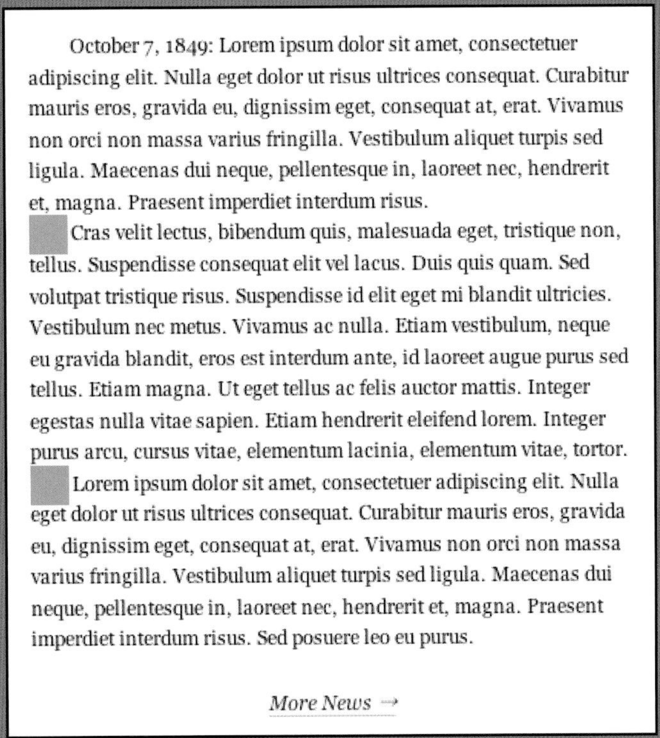

Figure 7-11. Each of these paragraph indents articulates a square of whitespace. Many typesetters find a square to be an ideal indent.

Adjacent selectors in an imperfect world

Using an adjacent selector is my logical next step:

```
p {
   margin: 0;
   }

p+p {
   text-indent: 2.1em;
   }
```

The p+p adjacent selector will address only a paragraph that is immediately preceded by another paragraph. In theory, this does *exactly* what I want it to, since the first paragraph is obviously not preceded by another paragraph, and will therefore ignore this rule. In a perfect world, this would have completed the task at hand, and I'd be at the bar by now. Sadly, though, Internet Explorer 6 does not support adjacent selectors, and now it renders all of my paragraphs as a single nebulous blob.

When faced with a similar problem while I was putting together my personal site, I solved it like so:

```
p {
   text-indent: 2.1;
   margin: 0;
   }

h2+p {
   text-indent: 0;
   }
```

The content area in question began with two headlines: a title (h1) and a date stamp (h2), followed by the first paragraph (p). The h2+p adjacent sibling selector achieved the desired effect in compliant browsers, and an indented first paragraph in Internet Explorer, a necessary compromise in a situation where the markup could not be altered.

This is not a viable option in my current situation, since #main's first paragraph is not preceded by another element, but there is also nothing stopping me from altering the markup ever so slightly. I need only to give the first paragraph a class of first:

```
<p class="first">First paragraph copy goes here.</p>
```

And then add one more rule to my original CSS:

```
p {
   text-indent: 2.1em;
   }

.first {
   text-indent: 0;
   }
```

Mission accomplished (Figure 7-12)!

> October 7, 1849: Lorem ipsum dolor sit amet, consectetuer adipiscing elit. Nulla eget dolor ut risus ultrices consequat. Curabitur mauris eros, gravida eu, dignissim eget, consequat at, erat. Vivamus non orci non massa varius fringilla. Vestibulum aliquet turpis sed ligula. Maecenas dui neque, pellentesque in, laoreet nec, hendrerit et, magna. Praesent imperdiet interdum risus.
>
> Cras velit lectus, bibendum quis, malesuada eget, tristique non, tellus. Suspendisse consequat elit vel lacus. Duis quis quam. Sed volutpat tristique risus. Suspendisse id elit eget mi blandit ultricies. Vestibulum nec metus. Vivamus ac nulla. Etiam vestibulum, neque eu gravida blandit, eros est interdum ante, id laoreet augue purus sed tellus. Etiam magna. Ut eget tellus ac felis auctor mattis. Integer egestas nulla vitae sapien. Etiam hendrerit eleifend lorem. Integer purus arcu, cursus vitae, elementum lacinia, elementum vitae, tortor.
>
> Lorem ipsum dolor sit amet, consectetuer adipiscing elit. Nulla eget dolor ut risus ultrices consequat. Curabitur mauris eros, gravida eu, dignissim eget, consequat at, erat. Vivamus non orci non massa varius fringilla. Vestibulum aliquet turpis sed ligula. Maecenas dui neque, pellentesque in, laoreet nec, hendrerit et, magna. Praesent imperdiet interdum risus. Sed posuere leo eu purus.
>
> *More News* →

Figure 7-12. A cohesive text block with elegant paragraph indents

This text block is shaping up nicely, but it still needs just a bit more. The last two ingredients of this typographic stew involve the creative use of capital letters, which will lend just enough visual interest to the page to complete the design.

Drop caps

Drop caps are one form of what is called a *versal*, a scribal tradition dating back to the earliest illuminated manuscripts of Europe's medieval period (Figure 7-13). A versal's purpose is to introduce the text with dignified fanfare. A drop cap does this by dramatically enlarging the first letter of the paragraph and carving out a space for it in the first few lines.

Figure 7-13. A page from a late 1470s Book of Hours, a common type of illuminated manuscript

As another elegant piece of insurance that my readers will be immediately drawn to what #main has to say, a drop cap will suit this page well.

Here are the properties I want my drop cap to include:

- The body text should wrap around it.
- It should be about six times the size of the text.
- The top should be flush with the top of the first line of text.
- The left side should remain flush with the text's left side, but the right and bottom sides should have a small margin to avoid butting up against the text.

Pseudo-elements in an imperfect world

Since I'm dealing directly with the first letter in my first paragraph (which already has a class of `first`), using the CSS `:first-letter` pseudo-element selector is a logical place to begin. Thus, rules for my drop cap will be addressed to `p.first:first-line`, and are easily translated line-for-line from my list of desired properties.

```
p.first:first-letter {
   float: left;
   font-size: 6em;
   line-height: .75em;
   margin-right: .1em;
   margin-bottom: .1em;
   }
```

In a rare twist, this code renders with reasonable consistency in all of my tested browsers, *except* for Firefox for Mac, which mysteriously inserts extra space at the top and bottom of my drop cap (Figure 7-14). No amount of fiddling with `line-height`, `padding`, or `margin` will make it behave consistently across browsers, and if the paragraph begins with an inline element like an em or strong (or a span, which I'll be adding later), the results are even more disparate. Sadly, I'll have to try a different solution.

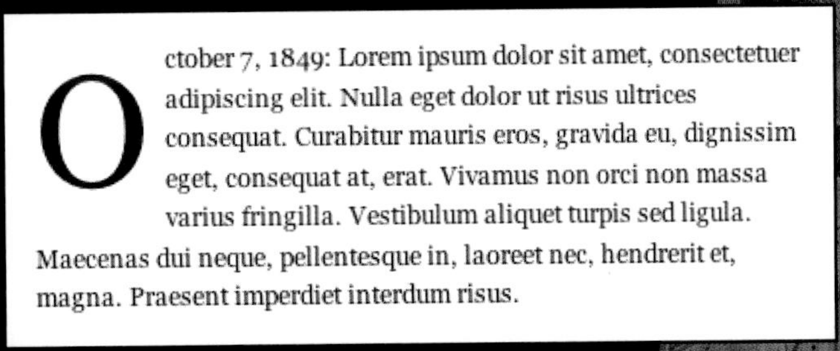

Figure 7-14. The Firefox `:first-letter` bug

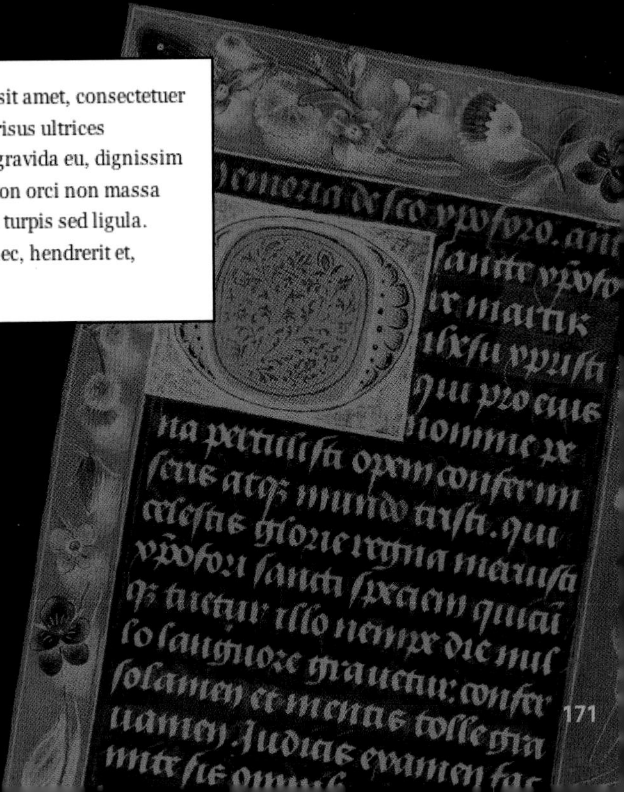

Span to the rescue

Another small adjustment to the markup will be necessary. I wrap my *O* in a span (with a class of drop) like this:

```
<p class="first"><span class="drop">O</span>ctober 7, 1849...</p>
```

And I give that class the exact same rules as before like this:

```
.drop {
  float: left;
  font-size: 6em;
  line-height: .75em;
  margin-right: .1em;
  margin-bottom: .1em;
  }
```

It works! My drop cap is in place (Figure 7-15).

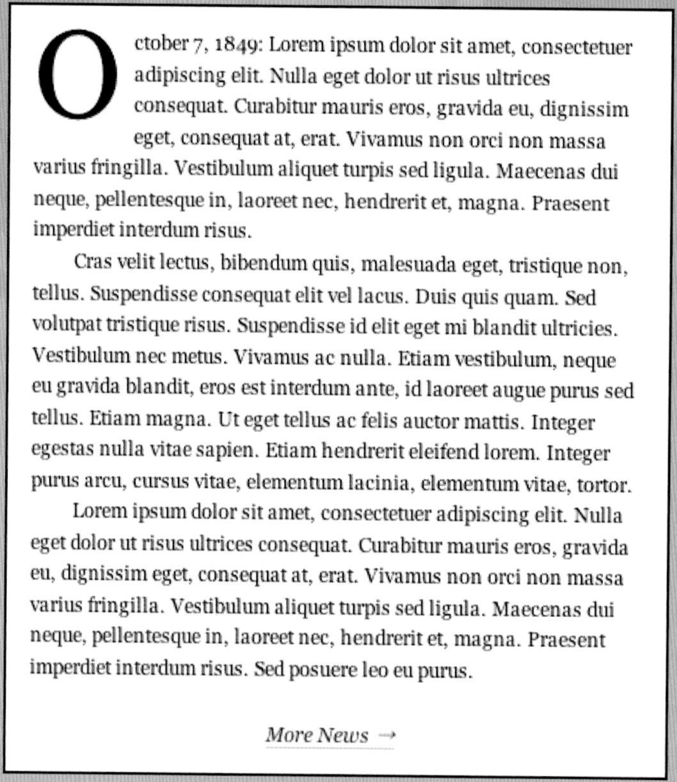

Figure 7-15. A pure CSS Georgia drop cap

Image replacement

But I'm still not happy. As much as I love Georgia, that big Georgia *O* is still not quite doing it for me. This page deserves something a bit more decorative, so I've created my own ornate capital *O* (Figure 7-16). This *O* is loosely based on the one found in Bodoni, an exquisite modern serif designed a year before Poe was born.

Figure 7-16. My custom versal

Rather than putting my versal image in the markup, I'm going to use an image replacement technique.

> *The particular image replacement technique I used is but one of many, most of which have been compiled by Dave Shea on his mezzoblue.com site (www.mezzoblue.com/tests/revised-image-replacement/). While I prefer this method for this example, others may be more appropriate for different situations, and I recommend reading up on them. You can also find more about image replacement techniques in Chapter 2, "Taming a Wild CMS with CSS, Flash, and JavaScript."*

Image replacement does exactly what it says: it replaces an element's HTML text with an image. In this example, it will be accomplished by sucking the text out of the element with a negative `text-indent`, and then dropping in my versal graphic as a background image.

```
.drop {
  width: 83px;
  height: 83px;
  float: left;
  text-indent: -9999px;
  background-image: url(o.gif);
  background-repeat: no-repeat;
  background-position: top left;
  margin-right: .1em;
  margin-bottom: .1em;
  }
```

My float and margins are intact from the previous example, my text is negatively indented to another galaxy, and the values for width and height correspond to the width and height of my versal graphic. It looks great in all of the browsers I'm testing, except for Internet Explorer. That browser has chosen to negatively indent my entire paragraph instead of just my span, causing the paragraph to completely disappear (Figure 7-17).

Cras velit lectus, bibendum quis, malesuada eget, tristique non, tellus. Suspendisse consequat elit vel lacus. Duis quis quam. Sed volutpat tristique risus. Suspendisse id elit eget mi blandit ultricies. Vestibulum nec metus. Vivamus ac nulla. Etiam vestibulum, neque eu gravida blandit, eros est interdum ante, id laoreet augue purus sed tellus. Etiam magna. Ut eget tellus ac felis auctor mattis. Integer egestas nulla vitae sapien. Etiam hendrerit eleifend lorem. Integer purus arcu, cursus vitae, elementum lacinia, elementum vitae, tortor.

Lorem ipsum dolor sit amet, consectetuer adipiscing elit. Nulla eget dolor ut risus ultrices consequat. Curabitur mauris eros, gravida eu, dignissim eget, consequat at, erat. Vivamus non orci non massa varius fringilla. Vestibulum aliquet turpis sed ligula. Maecenas dui neque, pellentesque in, laoreet nec, hendrerit et, magna. Praesent imperdiet interdum risus. Sed posuere leo eu purus.

More News →

Figure 7-17. Internet Explorer text-indent bug

Luckily, this problem is cleared up by simply declaring the span to be a block-level element:

```
.drop {
    width: 83px;
    height: 83px;
    display: block;
    float: left;
    text-indent: -9999px;
    background-image: url(o.gif);
    background-repeat: no-repeat;
    background-position: top left;
    margin-right: .1em;
    margin-bottom: .1em;
}
```

My custom-made drop cap is now in place (Figure 7-18)!

ctober 7, 1849: Lorem ipsum dolor sit amet, consectetuer adipiscing elit. Nulla eget dolor ut risus ultrices consequat. Curabitur mauris eros, gravida eu, dignissim eget, consequat at, erat. Vivamus non orci non massa varius fringilla. Vestibulum aliquet turpis sed ligula. Maecenas dui neque, pellentesque in, laoreet nec, hendrerit et, magna. Praesent imperdiet interdum risus.

Cras velit lectus, bibendum quis, malesuada eget, tristique non, tellus. Suspendisse consequat elit vel lacus. Duis quis quam. Sed volutpat tristique risus. Suspendisse id elit eget mi blandit ultricies. Vestibulum nec metus. Vivamus ac nulla. Etiam vestibulum, neque eu gravida blandit, eros est interdum ante, id laoreet augue purus sed tellus. Etiam magna. Ut eget tellus ac felis auctor mattis. Integer egestas nulla vitae sapien. Etiam hendrerit eleifend lorem. Integer purus arcu, cursus vitae, elementum lacinia, elementum vitae, tortor.

Lorem ipsum dolor sit amet, consectetuer adipiscing elit. Nulla eget dolor ut risus ultrices consequat. Curabitur mauris eros, gravida eu, dignissim eget, consequat at, erat. Vivamus non orci non massa varius fringilla. Vestibulum aliquet turpis sed ligula. Maecenas dui neque, pellentesque in, laoreet nec, hendrerit et, magna. Praesent imperdiet interdum risus. Sed posuere leo eu purus.

More News →

Figure 7-18. My gleaming drop cap

All caps

I am quite pleased with my drop cap. However, it is a bit visually jarring to have my paragraph go from such a bombastic introduction directly into much smaller lowercase text. I'll address this issue with one last bit of refinement, after which #main will be ready to meet its public.

If you haven't learned it in the typesetting world, you have probably learned it in the online world, especially in e-mail and instant messages: text set in all capital letters should be used with great caution. An errant mash of the Caps Lock key can give your audience members the impression that you are YELLING AT THEM, which isn't the best way to keep them coming back. With this rule in mind, all caps can still be used to great effect, and a restrained usage will make a logical bridge between my gigantic drop cap and the much smaller body text that it introduces. Since my date stamp—October 7, 1849 (the date of Poe's death)—already functions as a concise, self-contained opening to the text, it is a perfect candidate for the all caps treatment.

Your first instinct might be to merely set the text in all caps right in the markup, thereby avoiding the decidedly more laborious CSS process I am about to describe. This isn't a good idea for a number of reasons, and chief among them is the possibility that you may later wish to style this text differently. If this were a template from which many pages were built, it would be a lot easier to change one rule in a CSS file than to change the markup in dozens (or hundreds or thousands) of HTML documents. Also, as you'll see in the following example, there can be quite a bit more to consider while setting all caps text than merely typing with Caps Lock on.

I'll begin by adding one last span to my markup to target the date stamp:

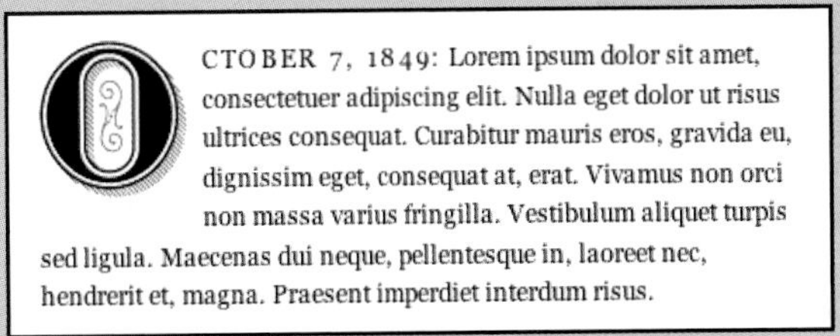

```
<p class="first"><span class="datestamp">
<span class="drop">O</span>ctober 7, 1849:</span> Lorem ipsum...</p>
```

Now I just need two simple, self-explanatory CSS rules to make my datestamp class behave in the desired fashion:

```
.datestamp {
   text-transform: uppercase;
   letter-spacing: .13em;
   }
```

Giving text-transform a value of uppercase will ensure that my text is set in all caps. It can also take the values lowercase (for all lowercase text) and capitalize (to capitalize the first letter of each word). As for letter-spacing, when setting text in all caps, a bit of extra letter spacing is key for legibility. Through a small amount of experimentation, I came to find the very precise 0.13em measurement to be ideal for this case (Figure 7-19).

Figure 7-19. #main's datestamp set in all caps Georgia

Text figures vs. titling figures

My paragraph introduction looks pretty good, but I've got one last fish to fry. One of the things that makes Georgia such a gem is that it is the only typeface in wide use on the Web that includes *text figures* (sometimes called *old style figures*) (Figure 7-20), which are essentially lowercase numerals. With ascenders and descenders just like lowercase letters, text figures are less disruptive to body text than their uppercase counterparts, called *titling figures*. Ideally, a typeface will include both text and titling figures, but typically only the latter is included. Georgia bears the odd distinction of instead including only text figures, and as a result, my uppercase date stamp has lowercase numerals. This won't do.

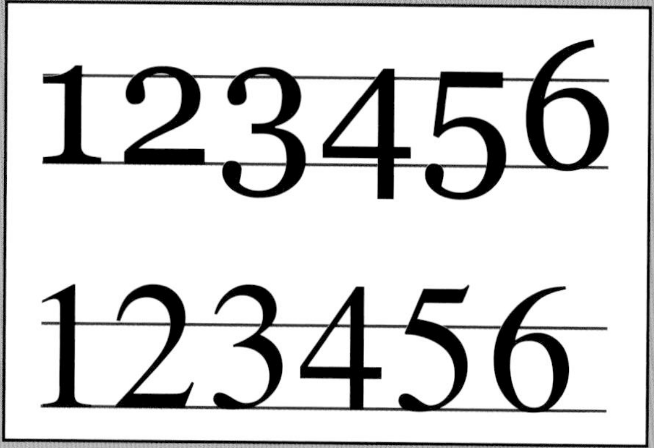

Times New Roman, with its similarity to Georgia and inclusion of titling figures, is the perfect solution to this problem. In addition, I find Times New Roman set in all caps to be slightly less heavy and oppressive than Georgia set in all caps. Ordinarily, I would avoid using such similar typefaces in the same document, but it works quite well in this case, since the idea here is to create the illusion of *one* typeface. With one more simple CSS rule, #main will finally be complete (Figure 7-21):

```
.datestamp {
    font-family: "Times New Roman", Times,
Georgia, serif;
    text-transform: uppercase;
    letter-spacing: .13em;
}
```

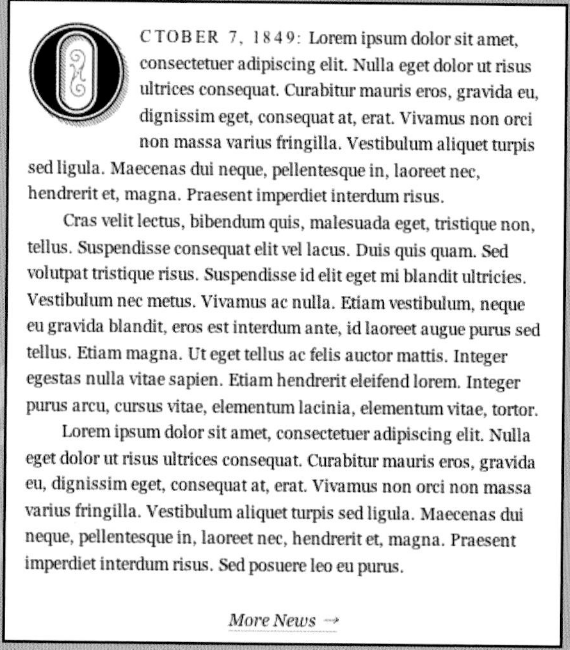

123456
123456

Figure 7-20. Georgia's text figures (top) vs. Times New Roman's titling figures (bottom)

OCTOBER 7, 1849: Lorem ipsum dolor sit amet, consectetuer adipiscing elit. Nulla eget dolor ut risus ultrices consequat. Curabitur mauris eros, gravida eu, dignissim eget, consequat at, erat. Vivamus non orci non massa varius fringilla. Vestibulum aliquet turpis sed ligula. Maecenas dui neque, pellentesque in, laoreet nec, hendrerit et, magna. Praesent imperdiet interdum risus.

Cras velit lectus, bibendum quis, malesuada eget, tristique non, tellus. Suspendisse consequat elit vel lacus. Duis quis quam. Sed volutpat tristique risus. Suspendisse id elit eget mi blandit ultricies. Vestibulum nec metus. Vivamus ac nulla. Etiam vestibulum, neque eu gravida blandit, eros est interdum ante, id laoreet augue purus sed tellus. Etiam magna. Ut eget tellus ac felis auctor mattis. Integer egestas nulla vitae sapien. Etiam hendrerit eleifend lorem. Integer purus arcu, cursus vitae, elementum lacinia, elementum vitae, tortor.

Lorem ipsum dolor sit amet, consectetuer adipiscing elit. Nulla eget dolor ut risus ultrices consequat. Curabitur mauris eros, gravida eu, dignissim eget, consequat at, erat. Vivamus non orci non massa varius fringilla. Vestibulum aliquet turpis sed ligula. Maecenas dui neque, pellentesque in, laoreet nec, hendrerit et, magna. Praesent imperdiet interdum risus. Sed posuere leo eu purus.

More News →

Figure 7-21. Completed #main

Small caps

There is one more typographic element that I've chosen to address, to apply in the #about paragraph on the right side of Poe's homepage. I want the first line to appear in small caps.

The basic markup of #about is very similar to #main.

```
<div id="about">

  <p class="first">Edgar Allan Poe lorem ipsum...</p>

  <p class="more"><a href="#" title="Edgar Allan Poe: About">
    More About Poe &rarr;</a></p>

</div>
```

Small caps are capital letters that are usually slightly taller than their typeface's x-height, which is the height of its lowercase letter *x*. Thus, they are effectively lowercase capital letters. They are commonly used for abbreviations, acronyms, and, as in this case study's example, to mark the beginning of a text in a more subdued manner than a versal would. For this purpose, the first few words or the entire first line of an introductory paragraph might be set in small caps.

Fair warning

To the untrained eye, small caps can easily be mistaken for merely shrunken versions of their uppercase counterparts. However, in a well-designed typeface, small caps are drawn separately from the uppercase letters, and the subtle differences between the two maintain the consistency of the letters' stroke weights (Figure 7-22). True small caps are easier to read at small point sizes and won't disrupt the flow of the text, whereas faux small caps (for example, 8-point uppercase type set amid a block of otherwise 12-point type) are almost always conspicuous and distracting.

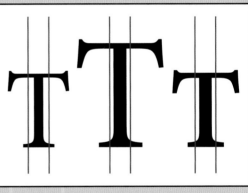

Figure 7-22. Note the difference in stroke width between the faux small cap (left), the full cap (center), and the true small cap (right).

When faced with the following set of CSS rules, a web browser will set the specified text in Georgia Italic, which is of course a different design from—and not merely a slanted bastardization of—Georgia Regular.

```
font-family: Georgia;
font-style: italic;
```

However, if I were to add a rule of `font-variant: small-caps`, the text couldn't be set in true small caps because Georgia has none to offer. Likewise, the vast majority of the most widely, publicly disseminated digital text faces do not include a set of small caps. As a result, web browsers use faux small caps by default. Before the dawn of screen font-smoothing technologies like Quartz (Mac OS) and ClearType (Windows), this wasn't much of an issue, since the subtleties of faux small caps' proportional differences were lost to the pixelated letters' low resolution (Figure 7-23). With screen font-smoothing becoming increasingly prevalent, though, we can no longer rely on the browser to cover up its own typographic *faux pas*. Faux small caps now look more or less the same on the screen as they do in print.

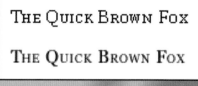

Figure 7-23. Pixelated small caps (top) vs. smoothed small caps (bottom)

Though faux small caps have been the object of legitimate scorn since long before the Web even existed, the argument could be made that they are acceptable on the Web, if only because true small caps simply aren't available yet. Conspicuous though they may be, they still certainly have the power to enhance and enrich the page. The decision of whether or not to use them is yours to make.

More pseudo-element selectors in an imperfect world

My last attempt at using a pseudo-element selector ended in heartache (remember `:first-letter`?), but, for the sake of small caps, I'm going to try again, this time with `:first-line`. Unsurprisingly, `:first-line` affects its targeted element's first line of text. In this case, the targeted element will be #about's first paragraph.

```
#about p.first:first-line {
    font-variant: small-caps;
    text-transform: lowercase;
    letter-spacing: .1em;
}
```

By now, these CSS rules should be fairly elementary, but there is one line that may have raised a questioning eyebrow. Why did I use `text-transform: lowercase`? The reasons are both preferential and practical. Small caps can, by their nature, function as either uppercase or lowercase letters. Accordingly, words that would ordinarily require capitalization (such as proper names) may or may not begin with a full capital letter when set in small caps. I usually prefer *not* to capitalize words set in small caps as a matter of consistency, since acronyms typically use small caps in place of the full caps that otherwise construct them. As for the practical concern, I don't want any more attention drawn to the artificiality of my faux small caps than is necessary. To have them sit alongside full caps invites comparison and further exposes their inauthenticity (as seen in Figure 7-23), so I prefer to keep them among their own faux kind if I can.

This may be sound reasoning, but Internet Explorer and Safari will hear none of it. Each has its own bug that prevents the intended effect from happening. Internet Explorer will not acknowledge any combination of `font-variant` and `text-transform` rules, and Safari will not acknowledge a `text-transform` rule applied to a pseudo-element selector. As a result, Internet Explorer and Safari both render the markup's capital letters as full caps. Firefox and Opera display the text correctly.

The Safari bug in particular makes it impossible for my intended effect to render consistently across browsers, as it's a combination of the pseudo-element selector `first-line` and the text transform rule `lowercase` that I'm trying to use here. Therefore, avoiding further changes to my markup and ensuring that my small caps remain only on the first line of text will require a compromise: Internet Explorer and Safari will display a potentially mixed bag of full caps and faux small caps. Looking at the finished page (Figure 7-24), I think I could definitely do a lot worse!

Edgar Allan Poe

http://wsc.robweychert.com/

HOME

ABOUT

NEWS

WORKS

CONTACT

CTOBER 7, 1849: Lorem ipsum dolor sit amet, consectetuer adipiscing elit. Nulla eget dolor ut risus ultrices consequat. Curabitur mauris eros, gravida eu, dignissim eget, consequat at, erat. Vivamus non orci non massa varius fringilla. Vestibulum aliquet turpis sed ligula. Maecenas dui neque, pellentesque in, laoreet nec, hendrerit et, magna. Praesent imperdiet interdum risus.

Cras velit lectus, bibendum quis, malesuada eget, tristique non, tellus. Suspendisse consequat elit vel lacus. Duis quis quam. Sed volutpat tristique risus. Suspendisse id elit eget mi blandit ultricies. Vestibulum nec metus. Vivamus ac nulla. Etiam vestibulum, neque eu gravida blandit, eros est interdum ante, id laoreet augue purus sed tellus. Etiam magna. Ut eget tellus ac felis auctor mattis. Integer egestas nulla vitae sapien. Etiam hendrerit eleifend lorem. Integer purus arcu, cursus vitae, elementum lacinia, elementum vitae, tortor.

Lorem ipsum dolor sit amet, consectetuer adipiscing elit. Nulla eget dolor ut risus ultrices consequat. Curabitur mauris eros, gravida eu, dignissim eget, consequat at, erat. Vivamus non orci non massa varius fringilla. Vestibulum aliquet turpis sed ligula. Maecenas dui neque, pellentesque in, laoreet nec, hendrerit et, magna. Praesent imperdiet interdum risus. Sed posuere leo eu purus.

More News →

EDGAR ALLAN POE lorem ipsum dolor sit amet, consectetuer adipiscing elit. Nulla eget dolor ut risus ultrices consequat. Curabitur mauris eros, gravida eu, dignissim eget, consequat at, erat. Vivamus non orci non massa varius fringilla.

More About Poe →

Figure 7-24. The effort was all worth it!

Conclusion

Make no mistake: the print world and the web world are different places, each with its own idiosyncrasies. They do have at least one very important thing in common, though, which is that they exist to help people communicate. While we should acknowledge and respect the fact that what works typographically for one might not work for the other, we should also respect the reader, who can benefit from many techniques whose utility is not inextricably tied to either medium. The techniques I've outlined in this chapter should have given you a good idea of some ways that you can enliven type on the Web.

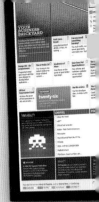

DOM Scripting Gems

What book on web standards would be complete without some DOM scripting examples? That's why I've dedicated the last part of this book to dynamic scripting techniques for improving your users' experience.

I've deliberately tried to choose techniques that aren't too scary for the more designy and less develop types among you—don't be afraid to get your hands dirty with some JavaScript!

Ian starts off by showing us his technique for saving the world: by using DOM scripting to specify that only the important parts of a web page get printed, we avoid wasted paper and hassle.

Next up, Cameron demonstrates that it's not that difficult to provide your users with a more dynamic interactive environment on your web pages by using a little well-placed scripting. During the course of his case study, he builds up a dynamic user interface that will adjust itself for optimum viewing, no matter what resolution/platform the user is using to visit your site. He also shows how to create an interface that the user can customize, by moving content around in different palettes.

Last but not least, Derek shows how to implement an attractive sliding site navigation menu that retains accessibility. I wanted to include some coverage of scripting and accessibility in the book, as it's a hot topic. Ajax especially can cause havoc for the accessibility of pages, and we need to be careful not to shut out users with disabilities.

8

Print Magic:
Using the
DOM and CSS
to Save the Planet

ian
lloyd

accessify.com

Ian Lloyd runs Accessify.com, a site dedicated to promoting web accessibility and providing tools for web developers. His personal site, Blog Standard Stuff, ironically, has nothing to do with standards for blogs (it's a play on words), although an occasional standards-related gem can be found there.

Ian works full-time for Nationwide Building Society, where he tries his hardest to influence standards-based design ("to varying degrees!"). He is a member of the Web Standards Project, contributing to the Accessibility Task Force. Web standards and accessibility aside, he enjoys writing about his trips abroad and recently took a "year out" from work and all things web (but then ended up writing more in his year off than he ever has). He finds most of his time being taken up by a demanding old lady (relax, it's only his old Volkswagen camper van).

Ian recently wrote his first book for SitePoint, entitled *Build Your Own Web Site the Right Way Using HTML & CSS* (in which he teaches web standards-based design to the complete beginner).

A printing technique is born

Saving the planet? What's that all about? Well, I'll be getting to that in due course. First, I want to take you back in time. OK, so it's only a month ago as I write this, but it's the point at which I got the inspiration for what you'll be reading in this chapter.

I was sitting at my desk at work, busy with something or other, when my colleague said to me, "Is there any way that you can get a web page to print only one specific part?"

"Oh yes," I replied, "That's easy—you can use print CSS styles to do that. Which part of the page do you want to print and which parts don't you want to print?"

"Well, that depends," he replied, preparing to throw the proverbial curveball. "We've got this great big long page of interest rates, but depending on the account the person has, they'll want a different section to be printed."

I mulled it over. I remembered that on some browsers it was possible to select a portion of a page and then print just that section, an option offered in the Print dialog box, but this was hardly ideal, as it required the user to know that option existed. Also, it's not available on all browsers. For the über-techy types, it would be possible to use a Greasemonkey[1] script to print a given selection, but that would probably account for 0.001% of our intended audience at a push. What my colleague was after was something that the browser simply did not offer in any obvious format. So I told him, "Sorry, you can't do that. I'm afraid that unless they know about highlighting a section and then choosing 'print selection,' it's not possible."

Then I got back to whatever pixels I was pushing around the screen at the time. However, the idea refused to go away, nagging at the back of my mind. I personally hate it when you want to print one section of a page and end up printing seven sheets of nonsense, six of which immediately get tossed. Couldn't there be a way of solving this problem and cutting down on wasted printouts? And then it came to me: a mixture of print CSS; some good, solid, and semantic markup; and some unobtrusive JavaScript might just achieve what he was after. So I got started on a proof of concept.

The basic idea

Knowing that it was possible to dynamically change the appearance of a web page as viewed on screen using the DOM, JavaScript, and CSS, I wondered whether the same theory could apply to print. There was nothing to suggest that this could not happen. I recalled reading Aaron Gustafson's article in A List Apart (http://www.alistapart.com), where he demonstrated a method for displaying footnotes, and I knew that there was some scope for this kind of behavior. I just wasn't sure just how "dynamic" this could be. The only one way to find out was to try it. So, I began with this idea:

For any given page that has specific sections that might need to be printed in isolation, such as the interest rates page that prompted my investigation, use JavaScript to dynamically switch the display property off or on (that's to say block or none), but *only* for the print view.

The other aims for this technique included

- The technique must be unobtrusive.[2] It should fit in the category of progressive enhancement,[3] and all the behavior should be controlled from a shared JavaScript file.
- It must look good, not just work.
- It has to be based on totally clean and valid markup.
- The purpose of the technique needs to be really obvious to the user.

Thankfully, all of these aims are achievable, as I will demonstrate in the following pages.

---

1. Greasemonkey is a Firefox extension that allows you to bolt on extra functionality to the browser. For more information, a good starting point is Dive Into Greasemonkey (http://diveintogreasemonkey.org/install/what-is-greasemonkey.html).

2. Unobtrusive scripts do not require inline event handlers, such as onclick or onmouseover, in the HTML. All scripting is centralized, making site-wide management and maintenance far easier (in a similar way to how using a shared style sheet centralizes the management of the site's presentation).

3. Progressive enhancement is an approach to web design that provides access to a basic version of your page to all, but adds an extra layer of behavior or styling (or both) to browsers that are up to the job. You can find out more about this technique and links to related articles at http://en.wikipedia.org/wiki/Progressive_Enhancement.

Preparing the foundations

With a clear final objective and some aims defined, I began work on a simple proof of concept. This is the part of the process where the visual effect looks a bit ugly but the functional parts get worked out, so don't worry—I'll be making it look pretty later in the chapter. I knew what the ultimate aim was (to apply it to the long-winded interest rates page that needs carving up for print), but to begin with, I created a dummy page that contained the basics.

Sectioning the page

The key to this technique is knowing which parts of the page you do and don't want to print. As I saw it, this could be done using CSS classes, and the obvious choice is to use a classname of section or, if you want to make it absolutely clear of the purpose, a classname like print_section.[4] So, here's a simple HTML page with some sections marked up (with just a sprinkling of CSS applied to help identify the boundaries):

```
<!DOCTYPE HTML PUBLIC "-//W3C//DTD HTML 4.01 Transitional//EN"➥
  "http://www.w3.org/TR/html4/loose.dtd">
<html>
<head>
<title>A sectioned-up web page</title>
<meta http-equiv="Content-Type" content="text/html; charset=utf-8">
<style type="text/css">
.print_section
{
  border:1px solid gray;
  background:#e1e1e1;
  margin:0 0 15px 0;
  padding:10px;
}
</style>
</head>

<body>
  <h1>Sectioned up page</h1>

  <div class="print_section">
    <h2>Section 1</h2>
    <p>This is section 1. Nothing much to see here, just a bunch of meaningless words.</p>
  </div>

  <div class="print_section">
    <h2>Section 2</h2>
    <p>This is section 2. You'd be better off watching paint dry than reading the content here.</p>
  </div>
```

---

4. If we were using XHTML 2.0, we could opt for using a section element. See www.w3.org/TR/xhtml2/mod-structural.html#edef_structural_section for more information.

```
<div class="print_section">
  <h2>Section 3</h2>
  <p>This is the final section. Hurrah!</p>
</div>

</body>
</html>
```

Figure 8-1 shows this dummy page.

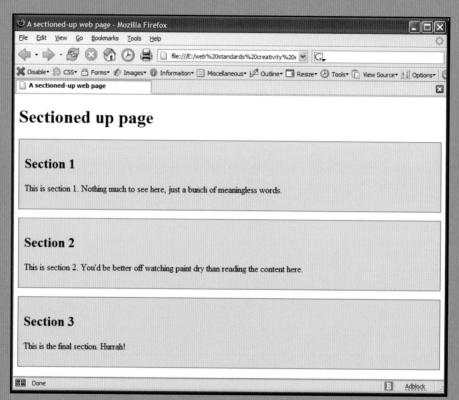

Figure 8-1. Sectioning the page, ready for printing

This would be the basic page (ignoring the placeholder content that I've used for the dummy page) that a visitor would see. Now the trick is to add in the extra layers of goodness on top for those browsers that are up to the job—progressive enhancement in action.

Identifying the sections

The basic structure of the page is there, but it needs something else if this technique is to work. How are we to magically toggle the appearance of these sections if we can't identify which section we're dealing with at any given time? The clue is in that question: *identify*, or id, the sections. Yep, we just have to add an id attribute to the sections, like so:

```
<div id="sect1" class="print_section">
  <h2>Section 1</h2>
  <p>This is section 1. Nothing much to see here, just a bunch of ➥
    meaningless words.</p>
</div>

<div id="sect2" class="print_section">
  <h2>Section 2</h2>
  <p>This is section 2. You'd be better off watching paint dry than ➥
    reading the content here.</p>
</div>

<div id="sect3" class="print_section">
  <h2>Section 3</h2>
  <p>This is the final section. Hurrah!</p>
</div>
```

This will have no effect on the visual side of things for the time being, but it will provide the hook that we're going to need for our JavaScript behaviors. Now let's get to the nuts and bolts of it.

Pseudocode first

Earlier in the chapter, I described in plain English what the technique should do. Now I'm going to veer into the pseudocode world and describe the order of events that are going to take place here.

The browser begins loading the page, and includes a piece of JavaScript in an external .js file that contains all the behavioral rules. When the page has loaded, the JavaScript kicks in and does the following:

1. First, it goes through the entire document looking for div elements and creates an array

2. Next, it goes through that array of div elements one by one. If the div element has a classname of print_section, it does the following:

    (a) It creates a button or link that will say Print this section or similar.

    (b) It then applies a behavior to that button. The behavior when clicked is to first check the id of the link that was clicked. If the id matches the current section (as the browser trawls through all the printable sections in the document), make that section visible (in the printed view). If the id of the link clicked does not match up (as the browser trawls through all the printable sections in the document), it hides the current section (again, only for print).

3. Bring up the Print dialog box in the browser, as shown in Figure 8-2. Unfortunately, it's not possible to avoid this step and get it to go *straight* to print. The user will still have one more button to click. In the Firefox example in Figure 8-2, it's the OK button.

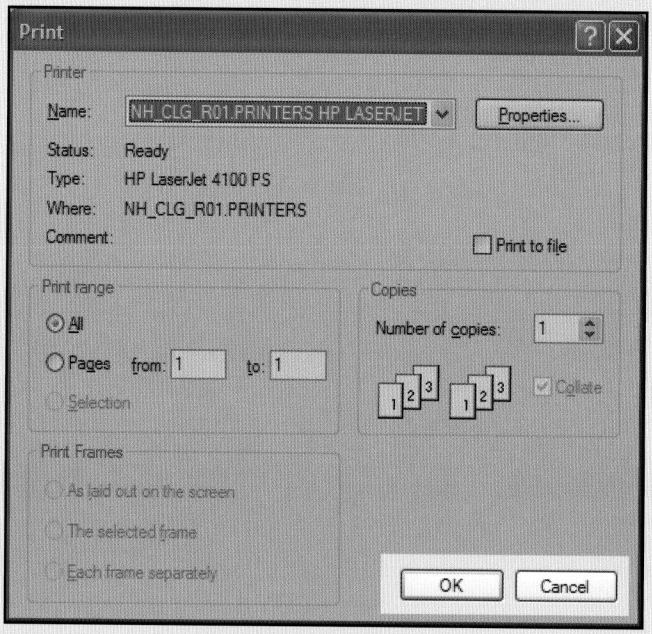

Figure 8-2. The Print dialog box appears before printing.

4. When the visual elements for each section are created and their associated behaviors are defined, they then get inserted into the page.

All of these steps should happen very quickly. Unless the web page is very long or there is an element on the web page that takes a lot longer to download than others (for example, an image from an external website that is running, like a dog, and not a greyhound at that), the user should not notice a jarring change in the page's appearance.

> *The reason why a single slow-loading element on a page can delay this effect is because the JavaScript runs after the page has loaded. This is because the* onload *event happens once everything on the page has been downloaded—all images, scripts, and CSS files linked to—rather than just the page's markup.*

So, that's the plan of attack with the dummy page. Let's look at some of the real code that's going to help us achieve this.

Event planning

The first thing that needs doing is setting up the page load events. Now there are many different ways of doing this, and just as many opinions about which method is the best (see http://tinyurl.com/ct2vy). My bet is that many of the readers of this book are at a level where they are quite capable of making up their own mind and can adapt the suggested addEvent function that I'm using (from Scott Andrew: http://tinyurl.com/qcmrd). However, even if this is not the case, and you, dear reader, have no idea what I'm talking about, fear not—it really is worrying too much about the smallest of details. Move along, nothing to see here, nothing to see . . .

The addEvent function primes the web page. It tells the browser what it needs to run (which JavaScript function) and when (on what event—for example, when the page loads or when something gets clicked). Here it is:

```
function addEvent(elm, evType, fn, useCapture)
{
  if(elm.addEventListener)
    {
    elm.addEventListener(evType, fn, useCapture);
    return true;
    }
  else if (elm.attachEvent)
    {
    var r = elm.attachEvent('on' + evType, fn);
    return r;
    }
  else
    {
    elm['on' + evType] = fn;
    }
}
```

Now if that looks like gobbledygook to you, don't worry. You don't need to understand everything it does or how. You simply need to know that it has been created to work around some cross-browser JavaScript issues, and it allows you to call it using three parameters:

- What element you are dealing with (elm)
- What the event is (click, load, focus) (evType)
- What JavaScript function you want it to do when that element has that event triggered (fn)

And here's an example of how you would call it:

```
addEvent(window, 'load', addPrintLinks, false);
```

Or, in plain English, when the window (or, to be precise, the document in this window) has loaded, please run the addPrintLinks function. This function has yet to be built, so just to test that it works, I've placed a simple alert there for the time being:

```
<script type="text/javascript">
  function addPrintLinks()
  {
    alert("Here's where the cool stuff will happen");
  }
  addEvent(window, 'load', addPrintLinks, false);
</script>
```

The alert looks like Figure 8-3.

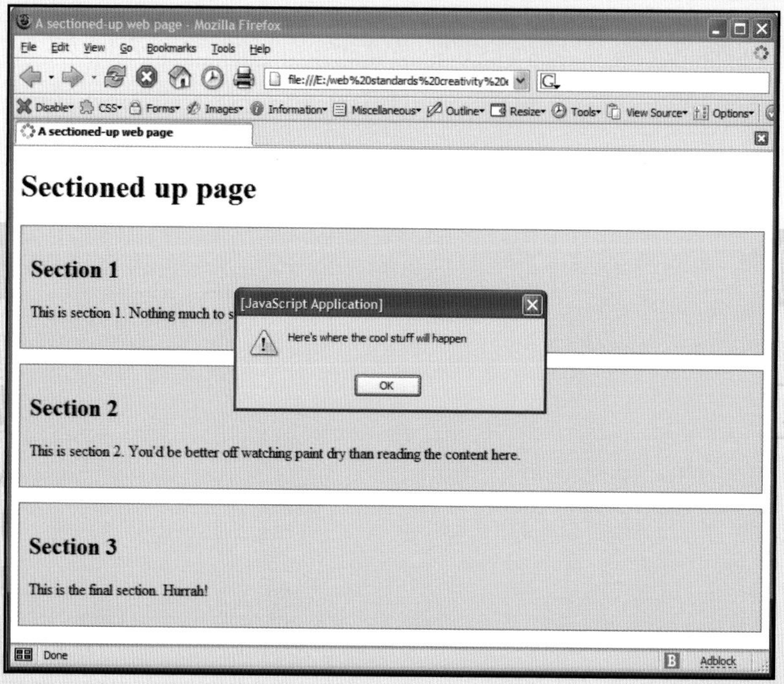

Figure 8-3. The alert placeholder in action

From pseudocode to real code

Having set out the steps required to make this work, let's take a look at the actual code that will do it (I'll quote from my earlier descriptions):

"The browser begins loading the page, and includes a piece of JavaScript in an external `.js` file that contains all the behavioral rules."

In the previous examples, I showed the scripts embedded in the page itself. It's now time to place the scripts in their own file and refer to them in the web page, like so:

```
<!DOCTYPE html PUBLIC "-//W3C//DTD XHTML 1.0 Strict//EN" ➥
  "http://www.w3.org/TR/xhtml1/DTD/xhtml1-strict.dtd">
<html xmlns="http://www.w3.org/1999/xhtml">
<head>
  <title>A sectioned-up page</title>
  <script type="text/javascript" src="print_sections.js"></script>
  <meta http-equiv="Content-Type" content="text/html; charset=iso-8859-1">
...
```

"When the page has loaded . . ."

That's our AddEvent part, mentioned previously. The addEvent function should be in the .js file, as is the following call to that function:

```
addEvent(window, 'load', addPrintLinks, false);
```

". . . the JavaScript kicks in and does the following:

First, it goes through the entire document looking for div elements and creates an array."

```
function addPrintLinks()
{
var el = document.getElementsByTagName("div");
for (i=0;i<el.length;i++)
  {//loop through the array of divs and do something cool
    ...
  }
}
```

Creating new print links for the page

"Next, it goes through that array of div elements one by one. If the div element has a classname of print_section . . ."

```
function addPrintLinks()
{
var el = document.getElementsByTagName("div");
for (i=0;i<el.length;i++)
  {
    if (el[i].className=="print_section")
    {//focus on only divs that are print sections
    ...
    }
  }
}
```

". . . it does the following:

It creates a button or link that will say Print this section or similar.

It then applies a behavior to that button."

Quite a bit of JavaScript is required to fulfill these aims, and here it is (with comments in the appropriate places explaining what each part is doing):

```
function addPrintLinks()
{
var el = document.getElementsByTagName("div");
for (i=0;i<el.length;i++)
  {
  if (el[i].className=="print_section")
    {
    // create the anchor element
    var newLink = document.createElement("a");
    // give it some text content
    var newLinkText = document.createTextNode("print this section only");
```

```
            // create a container for the link to
            // go in and give it a class
            var newLinkPara = document.createElement("p");
            newLinkPara.setAttribute("class","printbutton");

            // set up the 'print this section' link

            newLink.setAttribute("href","#");
            // the print button will need a unique ID
            // (this will be used to tell the function
            // what section is to be shown or hidden )
            var btId = "printbut_" + el[i].id;
            newLink.setAttribute("id",btId);
            // add the text for the link to the anchor element
            newLink.appendChild(newLinkText);
            // add the anchor element to the paragraph element
            newLinkPara.appendChild(newLink);

            //add the behaviors for the new link
            newLink.onclick = togglePrintDisplay;
            newLink.onkeypress = togglePrintDisplay;
            }
        }
    }
```

At this point, we've created the link that will be used to do the printout. It's been placed in a paragraph, but that paragraph has not yet been inserted into the document. It's currently in limbo—floating around in the browser's memory somewhere—but we'll be getting to that in just a moment. Carrying on with the pseudo-to-real code translations then:

"The behavior [of the link] when clicked is to first check the id of the link that was clicked. If the id matches the current section (as the browser trawls through all the printable sections in the document), make that section visible (in the printed view). If the id of the link clicked does *not* match up (as the browser trawls through all the printable sections in the document), it hides the current section (again, only for print).

Bring up the Print dialog box in the browser."

The behavior for the link was attached using these lines of script:

```
            newLink.onclick = togglePrintDisplay;
            newLink.onkeypress = togglePrintDisplay;
```

This means that when the link is clicked or when the link has focus and a keypress event is detected, the browser should run a new function called togglePrintDisplay.

Adding the behavior

Let's take a look at what's in the togglePrintDisplay function. I'll show it all in one go first, and then I'll step through the constituent parts to explain what's happening:

```
        function togglePrintDisplay(e)
        {
        var whatSection = this.id.split("_");
        whatSection = whatSection[1];
        var el = document.getElementsByTagName("div");
```

```
for (i=0;i<el.length;i++)
  {
  if (el[i].className.indexOf("print_section")!=-1)
    {
    el[i].removeAttribute("className");
    if (el[i].id==whatSection)
      {
      //show only this section for print
      el[i].setAttribute("className","print_section print");
      el[i].setAttribute("class","print_section print");
      }
    else
      {
      //hide the sections from printout
      el[i].setAttribute("className","print_section noprint");
      el[i].setAttribute("class","print_section noprint");
      }
    }
  }
if (window.event)
  {
  window.event.returnValue = false;
  window.event.cancelBubble = true;
  }
else if (e)
  {
  e.stopPropagation();
  e.preventDefault();
  }
window.print();
}
```

And here it is step by step. First, the function gets the id from the link that was clicked. The id should be something like printBut_sect2. It was created programmatically (grabbing the parent container's id of sect2 and appending it to the newly created button) earlier, like so:

```
var btId = "printbut_" + el[i].id;
```

Of course, it's possible to use shorter variable names, but I'm aiming for readability here. Note that you cannot begin an id with a number; hence, I used an underscore in the id value. It makes it pretty easy to retrieve the value later, as shown in the following snippet. We use a split function, splitting at the underscore. This creates an array with two values: printBut and the part we really want, sect2 in the following example.

Those two values are passed into a variable whatSection. We really want only the second part of that array, though. Because arrays start at 0, the second item in the array is referred to using [1]; hence, we get the information we want using whatSection[1]. That value is then passed into the whatSection variable (overwriting its previous array values; whatSection now ceases to be an array and becomes a string).

```
function togglePrintDisplay(e)
{
var whatSection = this.id.split("_");
whatSection = whatSection[1];
```

Now that we have the id we're looking for, we need to once again trawl through the document, looking for all the div elements, specifically the div elements that have a classname of print_section:

```
var el = document.getElementsByTagName("div");
for (i=0;i<el.length;i++) //loop through all the divs found
  {
  if (el[i].className.indexOf("print_section")!=-1)
    {
```

So, at this stage, we're looking at a div that has in its classname somewhere the value print_section. Note that there is a reason why I've chosen to use the indexOf method in the preceding bit of script to match the className attribute. In the next part, I'll combine the print_section classname with either a print or noprint classname, so a straight == comparison would not work. Onwards and upwards then.

First of all, we get rid of any className attributes found for the element that's currently being looked at (remember, we're looping through a collection), and then check the id we ascertained earlier. If the id matches up (for example, sect1, sect2), then we know that the button clicked relates to this div, and we can deal with it accordingly by setting a class of print, as well as reinstating the print_section classname (otherwise, this script would fail after its first use for any given page):

```
el[i].removeAttribute("className");
if (el[i].id==whatSection)
  {//if this is the section to be printed, set a 'print' classname
  el[i].setAttribute("className","print_section print");
  el[i].setAttribute("class","print_section print");
  }
else


  {
  // otherwise hide the section from printout
  el[i].setAttribute("className","print_section noprint");
  el[i].setAttribute("class","print_section noprint");
  }
  }
}
```

Note that there seems to be a bit of doubling of effort here: setting both the class attribute and the className attribute. This is a workaround to solve differences between the way Internet Explorer and other browsers handle things. It's not a *big* overhead, and hardly worth creating a new custom function to deal with it (which you could do if you felt so inclined).

The final part of the script is simply there to cancel the browser carrying out the default action of the element clicked. In the example here, the element I've chosen to fire up the printing functions is a link (or anchor, to be precise), which I gave an href attribute of #. Normally, a link with this attribute would call the same page again. If this happened in our page, when choosing the print button, the page would reload and appear to jump, which is not the desired effect. The following code stops the default action from taking place:

```
if (window.event)
  {
    window.event.returnValue = false;
    window.event.cancelBubble = true;
  }
else if (e)
  {
    e.stopPropagation();
    e.preventDefault();
  }
```

It is generally considered bad practice to use a link, stick an href of # in there, and then use the link for another purpose. So why the heck am I doing it? How can I justify these actions? Well, the reason that it's normally a bad idea is that a link written this way fails when JavaScript is switched off. However, we're using JavaScript to create this technique; therefore, there's absolutely no danger of this situation happening.

Another solution might be to dynamically write in buttons rather than a link. However, that itself presents some issues. First of all, this may limit your styling options (you have more CSS control over a link element than an input of type button or submit). Secondly, well, it's not really a form is it? And if you dynamically write in form buttons, you need to wrap a form element around it. Also, if it is a form, should you use an input of type button or submit? No form data is being submitted for processing, after all. So, I opted for an anchor. Somebody shoot me!

Finally, we call the Print dialog box. All the classnames have been changed—thus affecting their display—and so we're pretty much good to go:

```
window.print();
}//end of the togglePrintDisplay function
```

Writing the new links into the document

We're not quite done yet, though. The togglePrintDisplay function was called from the addPrintLinks function, and that first script wasn't quite completed yet. There was the small matter of inserting the buttons (contained in paragraphs) into the web page after it loaded. That's achieved with this line:

```
el[i].insertBefore(newLinkPara,el[i].firstChild);
```

Recap: what these scripts do

And now we're pretty much done. So to recap:

1. The page loads, and addPrintLinks runs.

2. addPrintLinks calls another function, togglePrintDisplay, where the behaviors are set.

3. When the behavior is set for each element required, addPrintLinks resumes, appending the new links into the web page.

Here are the finished scripts in their entirety:

```
function addEvent(elm, evType, fn, useCapture)
{
  if(elm.addEventListener)
    {
    elm.addEventListener(evType, fn, useCapture);
    return true;
    }
  else if (elm.attachEvent)
    {
    var r = elm.attachEvent('on' + evType, fn);
    return r;
    }
  else
```

```javascript
        {
        elm['on' + evType] = fn;
        }
}

function addPrintLinks()
{
var el = document.getElementsByTagName("div");
for (i=0;i<el.length;i++)
    {
    if (el[i].className=="print_section")
        {
        var newLink = document.createElement("a");
        var newLinkText = document.createTextNode("print this section ➡
            only");
        var newLinkPara = document.createElement("p");
        newLinkPara.setAttribute("class","printbutton");

        //set up the 'print this section' link
        var btId = "printbut_" + el[i].id;
        newLink.setAttribute("id",btId);
        newLink.appendChild(newLinkText);
        newLink.setAttribute("href","#");
        newLinkPara.appendChild(newLink);

        //add the behaviors for the new link
        newLink.onclick = togglePrintDisplay;
        newLink.onkeypress = togglePrintDisplay;

        //insert the para and the two links into the DOM
        el[i].insertBefore(newLinkPara,el[i].firstChild);
        }
    }
}

function togglePrintDisplay(e)
{
var whatSection = this.id.split("_");
whatSection = whatSection[1];
var el = document.getElementsByTagName("div");
for (i=0;i<el.length;i++)
    {
    if (el[i].className.indexOf("print_section")!=-1)
        {
        el[i].removeAttribute("className");
        if (el[i].id==whatSection)
            {
            //show only this section for print
            el[i].setAttribute("className","print_section print");
            el[i].setAttribute("class","print_section print");
            }
        else
            {
```

```
            //hide the sections from printout
            el[i].setAttribute("className","print_section noprint");
            el[i].setAttribute("class","print_section noprint");
          }
        }
      }
    if (window.event)
      {
      window.event.returnValue = false;
      window.event.cancelBubble = true;
      }
    else if (e)
      {
      e.stopPropagation();
      e.preventDefault();
      }
    window.print();
    }
  addEvent(window, 'load', addPrintLinks, false);
```

What about the CSS?

Wow, with all the talk of scripting, you might have forgotten that there's another very important aspect to this, and that's
the print CSS styles. The scripts change the classnames of the various elements in the document, but somewhere we need to
define the appearance of these items. The following CSS needs to be added to the document. The first part is purely cos-
metic (for the link—to make it appear "buttony"), but the important part is highlighted in bold:

```
  .print_section p.printbutton
  {
    float:left;
  }
  .print_section p.printbutton a
  {
    text-decoration:none;
    background:white;
    display:block;
    float:left;
    margin:3px;
    padding:10px;
    border:1px solid red;
  }
  @media print
  {
    .noprint, .printbutton
    {
      display:none;
    }
    .print
    {
      display:block;
    }
  }
```

The styles are limited to the print display by being contained inside the curly brackets after @media print. The toggling of display styles cannot affect the screen view (or other media types) because of this.

With all of this stitched together, the finished result looks like Figure 8-4.

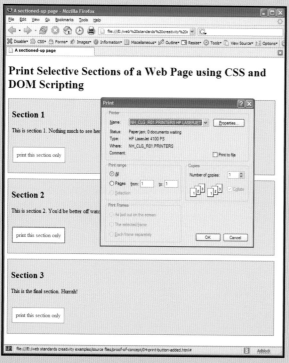

Figure 8-4. The finished prototype page

If the OK button were clicked, just one section of the page would be printed. In this example, it's section 2, as the print preview facility in Firefox demonstrates (see Figure 8-5).

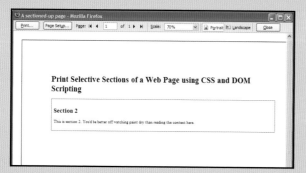

Figure 8-5. The functionality to print one section is working!

A couple of refinements

Before we move out of the proof-of-concept phase into practical application, there is a small issue to address. Consider this scenario:

What would happen if the user clicked a Print this section link but then hit Cancel. Perhaps the user wants to print the whole page after all?

If you check when the various events are triggered and what they do, you'll note there's a problem. By clicking the browser's print button after first activating one of the print section buttons, only the partial section will print. This is because the CSS displays have already been set, and the browser's print button will not affect this.

One solution is to write out two links: one that says print this section and another that says print the whole page. The idea is to stop people from veering up to their browser print button if they've just used the print this section button. Alternatively, you could create another function that reset the displays of each section to the default when a certain predictable event took place. For example, this could happen when the mouse pointer passes over a page header area, which it almost certainly would do if it were moving from a part of the page up to the top of the browser, as shown in Figure 8-6.

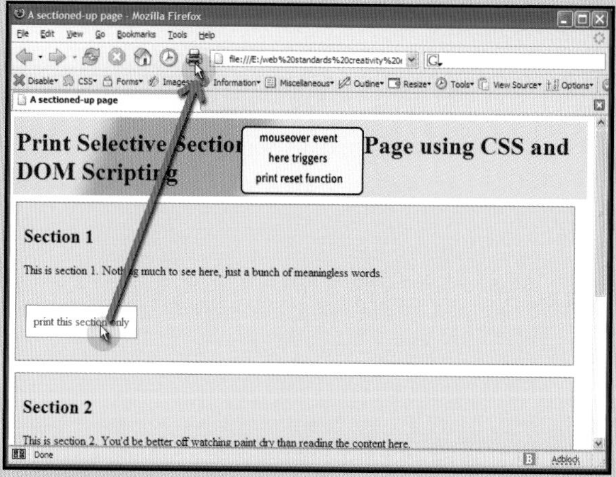

Figure 8-6. Resetting the display using a mouseover event that detects if the user gravitates towards the browser's print button

The following is the code required for my first solution (the simpler one of adding a second print button for each section). It's in the addPrintLinks function (additions shown in bold):

```
var btId = "printbut_" + el[i].id;
newLink.setAttribute("id",btId)
newLink.appendChild(newLinkText);
newLink.setAttribute("href","#");
newLinkPara.appendChild(newLink);

//set up the print all link
newLink2.setAttribute("href","#");
var bt2Id = "printall_" + el[i].id;
newLink2.setAttribute("id",bt2Id);
newLink2.appendChild(newLinkText2);
newLink2.setAttribute("href","#");
newLinkPara.appendChild(newLink2);

//add the behaviors for the new links
newLink.onclick = togglePrintDisplay;
newLink.onkeypress = togglePrintDisplay;
newLink2.onclick = printAll;
newLink2.onkeypress = printAll;
```

Note that the new links will call a new function named printAll. This is a variation of the togglePrintDisplay function (I copied, pasted, and amended it accordingly). This function simply runs through all the printable sections and resets the display so that they are visible for print purposes:

```
function printAll(e)
{
var el = document.getElementsByTagName("div");
for (i=0;i<el.length;i++)
  {
  if (el[i].className.indexOf("print_section")!=-1)
    {
      el[i].setAttribute("className","print_section print");
      el[i].setAttribute("class","print_section print");
    }
  }
if (window.event)
  {
    window.event.returnValue = false;
    window.event.cancelBubble = true;
  }
else if (e)
  {
    e.stopPropagation();
    e.preventDefault();
  }
window.print();
}
```

> It wouldn't take too much to abstract the original function (togglePrintDisplay) so that it could handle both the print some and print all scenarios, rather than having two separate functions. However, I've opted to keep them separate for now, mainly for clarity of reading.

The amended proof-of-concept page now looks like Figure 8-7.

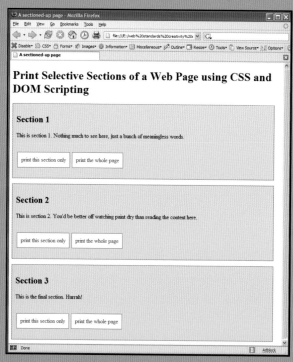

Figure 8-7. The finished prototype page, with refinements made

Note that you could combine the idea of adding a print the whole page link for each section with the earlier suggestion I made about having the print areas reset to show all when the mouse passes over a header area (or similar), for the proverbial "belt-and-braces" approach.

Let's see it in action, already!

Well, you've seen the theory behind the technique and seen it demonstrated on a basic page, but what about a practical application of the technique? As I mentioned at the beginning of the chapter, the inspiration came from a colleague who was asking about whether an entire page of interest rates really needed to be printed out when the person doing the printing is probably interested in only one part of it. Figure 8-8 shows that page.

Figure 8-8. As you can see, it's a long page!

Sliding in the code

In the proof-of-concept example, I placed all the functions in one single `.js` file. This included the addEvent function. If you are likely to use the addEvent function for more than one purpose across the site, it's probably better to split the `.js` file into two:

- A file containing the addEvent function (which can be used anywhere on the site for whatever purpose)
- Another file containing the print-handling functions (as it needs to be called only on pages that get this printing treatment)

So that's what I did for the practical application (the interest rates page in question can be found at www.nationwide.co.uk/savings/rates.htm (but please don't study the rest of the markup too closely, you might upset yourself—I don't have total control over what goes live, honest!). Here are the links to the JavaScript in the head of the document:

```
<script src="/_common_scripts/add_event.js" type="text/javascript">
</script>
<script src="/_common_scripts/print_sections_handler.js" ➥
  type="text/javascript"></script>
</head>
```

That's the behavior added in. Now what's needed is to add in the extra markup around the relevant sections on the page as it currently stands. Here's an example using one of the smallest sections (just two table rows) with the new markup that we need for the print functions to work:

```
<div id="sect4" class="print_section">
 <table cellpadding="4" cellspacing="0" width="100%">
  <thead>
   <tr>
    <th>accounts for over 65s</th>
    <th>interest tier</th>
    <th>AER %</th>
    <th>AER* %</th>
    <th>gross p.a. %</th>
    <th>net p.a. %</th>
    <th> </th>
   </tr>
  </thead>
  <tbody>
   <tr>
    <td class="textbottom" valign="top">
     <a href="/pdf/P8865_Sep05.pdf" target="_blank">
     Monthly Income 65+</a><br>passbook account
     with a guaranteed regular income for the over 65's
     <br><br><small>effective from: 01/09/2005</small>
    </td>
    <td>1+</td>
    <td><strong>4.50</strong></td>
    <td>n/a</td>
    <td>4.41</td>
    <td>3.53</td>
    <td>
     <a href="http://www.multimap.com/clients/places.cgi? ➥
       client=nationw_01" onclick="popUpWin(this.href,'console',
```

```
            600,500);return false;">apply in branch</a><br>
         <a href="http://www.nationwide.co.uk/pdf/P8865_Sep05.pdf"
         target="_blank"><img src="rates_files/pdf_icon.gif" ➥
         alt="view leaflet>view leaflet</a>
      </td>
   </tr>
 </tbody>
</table>
</div>
```

Each section on the page needs to be marked up in this way, with an id of sect#, where # is the section number.

The markup now has the necessary hooks for the script to grab and write in the print links. But how do these look? Well, a whole lot better than those shown in the proof of concept! Figure 8-9 shows a proposed design of the links in context.

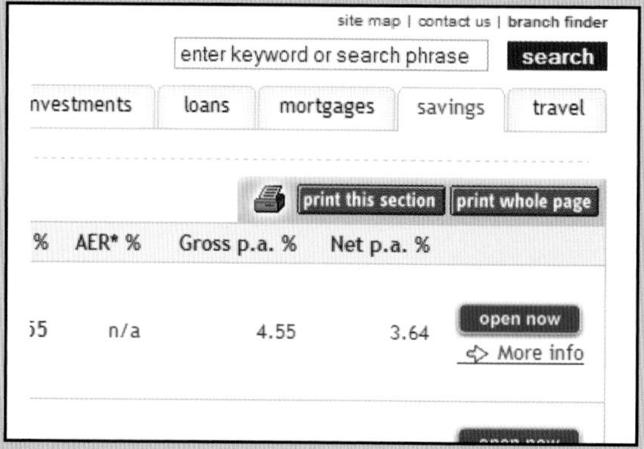

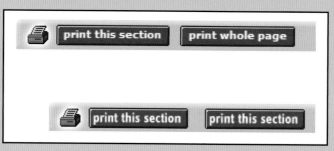

Figure 8-9. The print link design

Predictably, the design was put together in Photoshop, but very much with an idea for how it can be built. In the example in Figure 8-9, the link buttons could be created using images (and the script would need to be adapted so that it writes out an img element rather than text). Figure 8-10 shows the two approaches: the first set of links is HTML text over a background image, and the second is based on img elements.

Figure 8-10. The two appproaches to creating the link buttons

For the purposes of building on the proof-of-concept stage and doing a like-for-like translation, I am going to show how you do this using a combination of CSS background images and real text, rather than using img elements.

Important: The downside of this approach, I should warn you, is that when (or if) you scale text up on the page, the background image for the button will not scale accordingly, and text may break out of the button area, as shown in Figure 8-11. Writing out an img element gets around that problem, but I'll leave that to you to experiment with (it's really not a stretch to adapt the script to do this, honest!).

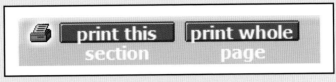

Figure 8-11. The effect of scaling up to maximum size in Internet Explorer when text sits on top of a button

Styling the print links

Regardless of the approach taken for the links, you'll need to apply some CSS. In the proof of concept, I used a paragraph, which contained the two links. This can be used to include a background image (the gray section in the images in Figure 8-10 that includes a printer), while the links themselves need the backgrounds. Figure 8-12 shows the constituent parts.

Figure 8-12. The background image and button used to style the print links

Before looking at the CSS, just to recap: the HTML for these buttons (once generated via the JavaScript and inserted into the DOM) is exactly as per the proof of concept. The bold markup shown here is the part that will be dynamically generated:

```
<div id="sect1">
  <p class="printbutton">
    <a href="#" id="printbut_sect1">print this section</a>
    <a href="#" id="printall_sect1">print whole page</a>
  </p>
  <table><!--table stuff goes here --></table>
</div>
```

To get it looking like the proposed design, the CSS needs to push the whole lot over to the right, apply the necessary backgrounds, and allow enough space to the left of the first link so the little printer icon is visible. Here's the CSS that lets us do this:

```css
p.printbutton
{
  background-image:url(print-button-para-bg.gif);
  background-repeat:no-repeat;
  background-color:#576374;
  float:right;
  padding:6px 0 0 40px;
}
#sect1 p.printbutton a
{
  background-image:url(print-button-bg.gif);
  background-repeat:no-repeat;
  padding:2px 0;
  margin:0 10px 0 0;
  color:white;
  text-decoration:none;
  width:110px;
  height:19px;
  font-weight:bold;
  font-size:x-small;
  display:block;
  float:left;
  text-align:center;
}
```

Pulling it all together

The scripts have been inserted in the document head, the styles for the generated links have been defined, and the page has had all the necessary ids applied that will make the technique work. Figure 8-13 shows the finished result as seen on screen (in the Windows version of Firefox).

Figure 8-13. The finished web page

Never mind all that—what about saving the planet?

Ah, that! I said I would return to the topic, which is all about saving paper, avoiding needless printouts. With the piece of JavaScript wizardry you've seen in this chapter doing its thing, users can now print just the part of the page that is of interest to them, and here's the proof. First, Figure 8-14 shows the results of a printout from the page before the script was applied—the "before."

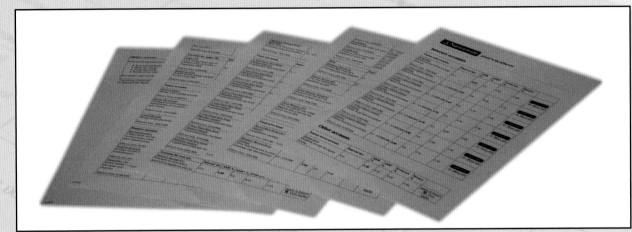

Figure 8-14. Phew—that's a lot of paper!

And Figure 8-15 shows the results after applying the script—the "after."

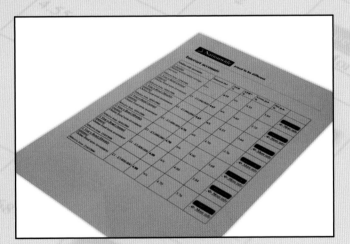

Figure 8-15. Much better!

The eagle-eyed among you will notice that the controls that appear on the page to selectively print certain sections are not showing on the printout. Well, why would you need them on a printout? You can't click them or do anything on paper, so these dynamically generated controls are switched off in the print style sheet, like so:

```
@media print
{
  p.printbutton
  {
    display:none;
  }
}
```

You could find many different uses for the technique, but essentially, it's handy wherever there's a large amount of content of which only a portion might sometimes need to be printed. The original posting on my personal site, where the technique was first put forward, is still up and available for comment (see http://tinyurl.com/p9tqb), including any suggestions that people have to improve the technique.

Conclusion

If there is one conclusion I would draw from this exercise, it's that it's all too easy to dismiss an idea on the basis that the browser can't do it. With the DOM, CSS, and JavaScript, you can custom-build functions to suit wildly inventive ideas and provide solutions to long-standing browser issues that looked like they never could be fixed. Print is often overlooked on the Web, but this need not be the case. Some fine-tuning can go a long way. And it can also save a tree or two in the process, which is all good.

9

Creating Dynamic Interfaces Using JavaScript

cameron
adams

www.themaninblue.com

Cameron Adams has one degree in law and another one in science. Naturally, he chose a career in web development. When pressed, he labels himself a "web technologist," because he likes to have a hand in graphic design, JavaScript, CSS, Perl (yes, Perl), and anything else that takes his fancy that morning. He runs his own business (www. themaninblue.com), and has done work for government departments, nonprofit organizations, large corporations, and tiny startups.

As well as helping his list of clients, Cameron has taught numerous workshops around the country and spoken at conferences worldwide, such as @media and Web Directions. He released his first book in 2006, *The JavaScript Anthology*, which is one of the most complete question-and-answer resources on modern JavaScript techniques.

Cameron lives in Melbourne, Australia, where, between coding marathons, he likes to play soccer and mix some tunes for his irate neighbors.

Different layouts for different needs

As the Internet becomes more pervasive, users are beginning to access web pages from a greater number of devices—laptops, desktops, PDAs, mobile phones, fridges . . . who knows what's around the corner? And with each new device comes a different design constraint. Mobile phones certainly don't have the screen space that a desktop computer has, so the way that users can—and should—view content will be vastly different.

Even on the same device, different users have different needs. Visitors come to your site to do different things, and your interface should be able to accommodate all of them. You want to be able to provide users with the optimal experience for their chosen device and purpose.

This chapter explores techniques for dealing with these design problems using JavaScript and CSS. I call these *dynamic interfaces*. We'll look at creating two types of layouts: resolution-dependent layouts and user-controlled modular layouts. All the source files for the examples are available to download from www.friendsofed.com/.

Resolution-dependent layouts

It's quite obvious that different devices have different display capabilities. Nowhere is this more apparent than when comparing mobile devices, such as PDAs, with their desk-locked cousins. The resolution on a PDA can be as low as 240×320, whereas a desktop monitor can go up to 2048×1536 and beyond. Even on desktops, the variance in resolution is astounding. Your parents could be browsing on a (now prehistoric) 800×600 system, while your power-user sister is on a 1280×960 screen. The difference between the two is huge, with an over 150% increase in available area. And the design requirements for each are equally different. Throw widescreen and dual-screen systems into the mix, and the possibilities explode.

With such large differences, it's no longer viable to say, "Well, just create a fluid layout that stretches for all resolutions." What we are talking about here is a fundamental difference in the way a page should be laid out. More information is going to be visible to someone with a higher resolution, so your design should take this into account. Less information will be visible to someone with a lower resolution, and your design should also be able to handle that.

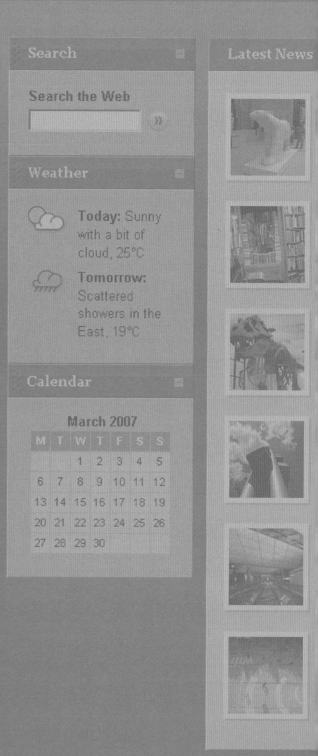

ow to get ahead without trying

avaScript is rife with unexplored nooks and crannies that can
even the most seasoned programmers. Billy Youkip
vestigates one of the deepest: the basic question of scope a
ntext.

ysterious rumblings

SON (JavaScript Object Notation) is a lightweight
ta-interchange format. It is easy for humans to read and writ
easy for machines to parse and generate.

ime to go underground

osures are one of the most powerful features of ECMAScript
avascript) but they cannot be properly exploited without
derstanding them.

ard rock climbing

rototype is a JavaScript framework that aims to ease
velopment of dynamic web applications. A unique, easy-to-u
olkit for class-driven development.

eginning of a new world

ie latest release of Dojo improves the already ground-breakir
3.x line with over a hundred improvements. 0.3.1 is a
aintainance release and is recommended for all users of Doj

hout & cheer

is whole memory thing seems to be more important and mo
mplicated than I thought. I have absolutely zero knowledge
ftware development and related skills, so I never worried abc
emory leaks

The trouble is that if you're trying to make your design one-size-fits-all, you'll encounter irreconcilable differences. At 1280×960, four columns of text may produce the most succinct, organized, and visible structure to your content, but giving four columns to someone on an 800×600 monitor will just produce a squished mess. Conversely, a single-column design that works quite comfortably at 800×600 will look painfully stretched at 1280×960.

Traditionally, one answer has been to simply limit the width of a page—lock it at a fixed width that produces nice, readable line lengths at a width of 800 pixels (or your chosen base resolution) and anything above. However, this is often unfairly constraining on those who are taking advantage of better-quality technology. Users with higher resolutions receive no benefit for their investment; they just get more space on either side of the content.

Recent statistics (www.thecounter.com/stats/2006/August/res.php) indicate that users with a screen resolution of 800×600 make up roughly 16% of the market, about 55% have a resolution of 1024×768, and about 21% are on a higher resolution than that (the actual statistics for any particular site will vary by audience). By designing to a resolution of 800×600, you're punishing the majority of your users for the circumstances of a minority, albeit a fairly large minority.

So is there a way to give users with larger screens the benefit of their hard-earned pixels without penalizing those on lower resolutions? Yes, by providing different designs to different sizes.

At first, this may sound like an inordinate amount of work. But thanks to the flexibility of standards-based layouts, it is quite possible—even easy—to use the exact same HTML markup and provide different designs to different resolutions by just changing the CSS.

As you can see by comparing the different layouts for the UX Magazine (www.uxmag.com) and White Pages (www.whitepages.com.au) websites, shown in Figures 9-1 through 9-4, the design aesthetics of a page do not have to alter greatly in order to accommodate different browser sizes. Most of the time, just a reorganization of the major content areas is enough to create a more flowing layout that maximizes screen real estate. Layouts optimized for wider screens usually result in a decreased page height, which brings more content above the fold, allowing users to see more of the page without scrolling. Assuming that your titles, menus, forms, and other website accessories are coded using some nice, robust CSS, they should all fit easily into either design.

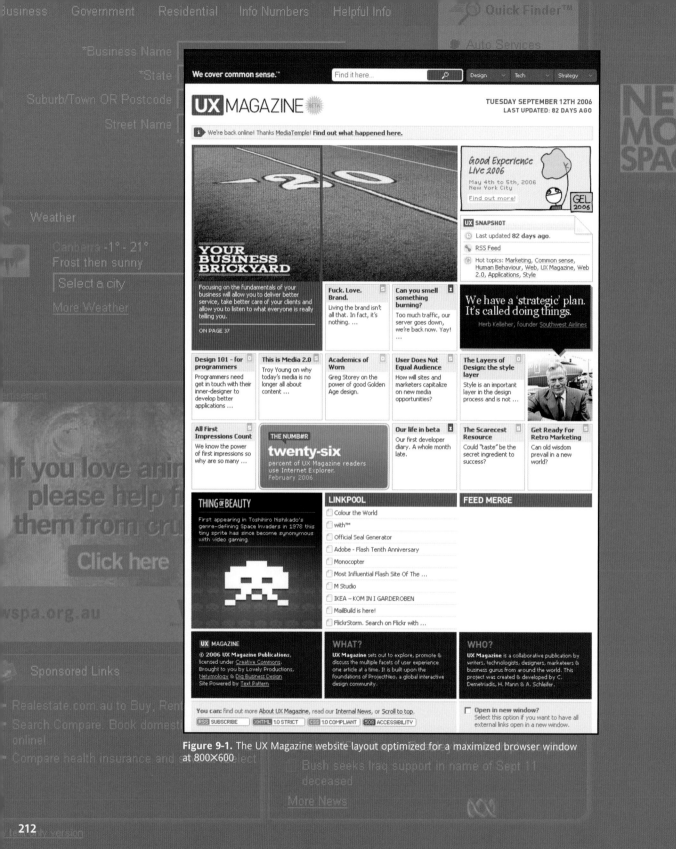

Figure 9-1. The UX Magazine website layout optimized for a maximized browser window at 800×600

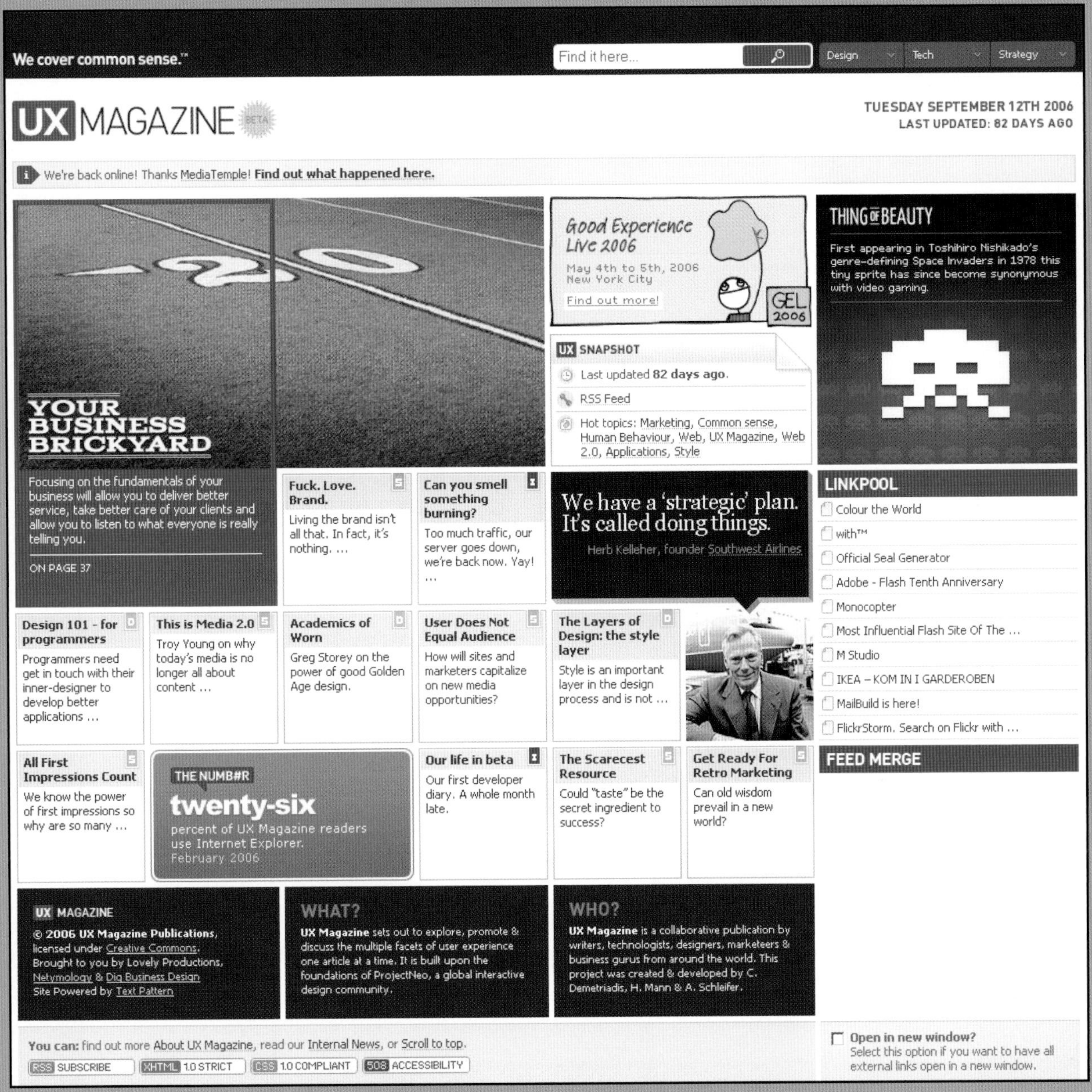

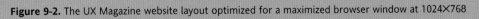

We cover common sense.™

Find it here...

Design   Tech   Strategy

UX MAGAZINE BETA

TUESDAY SEPTEMBER 12TH 2006
LAST UPDATED: 82 DAYS AGO

ⓘ We're back online! Thanks MediaTemple! **Find out what happened here.**

Good Experience
Live 2006
May 4th to 5th, 2006
New York City
Find out more!
GEL 2006

THING OF BEAUTY

First appearing in Toshihiro Nishikado's genre–defining Space Invaders in 1978 this tiny sprite has since become synonymous with video gaming.

YOUR BUSINESS BRICKYARD

Focusing on the fundamentals of your business will allow you to deliver better service, take better care of your clients and allow you to listen to everyone is really telling you.

ON PAGE 37

UX SNAPSHOT

🕐 Last updated **82 days ago**.
🔖 RSS Feed
◎ Hot topics: Marketing, Common sense, Human Behaviour, Web, UX Magazine, Web 2.0, Applications, Style

LINKPOOL

📄 Colour the World
📄 with™
📄 Official Seal Generator
📄 Adobe - Flash Tenth Anniversary
📄 Monocopter
📄 Most Influential Flash Site Of The ...
📄 M Studio
📄 IKEA – KOM IN I GARDEROBEN
📄 MailBuild is here!
📄 FlickrStorm. Search on Flickr with ...

Fuck. Love. Brand.
Living the brand isn't all that. In fact, it's nothing. ...

Can you smell something burning?
Too much traffic, our server goes down, we're back now. Yay! ...

We have a 'strategic' plan. It's called doing things.
Herb Kelleher, founder Southwest Airlines

Design 101 - for programmers
Programmers need get in touch with their inner-designer to develop better applications ...

This is Media 2.0
Troy Young on why today's media is no longer all about content ...

Academics of Worn
Greg Storey on the power of good Golden Age design.

User Does Not Equal Audience
How will sites and marketers capitalize on new media opportunities?

The Layers of Design: the style layer
Style is an important layer in the design process and is not ...

FEED MERGE

All First Impressions Count
We know the power of first impressions so why are so many ...

THE NUMB#R
twenty-six
percent of UX Magazine readers use Internet Explorer.
February 2006

Our life in beta
Our first developer diary. A whole month late.

The Scarecest Resource
Could "taste" be the secret ingredient to success?

Get Ready For Retro Marketing
Can old wisdom prevail in a new world?

UX MAGAZINE
© 2006 UX Magazine Publications, licensed under Creative Commons. Brought to you by Lovely Productions, Netymology & Dig Business Design Site Powered by Text Pattern

WHAT?
UX Magazine sets out to explore, promote & discuss the multiple facets of user experience one article at a time. It is built upon the foundations of ProjectNeo, a global interactive design community.

WHO?
UX Magazine is a collaborative publication by writers, technologists, designers, marketeers & business gurus from around the world. This project was created & developed by C. Demetriadis, H. Mann & A. Schleifer.

You can: find out more About UX Magazine, read our Internal News, or Scroll to top.

RSS SUBSCRIBE   XHTML 1.0 STRICT   CSS 1.0 COMPLIANT   508 ACCESSIBILITY

☐ **Open in new window?**
Select this option if you want to have all external links open in a new window.

Figure 9-2. The UX Magazine website layout optimized for a maximized browser window at 1024×768

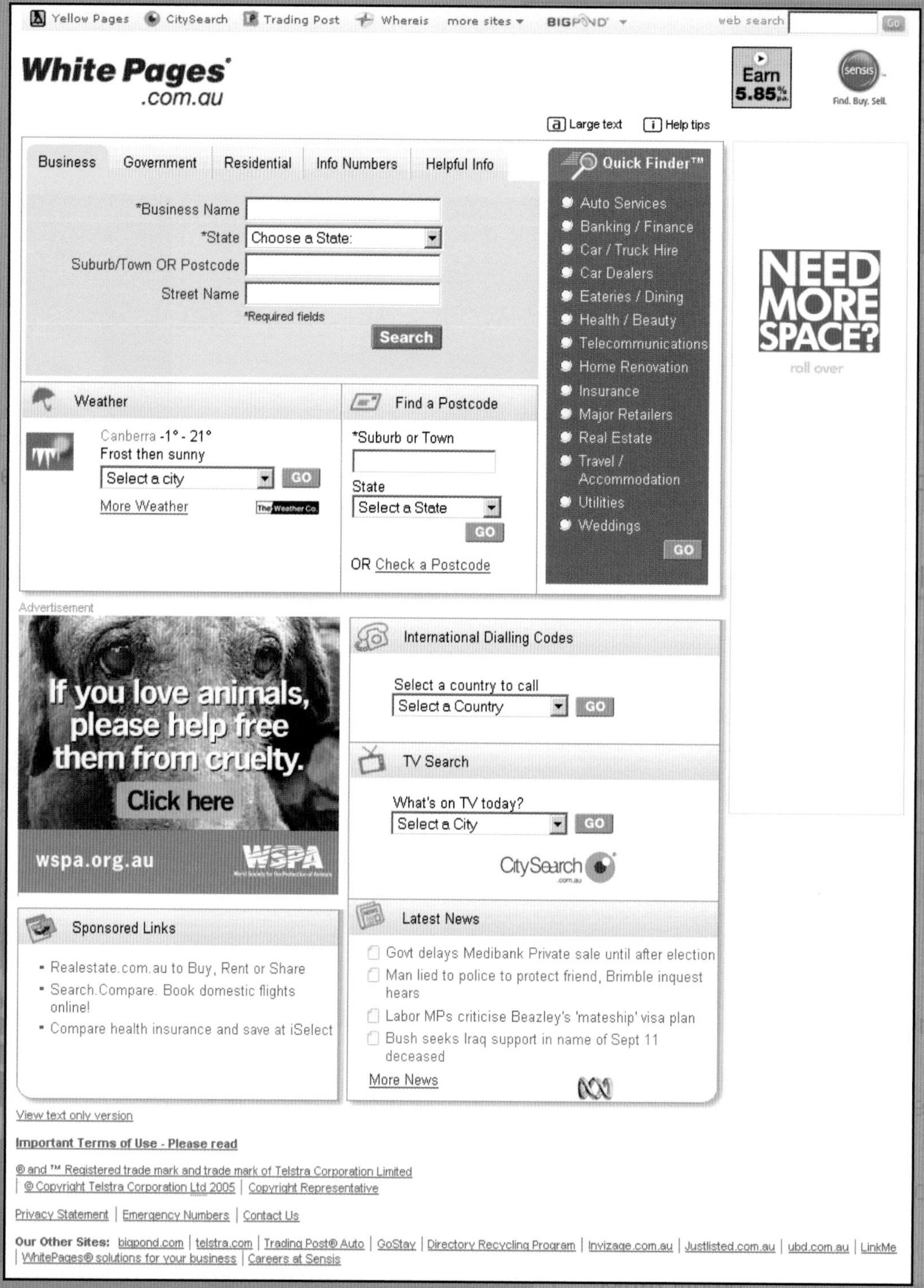

Figure 9-3. The White Pages website layout optimized for narrower browser windows (less than 1200px wide)

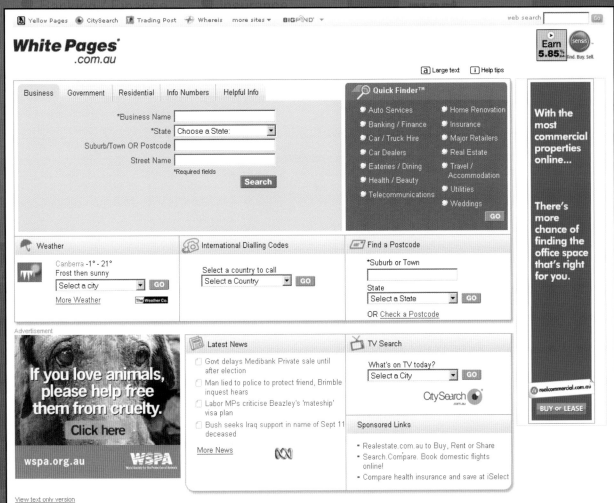

Figure 9-4. The White Pages website layout optimized for wider browser windows (greater than 1200px wide)

Browser size, not resolution

Although window size is quite often related to screen resolution, the two are not the same. Browser windows don't have to be maximized, so you can't assume that the browser size will match the screen resolution. From anecdotal evidence, users with 1024×768 and lower resolutions tend to browse with maximized windows, while those with higher resolutions are more likely to multitask with multiple, unmaximized windows.

The solution that I present here makes no assumptions based on screen resolution (even though it's called a *resolution*-dependent layout). We target layouts for the browser window, so if users on big screens happen to be browsing in a small window, they'll still get the optimal small window layout.

Resolution-dependent layout also doesn't just apply to fixed-width sites. You can still offer a fluid layout as part of your style sheet. This means you'll get the best of both worlds: a layout that not only accounts for the small inconsistencies between browser sizes (sidebars, scrollbars, maximized/unmaximized, and so on), but also handles big changes that give us enough extra room to warrant a reorganization of the content.

Multiple CSS files

The first step in creating a resolution-dependent layout is to create the different style sheets you'll need for the different resolutions.

Alternate style sheets and style-switching have been in common use for a while now. It's widely accepted that when users print out a page they require a different format than what they get on their screen. That's why we have alternate print style sheets. A lot of sites have alternate style sheets for larger text, high-contrast layouts, or just plain different looks. So what we're going to do here is make an alternate style sheet for a different resolution. This mostly entails changing the content for a greater page width.

As with any alternate style sheet, you first need to define what your base style is going to be. Which baseline demographic are you going to target? Currently, 800×600 is generally considered the lowest common desktop resolution, so we'll use this as our default size.

You next need to decide which resolution(s) will get an alternate style sheet. What resolutions will gain the most benefit from a different layout? You could provide many different layouts for many different resolutions, but to keep it simple here, we'll create only one alternate style sheet. We'll use 1024×768 as the switch for the alternate layout. It's not as radical a shift as 800×600 to 1280×1024, but it still provides enough real estate to warrant a change in layout.

DEPENDENT LAYOUT

Search this site

Home

Article Archive

Events Archive

The Laboratory

Downloads

Online Store

Contact Us

New Articles

How to get ahead without trying
JavaScript is rife with unexplored nooks and crannies that can trip up even the most seasoned programmers. Billy Youkip investigates one of the deepest, the basic question of scope and context.

Mysterious rumblings
JSON (JavaScript Object Notation) is a lightweight data-interchange format. It is easy for humans to read and write. It is easy for machines to parse and generate.

Time to go underground
Closures are one of the most powerful features of ECMAScript (javascript) but they cannot be properly exploited without

Figure 9-5 shows our basic design, optimized for 800×600. It's fluid, so it will work on smaller screens as well. Figure 9-6 shows our design for 1024×768 and higher resolutions.

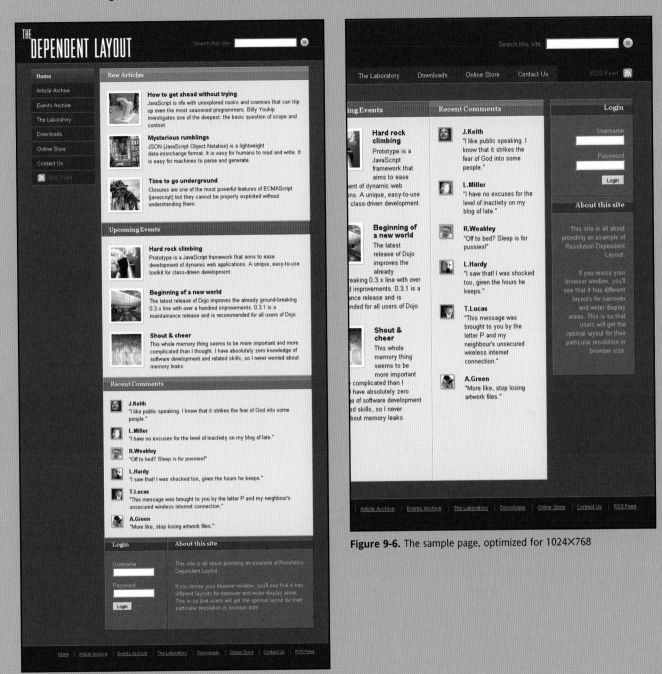

Figure 9-5. The sample page, optimized for 800×600

Figure 9-6. The sample page, optimized for 1024×768

There are two major changes between the two layouts:

- The content in the larger style is presented in four columns across the page, whereas the smaller style keeps the content in one column. A four-column layout better uses the space at higher resolutions and reduces the height of the page. At smaller screen sizes, the columns become too narrow to be useful, and so the single column produces better content width.

- The menus are positioned differently. When using a horizontal menu, we often run into problems on smaller screens as the number of menu items increases. Eventually, they will wrap onto two lines. To combat this, we change the orientation of the menu from horizontal to vertical and position it next to the content.

Both of these changes can be achieved relatively easily using CSS, by modifying widths and floating elements. For example, at 800×600, each of the three main content panels uses its default browser styling: a block element spanning 100% of its container. To get them to line up side by side in the 1024×768 style sheet, we make them float left and supply a width:

```
.panel
{
  float: left;
  width: 26.5%;
}
```

Both layouts use exactly the same HTML markup contained in resolution.htm, so the style sheet changes are the only ones you need to make.

Because an alternate style sheet is additive to the main style sheet, we go ahead and code the 800×600 style sheet as we would normally—it will be applied no matter what. To get our alternate wider style sheet, we extended the basic styles. We don't need to write an entirely new style sheet; we're just modifying and adding to the styles that already exist.

As you'll see in the downloadable files for this example, the basic style sheet, main.css, weighs in at (a nicely spaced) 442 lines. The alternate style sheet, wide.css, is considerably smaller, at 190 lines.

To include both style sheets on our page, we use link elements:

```
<link rel="stylesheet" type="text/css" ➥
  href="css/main.css" />
<link rel="alternate stylesheet" ➥
  type="text/css" href="css/wide.css"➥
  title="Wide" />
```

The main style sheet's rel attribute is set to stylesheet, so it will be applied to the page automatically. By setting the alternate style sheet's rel attribute to alternate stylesheet, we indicate to the browser that it shouldn't be applied unless specified. It's also important to include a title attribute for the alternate style sheet, so we can identify it later.

But how do we go about turning on the alternate style sheet when we need it?

Turning on the style

We have a few options for offering this new resolution-dependent style sheet to users, most of which are pretty ineffectual:

- Include the alternate style sheet in the HTML and hope that the user is using a browser that allows switching between alternate style sheets, and also *realizes* that there is an alternate style sheet, *and then* will bother to turn it on if it applies to him (ain't gonna happen).

- Use an in-page style sheet switcher. Create a widget on every page that allows the user to specify what style she would like the page to be viewed in (just like the one described by Paul Sowden in his article on A List Apart, http://alistapart.com/stories/alternate/). It's a bit like the native browser option, except it's more visible and is accessible to more browsers. However, in my experience, users aren't going to go out of their way to change the default appearance of a page, even if it's going to benefit them.

- Do it automatically. Supply the wider style sheet to browsers that can handle it. Give the users the best experience without them having to lift a finger.

You've probably guessed that we're going to take the third route, since that's what resolution-dependent layout is all about. The way to do this is to use some JavaScript that detects the window size as the page is loading and applies the wider style sheet if it will fit. If JavaScript happens to be turned off, the page won't explode. Instead, the user will get the basic style sheet, which if you've designed it properly, should still be perfectly usable. Just consider the alternate layout a bonus for people with larger screens and JavaScript turned on (which is a pretty hefty chunk of users).

The JavaScript should be placed after the style sheet declarations in the HTML:

```
<link rel="stylesheet" type="text/css" href="css/main.css" />
<link rel="alternate stylesheet" type="text/css" href="css/wide.css" title="Wide" />
<script type="text/javascript" src="scripts/resolution.js"></script>
```

This is important, because the JavaScript is going to run immediately and try to work on the style sheets, so if they haven't been included yet, you'll have problems.

The first thing to do inside resolution.js is to check the size of the browser window:

```
checkBrowserWidth();

function checkBrowserWidth()
{
  var theWidth = getBrowserWidth();

  if (theWidth == 0)
  {
    addLoadListener(checkBrowserWidth);

    return false;
  }

  if (theWidth >= 960)
  {
    setStylesheet("Wide");
  }
  else
  {
    setStylesheet("");
  }

  return true;
};
```

checkBrowserWidth() begins by getting the width of the browser using getBrowserWidth():

```
function getBrowserWidth()
{
  if (window.innerWidth)
  {
    return window.innerWidth;
  }
  else if (document.documentElement && document.documentElement.clientWidth != 0)
  {
```

```
      return document.documentElement.clientWidth;
    }
    else if (document.body)
    {
      return document.body.clientWidth;
    }

    return 0;
  };
```

There are actually a few ways of determining the width of the browser window, depending on which browser you're using, and each of the conditions in getBrowserWidth() matches one of these. Firefox, Mozilla, Safari, and Opera use window.innerWidth. Internet Explorer 6 and 7 use document.documentElement.clientWidth.

In a rather strange quirk that document.documentElement.clientWidth exists in Internet Explorer 5 and 5.5, but it is always set to 0, so we have to check for this and default to document.body.clientWidth if that's the case. The only problem with this is that the body element must exist before Internet Explorer 5.x can figure out the browser window width, so we have to reschedule the call to getBrowserWidth() once the page has been loaded. This is done in the first condition inside check-BrowserWidth(). If getBrowserWidth() returns 0, it means that the browser is probably Internet Explorer 5.x, so we create a new load event listener and wait for the page to load before doing any style sheet switching.

addLoadListener() is a generic page load event handler that abstracts around some of the differences in browser event handling:

```
  function addLoadListener(fn)
  {
    if (typeof window.addEventListener != 'undefined')
    {
      window.addEventListener('load', fn, false);
    }
    else if (typeof document.addEventListener != 'undefined')
    {
      document.addEventListener('load', fn, false);
    }
    else if (typeof window.attachEvent != 'undefined')
    {
      window.attachEvent('onload', fn);
    }
    else
    {
      return false;
    }

    return true;
  };
```

This and another abstracted event handler are included in event_listeners.js, because you'll probably use them regularly on other projects.

Most browsers won't have to go through the page load rigmarole, however. checkBrowserWidth() will receive the browser width immediately and be able to check it. This is done through a simple conditional—we check theWidth against our pre-determined value. In our example, we use 960 as a threshold because that's a nice, safe value for a maximized window size at a resolution of 1024×768 if we subtract some space for browser chrome like scrollbars. If you want your style sheet to change at a different resolution, just change this value to whatever you need.

If the window width is greater than or equal to 960 pixels, we activate the alternate style sheet by calling setStylesheet() with the appropriate style sheet title, in this case Wide:

```
function setStylesheet(styleTitle)
{
  var links = document.getElementsByTagName("link");

  for (var i = 0; i < links.length; i++)
  {
    if (links[i].getAttribute("rel") == "alternate stylesheet")
    {
      links[i].disabled = true;

      if(links[i].getAttribute("title") == styleTitle)
      {
        links[i].disabled = false;
      }
    }
  }

  return true;
};
```

setStylesheet() takes a style sheet title and iterates through all of the link elements in the page, checking whether their rel attribute matches alternate stylesheet. If that link is an alternate style sheet, its disabled property is set to true (turning any unselected style sheets off), and then the title attribute is checked to see whether it is Wide. If it is a match, disabled is set to false (turning on the style sheet).

After that loop has finished, the selected alternate style sheet will be switched on and all others turned off. The same function is used if the browser width is not greater than our threshold. We call setStylesheet() with an empty string (""), and this turns off all alternate style sheets because none of their titles will match.

Once all this has happened, the correct style sheet will be selected, and the page should now be displaying with the optimal layout for the user's browser size.

The last thing to do is to add in an event listener for when someone resizes the browser window. It's all well and good to detect the browser size when someone first visits a page, but if he changes the window size, we'll want to change the layout accordingly. To do this, we simply add an event listener for the window resize event that calls checkBrowserWidth() again:

```
attachEventListener(window, "resize", checkBrowserWidth, false);
```

Again, here I use a generic event handler (from event_listeners.js) that abstracts around some of the differences in browser event handling:

```
function attachEventListener(target, eventType, functionRef, capture)
{
  if (typeof target.addEventListener != "undefined")
  {
    target.addEventListener(eventType, functionRef, capture);
```

```
        }
        else if (typeof target.attachEvent != "undefined")
        {
            target.attachEvent("on" + eventType, functionRef);
        }
        else
        {
            return false;
        }

        return true;
    };
```

Optimizations for Internet Explorer 5.x

As noted earlier, Internet Explorer 5.x browsers will have to wait for the page to load before getting the browser width. This may cause a little visual flicker as the style sheets are swapped. In order to ameliorate this somewhat, we can set a cookie that stores the browser width upon the user's very first visit to the site, and then use this value upon repeat loads. This way, the user will get a flicker only on the first visit. To do this, we need to modify checkBrowserWidth():

```
    function checkBrowserWidth()
    {
        var theWidth = getBrowserWidth();

        if (theWidth == 0)
        {
            var resolutionCookie = document.cookie.match(/(^|;) res_layout[^;]*(;|$)/);

            if (resolutionCookie != null)
            {
                setStylesheet(unescape(resolutionCookie[0].split("=")[1]));
            }

            addLoadListener(checkBrowserWidth);

            return false;
        }

        if (theWidth >= 960)
        {
            setStylesheet("Wide");
            document.cookie = "res_layout=" + escape("Wide");
        }
        else
        {
            setStylesheet("");
            document.cookie = "res_layout=";
        }

        return true;
    };
```

Now, once the browser width has been determined and the style sheet has been switched, we also set a cookie called `res_layout` that stores the title of the applied style sheet. On repeat visits, if the browser width is returned as 0 (that is, it is Internet Explorer 5.x), we check whether a cookie value exists for `res_layout`, and if so, immediately set the style sheet accordingly. This eliminates the flicker. We still go on to add the load listener that recalls `getBrowserWidth()`, so if the user happened to change the size of her browser after the cookie was set, we can adjust the layout to the new width.

We've completed the resolution-dependent layout. Let's move on to another approach.

Modular layouts

It's one thing to provide a static choice of layouts depending on a user's browser size, but it's quite another to give users personal control over what they see on your page and where they see it.

Modular layouts provide users with a visual and behavioral framework that allows them to radically change the way that an interface is displayed on a web page in real time. Once the designer has divided the content into discrete content modules, those modules can be expanded and collapsed, their order reorganized, and their position on the page changed—all by the user.

Allowing the user to customize a page isn't something you should offer haphazardly. It's unlikely that someone will bother to spend the time investigating an interface and modifying it to his liking if he is going to spend only ten minutes there in his entire life. However, when you offer a service that aims to bring users back to your website often, and when they can gain some browsing or workflow efficiencies by customizing an interface, having a customizable layout can be quite an invaluable tool. The most likely candidate for a customizable layout is a web application, where users may want to perform only a subset of the tasks offered by an application, or where they regularly use specific functions in the application.

Figure 9-7 shows the default view of a sample page with a modular layout, which we'll build to demonstrate the dynamic layout techniques. The central content remains static. We'll focus on the auxiliary modules on either side.

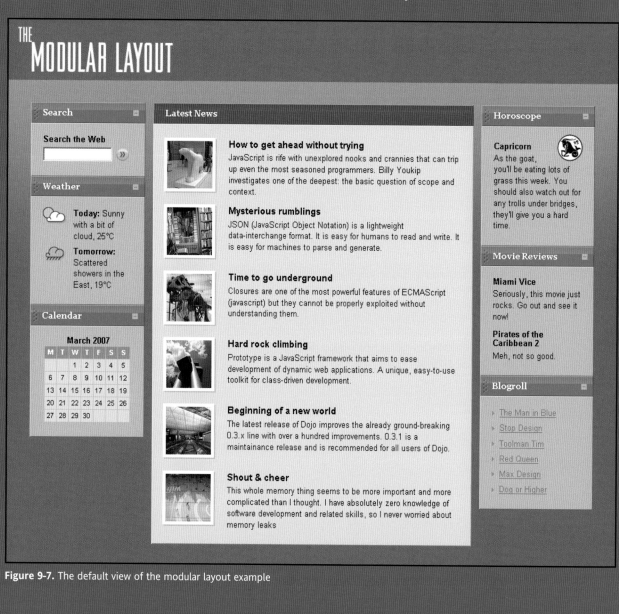

Figure 9-7. The default view of the modular layout example

Figure 9-8 shows a modified view of the interface, after a user has rearranged the modules to her liking through a combination of collapsing, reorganizing, and moving.

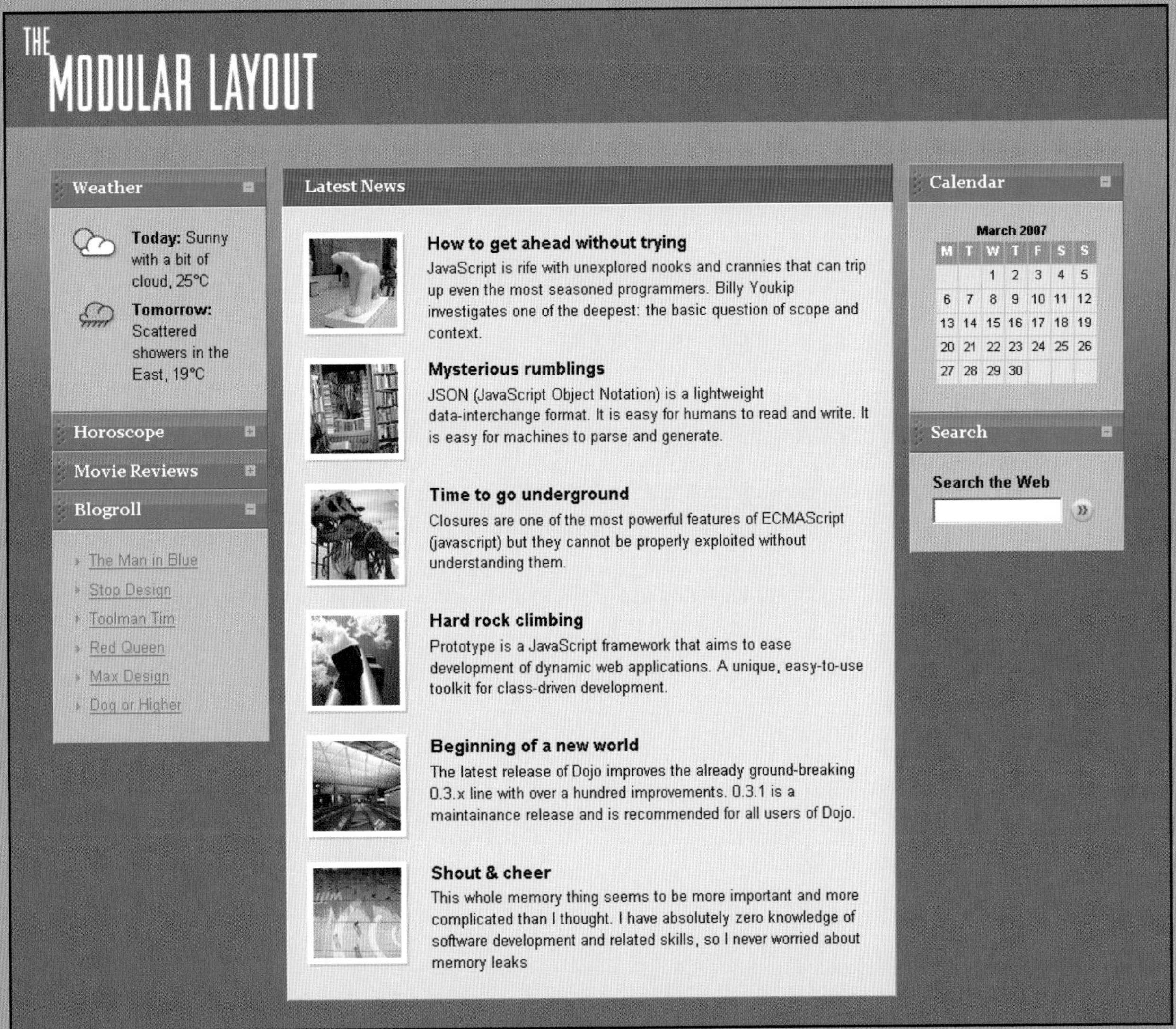

THE MODULAR LAYOUT

Weather

Today: Sunny with a bit of cloud, 25°C

Tomorrow: Scattered showers in the East, 19°C

Horoscope

Movie Reviews

Blogroll

- The Man in Blue
- Stop Design
- Toolman Tim
- Red Queen
- Max Design
- Dog or Higher

Latest News

How to get ahead without trying

JavaScript is rife with unexplored nooks and crannies that can trip up even the most seasoned programmers. Billy Youkip investigates one of the deepest: the basic question of scope and context.

Mysterious rumblings

JSON (JavaScript Object Notation) is a lightweight data-interchange format. It is easy for humans to read and write. It is easy for machines to parse and generate.

Time to go underground

Closures are one of the most powerful features of ECMAScript (javascript) but they cannot be properly exploited without understanding them.

Hard rock climbing

Prototype is a JavaScript framework that aims to ease development of dynamic web applications. A unique, easy-to-use toolkit for class-driven development.

Beginning of a new world

The latest release of Dojo improves the already ground-breaking 0.3.x line with over a hundred improvements. 0.3.1 is a maintainance release and is recommended for all users of Dojo.

Shout & cheer

This whole memory thing seems to be more important and more complicated than I thought. I have absolutely zero knowledge of software development and related skills, so I never worried about memory leaks

Calendar

March 2007

M	T	W	T	F	S	S
			1	2	3	4	5
6	7	8	9	10	11	12
13	14	15	16	17	18	19
20	21	22	23	24	25	26
27	28	29	30			

Search

Search the Web

Figure 9-8. A user-defined view of the modular layout example

The example we're using mirrors a portal page of sorts. Users might regularly visit this site to view an aggregation of different types of information, and the importance of certain information will vary among users.

All of the interface customization is, by necessity, done with JavaScript. This means that user agents that are not JavaScript-enabled will not be able to access the customization functionality. Those users will receive the default view of the page and be able to access all the information as if it were a normal static web page.

The markup

The high-level structure of the page content is fairly simple. The data modules on the left are contained in their own section, followed by the central content, then more data modules on the right:

```
<div id="modules1">
. . .
</div>
<div id="news">
. . .
</div>
<div id="modules2">
. . .
</div>
```

The most important thing to note here is that if the user moves content from one module area to the other, it must be placed into the appropriate container.

> The HTML for your web page doesn't have to strictly follow the template laid out in modular.htm. However, the JavaScript and CSS used in the example are tailored for that markup and would need to be tweaked according to the way your particular page is laid out.

Inside each of the module areas, we separate each of the modules into its own section, using a div with a class of module:

```
<div id="modules1">
  <div class="module">
    <h2>
      Search
    </h2>
    <div class="moduleContent">
. . .
    </div> <!-- END .moduleContent -->
  </div> <!-- END .module -->
```

Most of our JavaScript will be focusing on this h2 element, as it provides the handle with which to perform the expand/collapse and moving actions. We're not concerned with the HTML contained inside the moduleContent div, as that's specific to each module. We just want to abstract our framework to deal with each module block.

Expanding and collapsing modules

The ability to expand and collapse content is not a new concept, and it's actually quite simple. Probably the most important thing we can do is to keep it unobtrusive and accessible.

On the unobtrusive side of things, users who do not have JavaScript turned on should not be offered functionality that they cannot access. This means that the elements that allow for expanding/collapsing should be included via the JavaScript itself.

The JavaScript

When expand_collapse.js is included on the page, it sets up a page load listener, and then iterates through each of the modules and inserts the appropriate HTML elements:

```
addLoadListener(initExpandCollapse);

function initExpandCollapse()
{
  var modules = [document.getElementById("modules1"), document.getElementById("modules2")];

  for (var i in modules)
  {
    var h2s = modules[i].getElementsByTagName("h2");

    for (var i = 0; i < h2s.length; i++)
    {
      var newA = document.createElement("a");
      newA.setAttribute("href", "#");
      newA.setAttribute("title", "Expand/Collapse");
      attachEventListener(newA, "mousedown", mousedownExpandCollapse,false);
      newA.onclick = clickExpandCollapse;

        var newImg = document.createElement("img");
        newImg.setAttribute("src", "images/min_max.gif");
        newImg.setAttribute("alt", "Expand/Collapse");
        newA.appendChild(newImg);

      h2s[i].appendChild(newA);
    }
  }

  return true;
};
```

The page load listener is added using the addLoadListener() function from the same event_listeners.js file as the resolution-dependent layout example and calls initExpandCollapse() when the page is ready.

initExpandCollapse() starts by creating an array of the module elements of interest, and then iterates through that array to find all of the h2 elements. For each h2, we create a new anchor element that contains an img element (our little expand/collapse icon), and then we apply some behavior to that anchor. By using an anchor element instead of a span or a div, we make sure that the expand/collapse functionality is keyboard accessible. anchor elements are focusable via the keyboard and will receive a click event when the user activates them by pressing the Enter key.

We're capturing two events on the anchor tag: a mousedown and a click. The mousedown listener is required to counteract the mousedown that we'll use for dragging and dropping the content module. Essentially, we want to listen for clicks on the anchor, but whenever someone clicks a mouse button, it's also preceded by a mousedown. Because the anchor is inside the h2, that will trigger the h2's mousedown event, so we need to cancel the h2's mousedown event when the anchor's mousedown event fires. This is done via mousedownExpandCollapse():

```
function mousedownExpandCollapse(event)
{
  if (typeof event == "undefined")
  {
    event = window.event;
  }
```

```
    if (typeof event.stopPropagation != "undefined")
    {
      event.stopPropagation();
    }
    else
    {
      event.cancelBubble = true;
    }

    return true;
};
```

This short function is mainly about getting around browser differences in event handling. The first conditional checks whether an event object was passed to the function itself. This is normally done automatically by the event listener, but that doesn't happen with Internet Explorer 5.x. If the event object doesn't exist, we default to window.event, which is what Internet Explorer 5.x uses.

Next, we check whether the event object method stopPropagation() exists. This is the W3C standard method for stopping an event from bubbling upwards (that is, stopping the mousedown event on the anchor from also registering on the h2). If stopPropagation() exists, we call it. However, Internet Explorer uses a proprietary property of the event object called cancelBubble to stop event bubbling. If stopPropagation() doesn't exist, we set event.cancelBubble to true, and this has the same effect.

Now we need to deal with the click event. You might have noticed that to add the mousedown event listener to the anchor, we used the abstracting function from the resolution-dependent layout, attachEventListener(), but for the click event, we actually use one of the old event handlers, the onclick property. Because Safari doesn't allow us to stop the default action of click events added using the W3C event listeners, we need to revert to the dot property. In practice, this shouldn't cause much of a problem. We're adding the event handler to an element created by our own script, so it shouldn't have any other event information attached to it that might conflict.

The function that the click event handler points to is clickExpandCollapse():

```
function clickExpandCollapse()
{
  if (!hasClass(this.parentNode.parentNode, "collapsed"))
  {
    addClass(this.parentNode.parentNode, "collapsed");
  }
  else
  {
    removeClass(this.parentNode.parentNode, "collapsed");
  }

  return false;
};
```

This does a simple toggle of the class on the div that surrounds the h2. If that div doesn't have a class of collapsed, we add the class. If it does have a class of collapsed, we remove the class. This makes it easy to style the different views of a collapsed and expanded module purely through the CSS.

When dealing with element classes in clickExpandCollapse(), we always use these custom functions: hasClass(), addClass(), and removeClass(). These make it easier to work with multiple classnames on the same element. I've included the functions in their own library file, class_names.js, so they can easily be included in other projects:

```
function hasClass(target, classValue)
{
  var pattern = new RegExp("(^| )" + classValue + "( |$)");
```

```
    if (target.className.match(pattern))
    {
        return true;
    }

    return false;
};

function addClass(target, classValue)
{
    if (!hasClass(target, classValue))
    {
        if (target.className == "")
        {
            target.className = classValue;
        }
        else
        {
            target.className += " " + classValue;
        }
    }

    return true;
};

function removeClass(target, classValue)
{
    var removedClass = target.className;
    var pattern = new RegExp("(^| )" + classValue + "( |$)");

    removedClass = removedClass.replace(pattern, "$1");
    removedClass = removedClass.replace(/ $/, "");

    target.className = removedClass;

    return true;
};
```

It's not correct to do a direct string comparison on an element's class, because it can actually contain multiple classes, each separated by a space. This is the same reason you shouldn't do a direct assignment to the class, because you might overwrite existing classes. hasClass() checks whether the value you're searching for is one of the multiple classes. addClass() makes sure you don't overwrite any existing classes or add the same class more than once. removeClass() removes only the specified class while leaving all others intact.

Now that the click event is in place, every time that a user clicks the expand/collapse link for a content module, it will add or remove the collapsed class as necessary. And that finishes our expand/collapse behavior!

Styling with CSS

Now that we've added some new elements and classes to the page, it's time to style our expand/collapse widget. The expand/collapse anchor tag is nested inside the h2, so we can use that to get at it through CSS (from `main.css`):

```
.module h2
{
  position: relative;
}

.module h2 a
{
  position: absolute;
  top: 50%;
  right: 10px;
  width: 9px;
  height: 9px;
  overflow: hidden;
  margin: -4px 0 0 0;
  cursor: pointer;
}

.module h2 a img
{
  display: block;
}
```

In order to get the link aligned to the right of the h2, I've chosen to position it absolutely and use the right positioning property to put it 10px from the edge (you could just as easily float the element right).

The h2 itself is positioned relatively, and this has an important effect on the anchor. Normally, when you position an element absolutely, it will be positioned in relation to the entire page; for example, if you set its top to be 0, it will move to the top of the page. However, when you nest an absolutely positioned element (like our anchor) inside a relatively positioned element (like our h2), the anchor will now be positioned in relation to the h2. So when we set the anchor's right position, it will be positioned from the right of the h2.

The dimensions of the link are specific to the size of the image it contains. The size of the little plus and minus icons is 9px by 9px, so that should be the size of the link. Well, actually, the size of the *image* that contains the icons is 9px by 18px. That's because both icons are in the same image file, as shown in Figure 9-9.

By having both icons in the same image file, we can affect the display of the expand/collapse link just through the CSS. By limiting the link itself to the size of only one of the icons, and then applying the hidden value to the overflow property, we effectively crop out the rest of the image, making it look like only one icon. Then, inside `main.css`, we can move the image around inside its "box" to switch the icon from minus to plus:

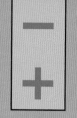

Figure 9-9. The two icons for expanding and collapsing combined in one image

```
.collapsed h2 a img
{
  position: relative;
  top: -9px;
}
```

By default, the minus icon will be showing, indicating that you can collapse the module. But once the module has been collapsed, we use the `collapsed` class to specify that the icon image should now be moved up 9px, relative to its containing element (the link), thereby showing the plus icon instead.

Showing and hiding the actual content of the module is even easier:

```
.collapsed .moduleContent
{
  display: none;
}
```

Now the expanding and collapsing styling matches the behavior, as shown in Figures 9-10 and 9-11, and we're all done!

Figure 9-10. The calendar module in its default, expanded view

Figure 9-11. The calendar module after it has been collapsed

Reorganizing modules

Expanding/collapsing is the easy part. What really puts a user in control is being able to dictate the layout of the modules themselves. We're going to allow users to grab a module by its title bar and drag it around—to move it up and down in its container position, or swap it over to the other module area. Because the reorganization behavior is entirely separate from the expand/collapse behavior, we can include it in a different file, modular.js, for easy maintenance.

Drag-and-drop event listeners

The first step in setting up our new behavior is to create the event listeners for the drag-and-drop actions:

```
addLoadListener(initModular);

function initModular()
{
  var modules = [document.getElementById("modules1"), document.getElementById("modules2")];

  for (var i = 0; i < modules.length; i++)
  {
    var h2s = modules[i].getElementsByTagName("h2");

    for (var j = 0; j < h2s.length; j++)
    {
      addClass(h2s[j].parentNode, "moduleDraggable");
      attachEventListener(h2s[j], "mousedown", mousedownH2, false);
    }
  }

  return true;
};
```

We add another page load listener using addLoadListener(), but this time it's calling initModular(), which, much like initExpandCollapse(), iterates through the module areas, finding each of the h2 elements. For each h2, we then add a new class, moduleDraggable, to its parent div and create a mousedown event listener on the h2. We place this class on the h2's parent div so that we can add in some styling tweaks once we know that JavaScript is enabled. We want to give the users a hint that the module is movable (otherwise, they might not be aware of this fact), so we use this CSS rule in main.css:

```
.moduleDraggable h2
{
  cursor: move;
}
```

This changes the cursor to a move cursor when the user hovers her mouse over a draggable h2 element, as shown in Figure 9-12.

The function called by the mousedown listener on the h2 does a lot of the work for the drag-and-drop behavior of the modules, by collecting information and setting up variables:

```
function mousedownH2(event)
{
  if (typeof event == "undefined")
  {
```

Figure 9-12. The mouse cursor changes appearance when it is hovered over a module's title bar.

```javascript
      event = window.event;
    }

    if (typeof event.target != "undefined")
    {
      dragTarget = event.target.parentNode;
    }
    else
    {
      dragTarget = event.srcElement.parentNode;
    }

    dragOrigin = [event.clientX, event.clientY];
    dragHotspots = [];

    var modules = [document.getElementById("modules1"), document.getElementById("modules2")];

    for (var i = 0; i < modules.length; i++)
    {
      var divs = modules[i].getElementsByTagName("div");

      for (var j = 0; j < divs.length; j++)
      {
        if (divs[j] != null && hasClass(divs[j], "module"))
        {
          var modulePosition = getPosition(divs[j]);

          dragHotspots[dragHotspots.length] =
          {
            element: divs[j],
            offsetX: modulePosition[0],
            offsetY: modulePosition[1]
          }
        }
      }

      var modulePosition = getPosition(modules[i]);

      dragHotspots[dragHotspots.length] =
      {
        element: modules[i],
        offsetX: modulePosition[0],
        offsetY: modulePosition[1] + modules[i].offsetHeight
      }
    }

    var position = getPosition(dragTarget);

  var ghost = document.createElement("div");
    ghost.setAttribute("id", "ghost");
    document.getElementsByTagName("body")[0].appendChild(ghost);
```

```
ghost.appendChild(dragTarget.cloneNode(true));
ghost.style.left = position[0] + "px";
ghost.style.top = position[1] + "px";

attachEventListener(document, "mousemove", mousemoveDocument, false);
attachEventListener(document, "mouseup", mouseupDocument, false);

event.returnValue = false;

if (typeof event.preventDefault != "undefined")
{
    event.preventDefault();
}

return true;
};
```

After it does the normal event object abstraction, `mousedownH2()` then goes about finding exactly which element was clicked. This should be theoretically possible just by referencing the `this` object, but unfortunately, Internet Explorer doesn't assign this object correctly when events are added using the W3C event model. Instead, we have to rely on the event object's target element property, which can be inaccurate if there are elements nested inside our event target, but it's fine here because the h2 is the deepest element in this branch. Naturally, Internet Explorer doesn't call this element `target`, as other browsers do; it's `srcElement` in Internet Explorer. So we have to check whether `event.target` exists (the standard property), and if it doesn't, use `event.srcElement` (the Internet Explorer property).

Once these differences have been sorted out, we create a reference to the parent node of the target element (the div surrounding the h2) in a global variable called `dragTarget`, so that we can use it later in other functions.

After the target has been discerned, we then create some global variables that will help track what's happening as the user drags the module around. `dragOrigin` stores the coordinates of the original mousedown event. Whenever an event is fired, `event.clientX` and `event.clientY` record the two coordinates that define the place on a page where an event occurred; in this case, where the user pushed down the mouse button. It's important to store this original location, because when the user moves her mouse, we want to know how far she moved it from where she clicked originally.

A map of the page

`dragHotspots` is an array that stores the locations of all the possible places you could drag a module. You can think of it as a sort of map. When users drag a module around, they aren't changing its position to an arbitrary point on the page; instead, they are actually changing its position relative to the other modules. So, instead of specifying a module's destination in terms of absolute coordinates, we are trying to describe its destination in terms of its location among the other modules: "move the search module beneath the calendar module, but above the horoscope module." In order to do this, we need to create a map of the page indicating where all the other modules are. That way, when the dragged module is moved around the page, we know whether the dragged module should be above or below each of the static modules. All that calculation is done by the mousemove handler, though. For now, we're just concerned with creating the map.

We could create the map inside the mousemove handler, but every time the mouse moved, the calculations would have to be done again. Creating the map just once—when the mouse button is pressed—is more efficient.

To create the map, we look inside each of the module areas and iterate through all of the divs that have a class of module. For those divs, we create a new object in the `dragHotspots` array that holds a reference to the module (`element`), the horizontal page offset of the module's top-left corner (`offsetX`), and the vertical page offset of the module's top-left corner (`offsetY`). Those last two properties get their values from the `getPosition()` function, which takes an element and returns

```
function getPosition(theElement)
{
  var positionX = 0;
  var positionY = 0;

  while (theElement != null)
  {
    positionX += theElement.offsetLeft;
    positionY += theElement.offsetTop;
    theElement = theElement.offsetParent;
  }

  return [positionX, positionY];
};
```

Getting the position of an element on a page is overly complicated, but there's nothing to be done about it. An element can discern its position only in relation to its "offset parent" (which varies according to the way it is positioned, floated, and so on). To get its absolute location on the page, we have to recursively work our way up the offset parent tree (using element.offsetParent), getting the positions of each of the offset parents along the way and adding them together to return a total.

Once each of the modules inside a module area has been added to dragHotspots, there's a special case where we add the module area itself to dragHotspots. This is so we can recognize when the dragged module is below all other elements in the module area; in which case, we move it right to the end.

The ghost

After the map is created, we need to create the visual element that will indicate to users that they are dragging something. It's actually a copy of the module that the user is dragging, and we make it look ghostly by changing its transparency, so I call it the ghost.

We get the current position of the dragged module using getPosition(), and then we create the new ghost element. It's an absolutely positioned empty div wrapped around a direct copy of the dragged module. The empty div acts as a substitute for the constraints of the module area div, giving the module a width to fill; otherwise, it would expand to a width of 100%. Because it's positioned absolutely and inserted at the end of the body element, it's free to move wherever the user's mouse cursor moves.

The copy of the dragged module is created using the cloneNode() method. cloneNode() takes one argument that specifies whether you want the contents of the node to be copied as well, or just the node itself. By calling dragTarget.cloneNode(true), we are saying we want a copy of dragTarget *and* its contents. We add that copy to the empty shell and then position it over the original module, so it looks like the user is dragging the ghost out of its body. By applying a bit of CSS opacity, we can give the ghost its ghostly appearance:

```
#ghost .module
{
  opacity: 0.65;
  filter: alpha(opacity=50);
}
```

You can see the result in Figure 9-13.

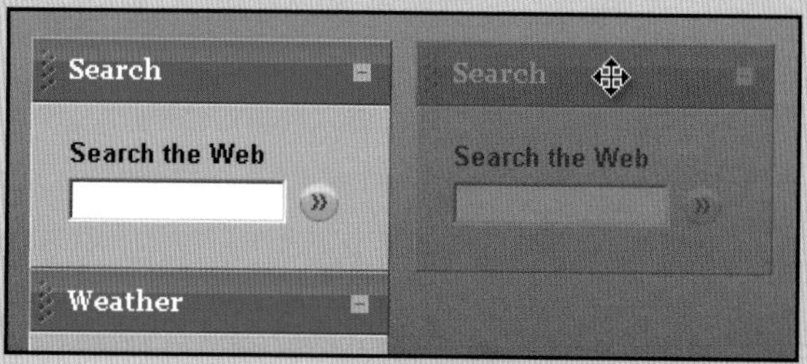

To track where the user is moving the mouse while the button is pressed, we need to add a mousemove listener to the entire document. We add a mouseup listener to tell us when the user has released the mouse button.

Figure 9-13. The ghost copy of a module next to its original

Now we're fully prepared for users to drag modules around. The last thing that mousedownH2() does is to stop the default action of the mousedown. This prevents the browser from doing what it normally does when the user presses down the mouse button. In a drag-and-drop situation, it stops text on the page from being selected while the ghost is being dragged.

As the user moves the mouse around, the document mousemove event listener will be constantly calling mousemoveDocument():

```
function mousemoveDocument(event)
{
  if (typeof event == "undefined")
  {
    event = window.event;
  }

  var ghost = document.getElementById("ghost");

  if (ghost != null)
  {
    ghost.style.marginLeft = event.clientX - dragOrigin[0] + "px";
    ghost.style.marginTop = event.clientY - dragOrigin[1] + "px";
  }

  var closest = null;
  var closestY = null;

  for (var i in dragHotspots)
  {
    var ghostX = parseInt(ghost.style.left, 10) + parseInt(ghost.style.marginLeft, 10);
    var ghostY = parseInt(ghost.style.top, 10) + parseInt(ghost.style.marginTop, 10);

    if (ghostX >= dragHotspots[i].offsetX -➡
    dragHotspots[i].element.offsetWidth && ghostX <=➡
    dragHotspots[i].offsetX + dragHotspots[i].element.offsetWidth)
    {
      var distanceY = Math.abs(ghostY - dragHotspots[i].offsetY);

      if (closestY == null || closestY > distanceY)
      {
        closest = dragHotspots[i];
        closestY = distanceY;
      }
    }
  }

  if (closest != null)
  {
    var ghostMarker = document.getElementById("ghostMarker");

    if (ghostMarker == null)
    {
      ghostMarker = document.createElement("div");
      ghostMarker.id = "ghostMarker";
```

```
          document.getElementsByTagName("body")[0].appendChild(ghostMarker);
        }

        ghostMarker.marked = closest.element;

        ghostMarker.style.left = closest.offsetX + "px";
        ghostMarker.style.top = closest.offsetY + "px";
      }
      else
      {
        var ghostMarker = document.getElementById("ghostMarker");

        if (ghostMarker != null)
        {
          ghostMarker.parentNode.removeChild(ghostMarker);
        }

      }

      event.returnValue = false;

      if (typeof event.preventDefault != "undefined")
      {
        event.preventDefault();
      }

      return true;
    };
```

The first order of business for this function is to change the position of the ghost so that it looks like it's following the user's mouse cursor. We do this by calculating how far the user has moved from the original mousedown point, and then setting the margins on the ghost div to reflect this difference. The current coordinates of the mouse cursor are again obtained using event.clientX and event.clientY, and the global dragOrigin variable is used for the original mousedown coordinates.

mousedownDocument() then needs to use our map of the other modules to figure out the new insertion point of the dragged module. We know the location of the ghost div, and we know the location of each of the static modules' top-left corners, so it's quite easy to figure out which static module the ghost is nearest. We want to insert the dragged module before that static module.

For each entry in dragHotspots, we do a quick test of the horizontal position of the ghost. If no part of the ghost is within the width of the module area where the static module is located, we don't want to consider it as a viable destination for the dragged module. So we check whether the *right* edge of the ghost is right of the static module's left edge and whether the *left* edge of the ghost is left of the static module's right edge. This means that some part of the ghost is overlapping the width of the module area.

Then we can concern ourselves with the vertical distance between the ghost and the static module. To do this, we measure the difference between the top of the ghost and the top of the static module, and then compare it with the minimum value already found. If the distance to the current static module is less than the current minimum value, that becomes the new minimum value. After all the dragHotspots entries have been checked against, we know whether there is a suitable location for the dragged module to be inserted at, and if so, where.

If there was a suitable location, we need to show this to the users, so that they know where the dragged module will be inserted if they release the mouse button. To do this, we create a new element called ghostMarker, which is simply a thin, square block that sits at the top of the candidate insertion point. The ghost marker is an absolutely positioned child of the body element, so to position it, we use the coordinates of the closest static module. As you can see in Figure 9-14, with a bit of CSS styling, the ghost marker gives a good indication of where the dragged module is going to be inserted.

To make it easy for later insertion of the dragged module, we also create a new property of ghostMarker that records which static module it is marking: ghostMarker.marked.

Figure 9-14. The ghost marker showing where the dragged module will be inserted

If there wasn't a suitable location for the dragged module to be inserted—the user didn't drag the ghost close enough to one of the static modules—then we actually remove ghostMarker. So if the user moved the ghost from a suitable location to an unsuitable one, it won't still indicate that he can reposition the dragged module.

The last operation in mousemoveDocument() again stops the default action that the browser would normally perform for a mousemove, preventing unwanted actions from occurring while the user is dragging.

The repositioned module

When the user has decided where he wants to place the dragged module, or that he doesn't want to move it, he will release the mouse button. This is captured by mouseupDocument():

```
function mouseupDocument()
{
  detachEventListener(document, "mousemove", mousemoveDocument, false);

  var ghost = document.getElementById("ghost");

  if (ghost != null)
  {
    ghost.parentNode.removeChild(ghost);
  }

  var ghostMarker = document.getElementById("ghostMarker");

  if (ghostMarker != null)
  {
    if (!hasClass(ghostMarker.marked, "module"))
    {
```

```
            ghostMarker.marked.appendChild(dragTarget);
        }
        else
        {
            ghostMarker.marked.parentNode.insertBefore(dragTarget, ghostMarker.marked);
        }

        ghostMarker.parentNode.removeChild(ghostMarker);
    }

    return true;
};
```

Most of the heavy lifting has already been done, so this function just tidies things up. First, it removes the mousemove event listener from the document, as we no longer need to know when the user is moving the mouse. After that, we remove the ghost element, as we want to stop displaying the copy.

Then we decide where to place the dragged module. If ghostMarker still exists, it means that the user released the mouse button when there was a valid place to move the dragged module. Using the ghostMarker.marked property, we can see which element to insert the dragged module before. We need to check whether the marked module is actually a module, or whether it was the extra placeholder we put in for the end of the module area. If it's an actual module (it has a class of module), we can use the insertBefore() method to move the dragged module before the marked module. If it was a module area, we use appendChild() to place the dragged module at the end of the area. Either way, we remove the ghost marker, and the dragged module now ends up in its new location, just where the user wanted! If ghostMarker no longer exists, we know that there's nowhere for the dragged module to move to, so we can quietly finish.

Figure 9-15 shows the whole process of a user dragging a module from one module area to another.

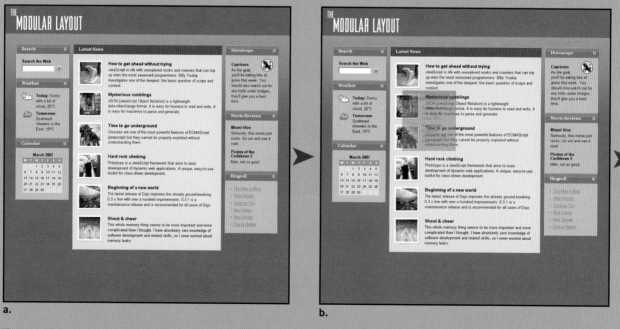

Figure 9-15 (a-d). Dragging a module to another module area

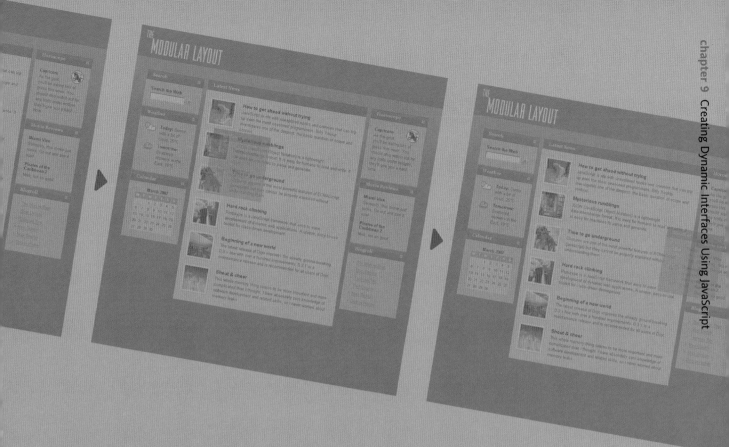

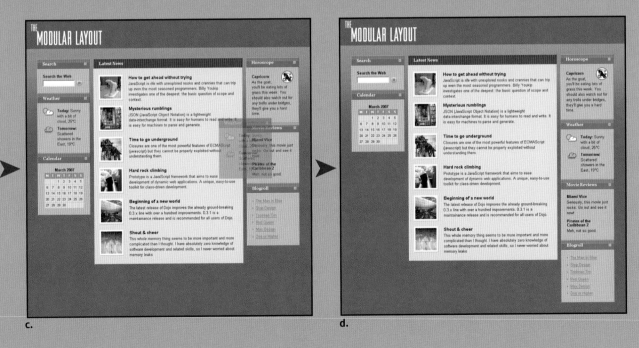

c.

d.

Keeping track of changes

The techniques explained in this example create a page that users can customize to their heart's delight. But it will be in vain if they return to the page the next day and it hasn't kept any of their changes.

Although it would be possible to download the page from the server and rearrange the modules via JavaScript, this is a rather clumsy process, and would probably result in users seeing the default layout before the page switches to their custom layout.

The best solution is to assemble the custom layout on the server and serve it to the users as they arranged it. The easiest way to achieve this is to store a cookie in the user's browser that tells the server the order of the user's layout, and the server can use this to assemble the proper page.

All we have to do is keep track of which modules are in which module area and their order. To do this, we need to make sure that each of the modules has a unique ID, in our markup. Once that's done, we can modify the mouseupDocument() function to write some cookies that contain the preference data. This updated function is included in modular_cookie.js (which you could include instead of modular.js):

```
function mouseupDocument()
{
  detachEventListener(document, "mousemove", mousemoveDocument, false);

  var ghost = document.getElementById("ghost");

  if (ghost != null)
  {
    ghost.parentNode.removeChild(ghost);
  }

  var ghostMarker = document.getElementById("ghostMarker");

  if (ghostMarker != null)
  {
    if (!hasClass(ghostMarker.marked, "module"))
    {
      ghostMarker.marked.appendChild(dragTarget);
    }
    else
    {
      ghostMarker.marked.parentNode.insertBefore(dragTarget, ghostMarker.marked);
    }

    ghostMarker.parentNode.removeChild(ghostMarker);

    var modules1 = document.getElementById("modules1");
    var modules1Modules = [];
    var divs = modules1.getElementsByTagName("div");

    for (var i = 0; i < divs.length; i++)
    {
      if (hasClass(divs[i], "module"))
```

```
        {
            modules1Modules[modules1Modules.length] = divs[i].getAttribute("id");
        }
    }

    document.cookie = "modules1=" + modules1Modules.join(",");

    var modules2 = document.getElementById("modules2");
    var modules2Modules = [];
    var divs = modules2.getElementsByTagName("div");

for (var i = 0; i < divs.length; i++)
    {
        if (hasClass(divs[i], "module"))
        {
            modules2Modules[modules2Modules.length] = divs[i].getAttribute("id");
        }
    }

    document.cookie = "modules2=" + modules2Modules.join(",");
    }

    return true;
};
```

Now when a module is repositioned, two cookies are written. For each module area, the divs with a class of module are found and their IDs added to an array. The array will reflect the order of the modules, as getElementsByTagName() returns elements in source order. Once the array has been completed, it is written into a cookie—either modules1 or modules2, depending on the circumstances, with each of the IDs separated by a comma.

When these cookies are passed to the server, you should be able to use them to check the order of the modules and write them into the web page in the appropriate order.

Conclusion

The diversity of user needs—whether technological or task-based—is challenging the traditionally static form of the Web. Creating dynamic interfaces is one of the ways that you can help to meet those needs. The two techniques I've described here demonstrate how the flexibility of standards-based web pages can change the way in which we design for the Web.

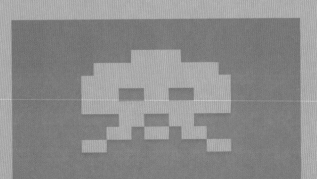

10 Accessible Sliding Navigation

derek
featherstone

boxofchocolates.ca
furtherahead.com

Engaging, surprising, and inspiring, **Derek Featherstone** has a gift for taking a fresh look at virtually every aspect of web development and teaching it in a way that renews our passion for making the Web better for everyone. Featherstone is an internationally known authority on accessibility and web development, and a respected technical trainer and author.

Creator of in-depth courses on HTML, CSS, DOM scripting, and Web 2.0 applications, Derek never fails to champion the cause of Web Standards and universal accessibility. Through his company, Further Ahead (www.furtherahead.com), he has been an in-demand consultant to government agencies, educational institutions, and private-sector companies since 1999. His wealth of experience and insight enables him to provide audiences with immediately applicable, brilliantly simple approaches to everyday challenges in website design.

Derek serves as the Lead for the Accessibility Task Force and is a member of the DOM Scripting Task Force of the Web Standards Project. He also comments on a variety of subjects at his popular blog and personal site, www.boxofchocolates.ca.

The killer feature

Admit it. You want it. You know, the killer feature on your website that makes the blogosphere say "aaaaaaahhh-hhh." The one that wins you the reboot award. The one that makes your website stand out from the rest. OK, forget that. What about the one that makes life easier for your visitors by providing them with easier access to information and links?

We're talking about today's replacement for the old-school Dynamic HTML menu systems that provided access to all of your categorized and subcategorized links in a few easy mouseovers and a click. This replacement is the *sliding navigation system*, which displays nicely categorized links.

Shaun Inman's blog (www.shauninman.com) showcased this technique in his 2005 redesign, complete with a single sliding navigation and search tab that hides and exposes the details of his site. His blog categories, recent posts, search box, and other goodies remain tucked away until called into action by some dutiful JavaScript.

Another recent trend in website design is the information-rich footer. Derek Powazek "embraced his bottom" (www.powazek.com/2005/09/000540.html) in his 2005 redesign, making the footer of his site very prominent and useful, rather than obscure and filled solely with a copyright statement (see Figure 10-1). He has one of the best bottoms—er, footers—in the business. It is designed with purpose and intent to motivate, provide more information, and give context for visitors.

In this chapter, we'll implement a site that combines sliding navigation with the information-rich footer into a system that adds detail and usability enhancements to the traditional "tabbed" navigation found on many of today's websites. And, as you should expect, it will take accessibility into account from the beginning.

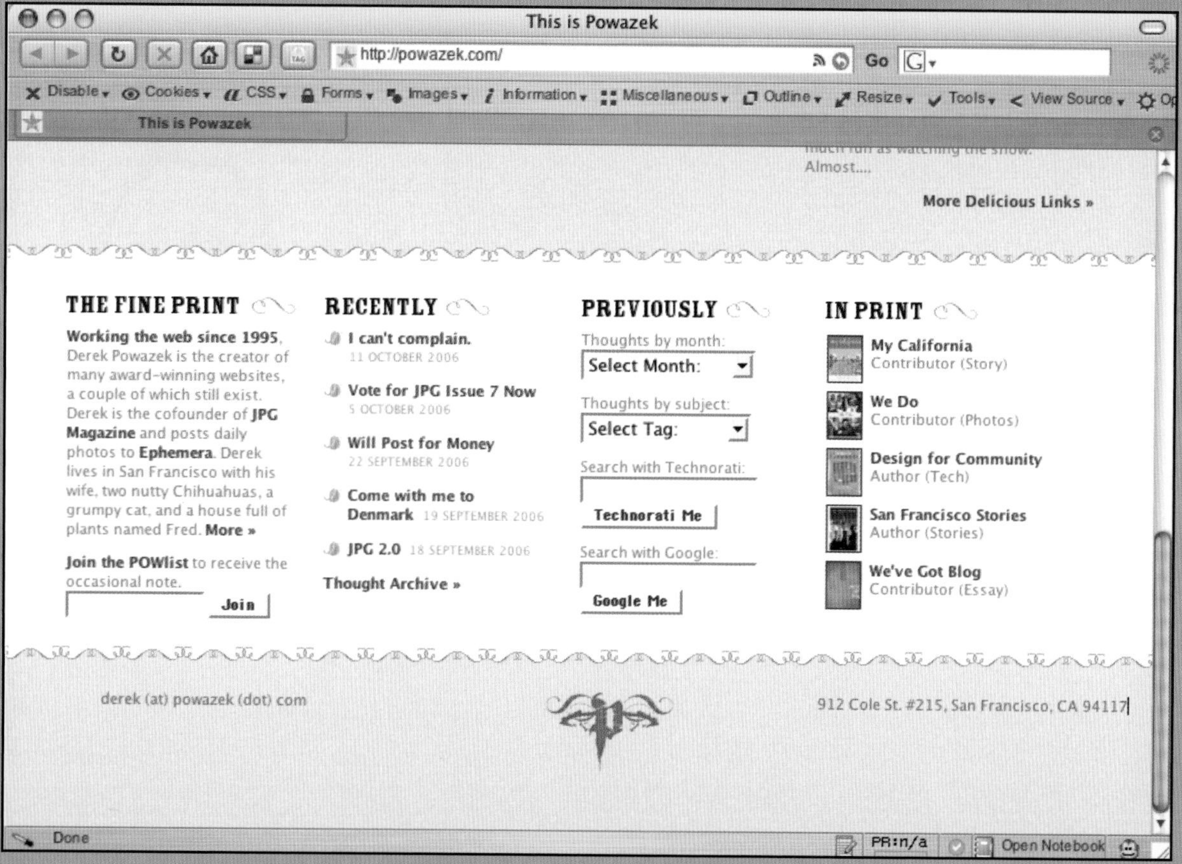

Figure 10-1. The footer from Derek Powazek's blog. More than your average footer, Derek's is designed to be useful and provide the visitor with more context and blog-related functionality.

Accessibility basics

Web accessibility might best be described as a set of guiding principles or guidelines that help us to make websites that work for all different types of users, regardless of their ability. We strive to take these differing levels of ability into account when we code our websites:

- Vision impairment (varying degrees of blindness, low vision, and color blindness)

- Mobility or dexterity impairment (requiring use of voice-recognition software or hardware aids to facilitate keyboard usage or to help compensate for different levels of fine motor control)

- Auditory impairment (requiring captioning and/or transcripts for multimedia audio and video, for example)

- Cognitive disabilities (including varying degrees of dyslexia, autism, and other learning impairments)

To take this wide range of abilities into account, we need to do some simple things. We make sure that images have appropriate alt text so that people who are visually impaired have alternative representations that their screen reader software can read to them. We implement solutions that allow users to resize the text on their page so that they can read it more easily. We have appropriate color contrast between foreground and background colors. We label our form fields, We use structured markup to ensure that the elements we have on the screen use the best possible HTML elements available—headings, paragraphs, lists, tables, form buttons, and so on.

One of the long-standing problems with building accessible websites is that we, as developers, designers, and content creators, have very little hands-on experience working with people with disabilities to understand their true needs and how we can avoid putting accessibility barriers in their way. Enter the World Wide Web Consortium's Web Accessibility Initiative (www.w3.org/WAI).

Accessibility guidelines

The Web Accessibility Initiative (WAI) strives to make the Web more accessible to everyone and has a set of guidelines that can be used to help developers build accessible websites. Don't worry; it isn't all up to us. WAI has also produced guidelines for browser makers and authoring tool vendors so that they can ensure that the tools that people use facilitate accessibility. These other guidelines—the User Agent Accessibility Guidelines (UAAG) and the Authoring Tool Accessibility Guidelines (ATAG)—are important, but beyond the scope of what we do as developers. Our attention should be firmly placed on the Web Content Accessibility Guidelines (WCAG).

WCAG (www.w3.org/WAI/intro/wcag.php) is a set of guidelines that give us some starting points for creating accessible websites. This does not mean, however, that simply following the guidelines will guarantee our sites will be accessible. In order to create accessible websites, we need to generally follow the principles found in the guidelines, and then test our resulting web pages with people using assistive technology. This ensures that we get the best of both worlds. We achieve technical compliance by adhering to the guidelines, and through testing with people with disabilities, we create something that is actually usable to them.

The example presented in this chapter examines many of the principles of WCAG and includes the results of testing with various screen readers, voice-recognition software, and a screen magnifier.

> For a detailed and in-depth look at accessibility, read Web Accessibility: Web Standards and Regulatory Compliance (friends of ED, ISBN: 1-59059-638-2).

Accessibility and JavaScript

For years, both accessibility and JavaScript have been the realm of the expert who is well-versed in a niche subject area. Work in this area has been hindered by the long-standing myth that has been handed down from generation to generation of web developers. This myth is very simply stated: To make sure that your web page is accessible, it must work with JavaScript on or off.

This misconception is in large part due to WCAG checkpoint 6.3 (www.w3.org/TR/WCAG10/wai-pageauth.html#tech-scripts), which states:

> *Ensure that pages are usable when scripts, applets, or other programmatic objects are turned off or not supported. If this is not possible, provide equivalent information on an alternative accessible page.*

In 1999, when WCAG 1.0 was published, this was a reasonable guideline. Screen readers and browsers were not nearly as advanced as they are today. It was widely accepted (and propagated) that screen readers just didn't understand JavaScript. The on/off scenario used to be reasonably accurate.

Today's screen readers *do* understand much of the JavaScript that is supported in today's browsers, yet many people are still holding on to the idea that this isn't possible. They cling to the assumption necessary for WCAG checkpoint 6.3: accessibility and scripting as a binary on/off scenario.

Enter the modern era of web accessibility and assistive technology. Yes, some people with disabilities may use browsers that can't handle scripting, or even turn off JavaScript, but the majority of the population is likely to be using a regular browser with scripting support. It is no longer a black and white matter. Ensuring that a page works with scripting on or off is more about *interoperability*—providing at least basic functionality in either state—than it is about *accessibility*.

So the trick to creating accessible JavaScript is not solely about ensuring that our solutions work with JavaScript on or off. We must also make sure that our solutions are compatible with users of varying abilities and with assistive technologies. Keep this in mind as we progress through the rest of the chapter.

The accessible solution

We know from our experience that basic accessibility for people with disabilities and basic interoperability with different devices are provided by a standards-based approach to web development: structural HTML, CSS for presentation, and a final layer of JavaScript on top to provide behavior. This approach will be used in this chapter's example to ensure that we've covered the basics. We'll use semantic HTML, design with CSS, and deliver a solution that works with both JavaScript on or off. Once we have done that, we'll add some more scripting to make sure that the system works well for people using a variety of assistive technologies.

Before we start getting into code, let's take a look at a brief overview of the solution as well as the files that make it all happen (these are available for download from this book's page on www.friendsofed.com):

- Base HTML file, wscslide.html
- Style sheet, wscslide.css
- JavaScript functions, wscslide.js

Figure 10-2 shows a simple wireframe of the effect we are trying to achieve with our sliding navigation. The initial position for the navigational panes when the page loads and before any JavaScript has taken effect is at the bottom after the content. Once the main navigational link for Recent Posts has been activated, we use some basic JavaScript to change the CSS that is applied to the navigational pane to visually place it just below the navigation.

Once we have achieved that, we'll use some additional JavaScript to set the height of that pane to 0, and then create a sliding effect by changing that height one step at a time, returning the height to its original value. For example, if the original height of the Recent Posts pane is 180px, we'll set the height to 0, and then change it to 90px, then 135px, then 158px, and so on, until the height is back to its original size of 180px.

In the finished solution, the initial state for the navigational panes will appear as shown in Figure 10-3.

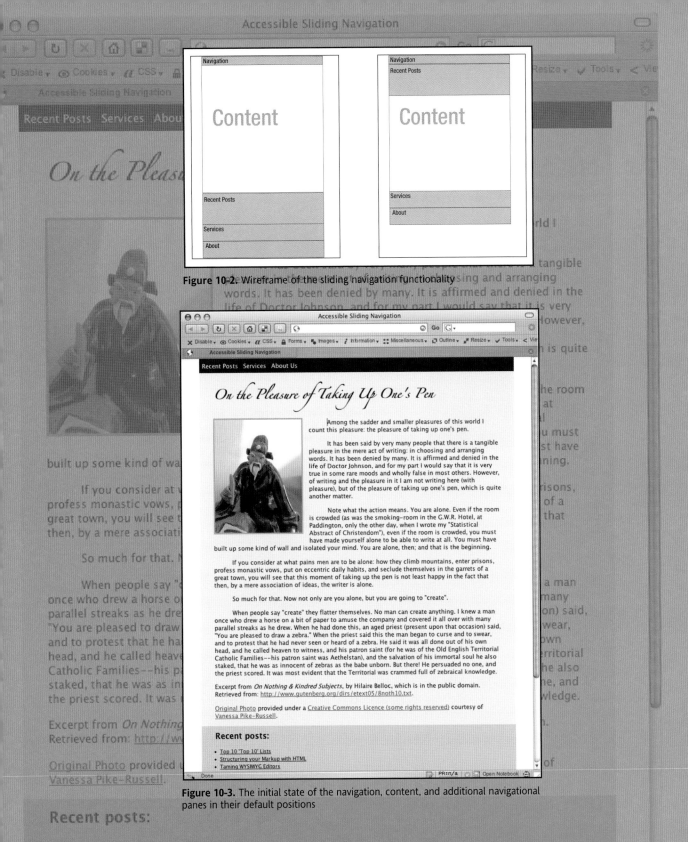

Figure 10-2. Wireframe of the sliding navigation functionality

Figure 10-3. The initial state of the navigation, content, and additional navigational panes in their default positions

After the main link is clicked, the navigational pane will slide into its final position, as shown in Figure 10-4.

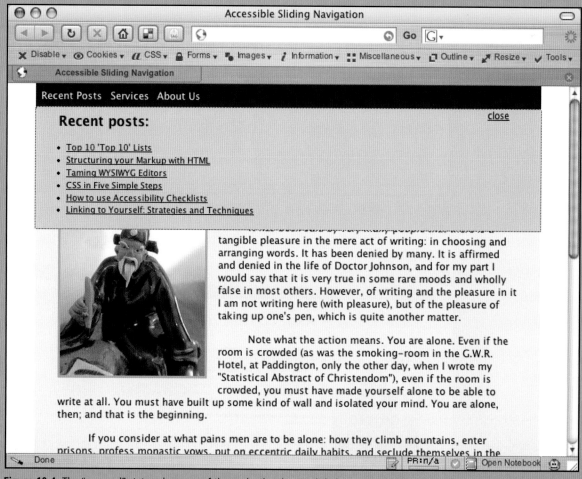

Figure 10-4. The "exposed" state, when one of the navigational panes is in its new position, visually just below the main navigation

These represent the two "states" for each tab: when the information is hidden and when it is exposed (this will be important later when we examine the CSS and JavaScript portions of the solution).

Starting with pristine HTML

In order to make any site or web application work, we need a solid foundation of content and functionality that is provided via clean HTML. Not only should the HTML be meaningful in terms of its content, but it should also be meaningful in terms of its functionality. Though most people tend to consider HTML only as content, it does provide basic functionality through form fields and links. Later in the chapter, we'll use these links as the basis for the interactive part of the scripting.

We need to implement three main areas of HTML for this solution:

- Navigation area
- Main content
- Additional content in the footer

The navigation will consist of a single unordered list, with each item containing a link to the relevant footer section. Note that these hrefs simply point to another portion of the page.

```
<ul id="nav">
<li><a href="#drop-posts">Recent
Posts</a></li>
<li><a href="#drop-services">Services</a></li>
<li><a href="#drop-about">About Us</a></li>
</ul>
```

For the purposes of this implementation, the main content is largely irrelevant. Its main purpose in this example is to make sure that the footer content is not visible when visitors first get to the page.

The footer content is fairly straightforward and includes several sections. In this case, we're using an About section, a Recent Posts section, and a Services section. Each of these content areas provides a glimpse into the full content that is available when viewing that section in detail, providing an abstract of sorts. We are wrapping each footer section in its own <div></div> to provide the appropriate styling later.

Note that the hrefs for the links in the Recent Posts pane are left blank purely for convenience in this example. Including blank links such as these in your document can be confusing to all users and especially those with disabilities, particularly those using screen reader software.

```
<div id="drops">
<div id="drop-posts">
 <h2>Recent posts:</h2>
 <ul>
  <li><a href="">Post 1</a></li>
  <li><a href="">Post 2</a></li>
  <li><a href="">Post 3</a></li>
  <li><a href="">Post 4</a></li>
  <li><a href="">Post 5</a></li>
  <li><a href="">Post 6</a></li>
 </ul>
</div>

<div id="drop-services">
 <h2>Services</h2>
 <p>things about services go here</p>
</div>
```

```
<div id="drop-about">
 <h2>About Us</h2>
 <p>Stuff about you goes here</p>
</div>

</div>   <!-- ends drops -->
```

The ids for each div are just used for clarity in this example are not necessarily the best choices. Placing an id of drops on the div that contains all the additional navigation panes signifies a very specific function. If we were to later change this site so it no longer uses sliding navigation, the name drops might be confusing. It would be better to give the wrapper div an id that it is more indicative of its function, such as supplemental. Nevertheless, to identify the behaviors we are implementing in this example, we'll keep the id as drops.

Also note that we have added headings to each footer section to provide a kind of "marker" for the section. For the sake of the examples, we'll mark these as <h2> elements. You will need to decide if <h2> is appropriate for your usage or if some other lower-level header is a better fit.

These code blocks will serve as our base for the rest of the implementation. We will modify it as we add styling and functionality.

Adding the presentation

The CSS for the example is fairly straightforward, and a lot of it is for dressing up the example. We add in some styling to lay out the basic page, specify the colors and background image, and format the text. With that in place, we can focus on the footer itself and the styles we'll need to have the navigation "slide" down from the top.

Finalizing the CSS will take some work, but the core layout remains the same. For this version of the sliding navigation, we use absolute and relative positioning to move the navigation panes from the bottom of the page to the top. It is this action that forms the core CSS "switch" for making the navigation possible and for keeping it accessible. The main mechanism is simply a link to another part of the page that contains the information we want. When a pane is exposed, it will take its place at the top of the page, as with the Recent Posts pane shown earlier in Figure 10-4.

Switching between CSS states with JavaScript

In the days when JavaScript was vilified for the way it was used on the Web, in-line scripting, event handlers, and modification of style properties were simply how things were done. These ad hoc changes usually had something to do with modifying and defining absolutely everything on the fly—height, width, background color, and various other style properties.

> We have progressed significantly from those dark days and work hard to separate our HTML from our CSS and our JavaScript. Modern techniques strive to ensure that our pages work with JavaScript both on and off. This is referred to as "unobtrusive scripting" and is the standard you'll find elsewhere in this book, as well as in other modern scripting books, such as Jeremy Keith's book DOM Scripting (friends of ED, ISBN: 1-59059-533-5).

In our current crop of web browsers, we have a much more predictable environment in which to work. This predictability provides us with the ability to change properties beyond height and width, and get creative with things like switching between predefined states that include CSS positioning. With all the changes to CSS that are needed stored in a series of CSS rules, we can simply use some JavaScript to change the class of the appropriate containing element as required.

For the purposes of our sliding navigation we have two core states:

- On initial page load, our navigational panes appear at the bottom of the page (see Figure 10-3).
- When a navigational item is activated (either with the keyboard or the mouse), the navigational pane moves to the top of the page (see Figure 10-4).

We use JavaScript to change the class of the navigational pane to be "exposed," which gives it the proper positioning at the top of the page just below the navigation. We create a style rule that positions any of the panes in the correct place (from the style sheet, wscslide.css):

```
/* apply to any div with class="exposed"
   that is in the <div id="drops"> */
div#drops div.exposed {
  position: absolute;
  top: 0;
  left: 0;
  padding: 0; /* added to remove doubled-up padding when positioned */
}
```

Note that this works because we are positioning these panes within the nearest relatively positioned parent, div#inner-wrap:

```
div#inner-wrap {
  background-color: #ccc;
  color: #000;
  position: relative;
  margin: 0;
  padding: 0.5em 0;
}
```

We also use JavaScript to remove the class exposed to return the pane to the bottom of the page.

We could incorporate the JavaScript to do this in many ways. In order to maintain our solid HTML base, we use JavaScript that intercepts, or "hijacks," the click on the navigational items and toggles the state of the navigational panes. It employs a function called toggle, which switches between an exposed navigational pane and its original state. It would be best to assign these dynamically to each of the navigational items, but for the sake of clarity, this ultimately results in the following for our navigational links:

```
<a href="#drop-posts" onclick="return toggle('drop-posts');">
  Recent Posts
</a>
```

Here is a quick look at the first version of the toggle function from wscslide.js:

```
function toggle(element) {

    var inner = document.getElementById('inner-wrap');

    /* if the scripting isn't supported, we want to return true so that
        default behavior of clicking the link works (i.e., take the user
        to the bottom part of the page)
    */

    if (!document.getElementById) return true;

    var elt = document.getElementById(element);

    // do a test on the className property on the element to
    // check for the exposed class

    if (/exposed/i.test(elt.className)) {
        // exposed state was found, so remove it

        elt.className = elt.className.replace(/exposed/g,'');
    } else {
        // add exposed to current class to respect any
        // styles/classes that already exist

        elt.className += " exposed";
    }

    return false;
}
```

> In this case, the core functionality is provided by the hrefs. Ensuring that they are in place means that we achieve a base level of interoperability with scripting either on or off. Don't confuse this with accessibility for people with disabilities. We'll address accessibility later after we've taken care of the basic interoperability needs.

The critical component of this script is that we're using scripting to take over for the functionality provided by the `<a href="#drop-posts">` links in the HTML. This ensures that a person using a browser without scripting support will be taken to the correct part of the page.

This serves as the base for the rest of the scripting. With this main toggle in place, we can add in our sliding behaviors.

Adding sliding behaviors

Now that we have used scripting to toggle between the exposed and the normal position for each of the navigation panes, we can add in scripting that slides the navigation out from "under" the main navigation. We accomplish this by changing the height of the pane to 0 when the exposed state is activated and writing a function that reveals the navigational pane by changing its height.

> As an alternative, when we activate the exposed state, we could put an appropriate padding-top on the content div to allow the navigational pane to sit on top of the content. Using a negative value for the CSS top property, we could hide the navigational pane under the navigation at the top and use JavaScript to slide the div#inner-wrap down the appropriate distance. However, during early testing of this solution, some testers reported a "choppy" sliding behavior. This was, in part, due to sliding a div that essentially contained all the content on the page. As the size of the page grew, the sliding just wasn't smooth.
>
> Both this solution and the one used in the example require additional scripting, but neither have significant impact on accessibility from a technical perspective. (Although there may or may not be issues with sliding navigation in general, for people with cognitive disabilities, for example.)

The finished script includes several additional features that make it work well:

- Simple error-checking to prevent the user from clicking twice on a tab. Once a navigational pane is "moving," the function simply returns rather than calling it again.
- A basic reset function that can be used to reset the tabs to their original state.
- A constant SLIDEINTERVAL, which lets us define the speed at which the Reveal function will be called repeatedly. In this case, we call it every 65 milliseconds.

We could take an extensive tour through this script, looking at the changes that we've made in a step-by-step manner. For example, we could look in detail at the animation strategy. However, I want to focus specifically on the accessibility side of things in detail and leave most of the core script to speak for itself. You'll find comments throughout the script to detail what is happening. Here is the listing for the final core script, wscslide.js:

```
var slideready = false;
var SLIDEINTERVAL = 65;
var revealTimer = null;
var moving   = false;

window.onload = function() {
  slideready = true;
}

function toggle(element) {
  if (!slideready || moving) return false;
  reset(element);
  if (!document.getElementById) return true;
  var elt = document.getElementById(element);
  var initialheight= elt.offsetHeight;
  Reveal(element, initialheight);
  //return false;
}
```

```
/* reset function used to set all navigation pane divs back to their
   initial state */

function reset(element) {
  var elt = document.getElementById('drops');
  var elts = elt.getElementsByTagName('div');
  var exposed = document.getElementById(element);
  for (i=0; i< elts.length; i++) {
    // we only want to reset divs that are acting as navigation panes
    // and exclude the current one that has been set to "exposed"
    if (!/drop-/i.test(elts[i].id) || (exposed ==  document.getElementById(elts[i].id))) {
      continue;
    }
    thiselt = elts[i];
    thiselt.className = thiselt.className.replace(/exposed/g,'')
    // set style back to overflow: hidden to remove visual artifacts
    // when switching from one tab to another
    thiselt.style.overflow = "hidden";

  }

  return;

}

function changeHeight(elt, dH) {
  var thiselt = document.getElementById(elt);
  // is this a reveal up or down? if up, the final target height is 0
  var targetHeight = (dH < 0) ? 0 : dH;

  // the current height of the element
  var currHeight = thiselt.offsetHeight;

  // the change in height required - to smooth the transition we reveal
  // half of the remaining height of the pane with each iteration
  var dHeight = Math.ceil((targetHeight - currHeight) / 2);

  newHeight = currHeight + dHeight;

  // if the difference is less than 1 pixel we'll stop moving,
  //clear the interval and set the height to the exact height
  // we started with
  if (Math.abs(dHeight) <= 1) {
    clearInterval(revealTimer);
    moving = false;
    newHeight = targetHeight;

  }
```

IN PRINT

My California
Contributor (Story)

We Do
Contributor (Photos)

Design for Community
Author (Tech)

San Francisco Stories
Author (Stories)

We've Got Blog
Contributor (Essay)

```
    // set the height to a new value
    thiselt.style.height =  newHeight + "px";

    // if the height is now zero, we need to remove the "exposed" state
    // set the height back to the original height and clear the JS set
    // value for height so that it is reset to the value found in the
    // original CSS
    if (thiselt.offsetHeight == 0) {
      thiselt.className = thiselt.className.replace(/exposed/g,'');
    //force a repaint for getting around Safari rendering issue
      thiselt.innerHTML = thiselt.innerHTML + '';
      thiselt.style.height = '';
    }
  }

  function Reveal(elt, dH) {
    // prevent the function from doing anything if it is already active
    if (moving) return;
    var thiselt = document.getElementById(elt);
    if (/exposed/i.test(thiselt.className)) {
      // if we are exposed, we want to slide the pane up instead of down
      dH = -dH;
// if we are sliding up, then we want to reset the overflow to hidden
      thiselt.style.overflow = "hidden";
    } else {
      // this opens the tab and respects classes that already exist
      thiselt.className += " exposed";
    }
    moving = true;
    // run the changeHeight function at the specified interval;
    // will run until we clear the interval
    revealTimer = setInterval("changeHeight('" + thiselt.id "','" + dH + "')", SLIDEINTERVAL);
  }
```

Where does the accessibility come in to it?

The core of this script is accessible because it is interoperable. That gives us the following benefits:

- It works with scripting on or off.
- It uses the core behaviors inherent to HTML, namely simple links to other spots on the same page.
- We are (generally speaking) changing the CSS only for components of the page, and we aren't changing any CSS using display: none (which is notorious for removing elements from the internal DOM of a screen reader; see http://css-discuss.incutio.com/?page=ScreenreaderVisibility for a discussion of this often frustrating behavior).
- All links allow for keyboard activation. We didn't do anything to enable that; it is built-in behavior. In our scripting, we made sure not to do anything that *takes away* keyboard functionality.

This is good news, but it doesn't mean that we are free and clear of further obligation. To make sure that this solution is really accessible, we need to do some additional testing. Let's take a look at some of those tests.

Low vision

The CSS is constructed so that text is scalable in all browsers. The height of the navigational panes is never defined to be a static number; it is allowed to be flexible. The height of each navigational pane is determined when the script runs. This means that if a user opens and closes a pane, resizes the text, and then opens and closes the pane again, the script and the CSS automatically adjust to accommodate the sizing. We declared background and foreground colors in pairs, so that when a pane is opened and text is resized, it will still be readable, even if it falls out of the pane in which it is contained. Figure 10-5 shows a page with the text resized.

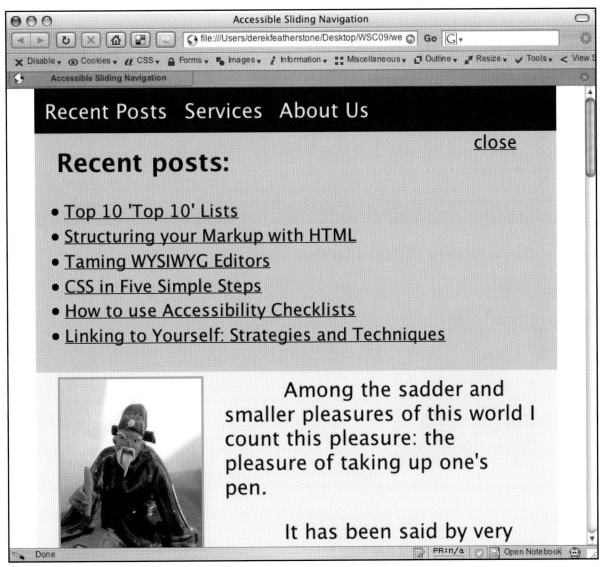

Figure 10-5. Flexible sizing allows for the fonts and the navigational pane itself to be resized, without breaking the design.

Voice recognition

This particular solution appears to work well with voice-recognition software (Dragon NaturallySpeaking was used for testing), with one minor exception. A voice-recognition user has the ability to focus on the links in a page. They may say "link" and be presented with numbered choices, as shown in Figure 10-6.

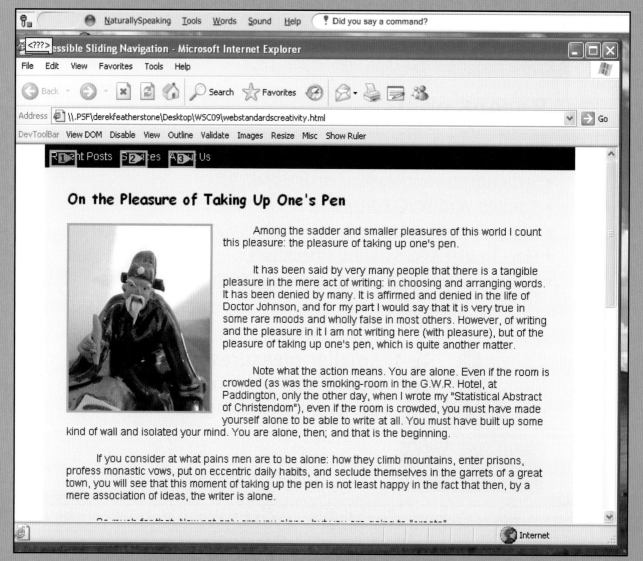

Figure 10-6. Using the link functionality in Dragon NaturallySpeaking to select the navigational links

If the person using the site then opens a navigational pane, the links that were off the screen will not be available using the numbered mechanism. The user could then repopulate the links array by saying "link" again, to give a numbered link choice, as illustrated in Figure 10-7.

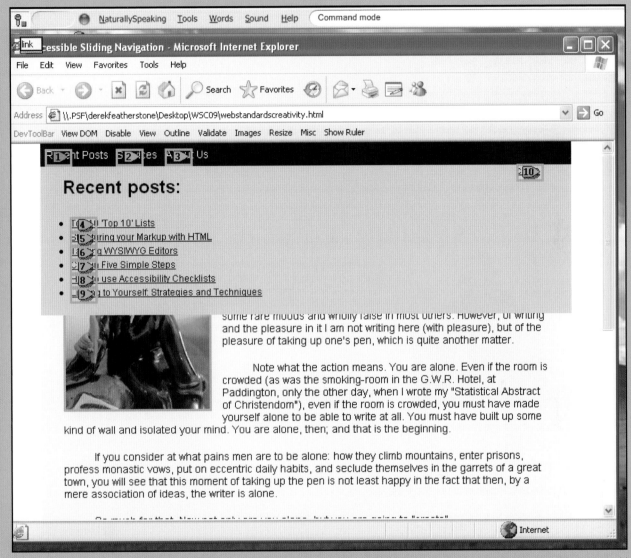

Figure 10-7. When the navigational pane opens, the links contained within the pane are not available using the links array. The user would be required to say the command "link" again to repopulate the array, as seen here.

If the user does repeat the "link" command, and then closes the navigational pane (or changes to another pane), he ends up with a visual "artifact" where each of the links used to be (see Figure 10-8 for an example). This can be remedied by manually repopulating the links array.

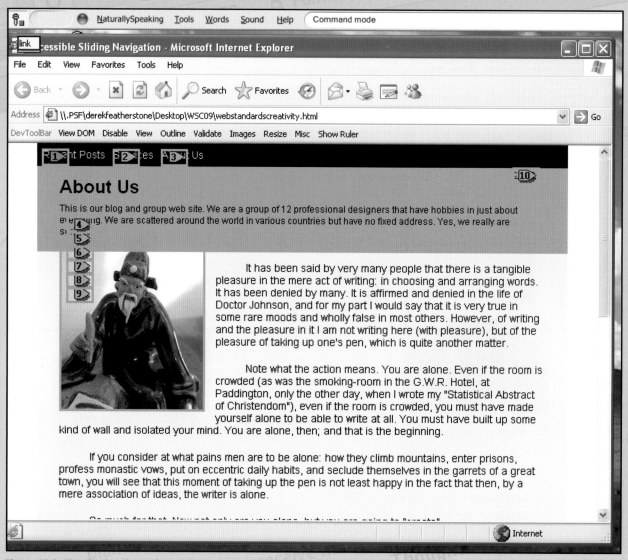

Figure 10-8. The visual artifacts of the links array. When using DOM scripting effects to move or generate content within the page, the links array does not automatically update. It requires the user to update it manually by giving the appropriate command, such as "link."

Screen readers

Testing this solution with screen readers reveals a problem. If we return `false` when hijacking the `href`s (a common practice to avoid the page "jumping" to the internal anchor/`id` that the `href` points to), then we leave the screen reader's "cursor" where it is. While we move the related navigational pane to the top visually, we are not providing the same access to a screen reader. In fact, returning `false` removes functionality from the screen reader user—we've created a barrier by not allowing the in-page jump.

How do we solve that problem? This is where we must examine accessibility and JavaScript again. If we had simply stopped at making sure that our pages were usable with scripting on or off, we wouldn't have realized the problems we are creating for screen reader users. To reiterate, the scripting on/off scenario is more about basic interoperability than it is about accessibility for people with disabilities.

One possibility is to not return `false`, and allow the history stack to take its course. In some cases, it may even be desirable to do so. However, this would mean that we get the visually jarring "jump" within the page and also end up hiding the main navigation, removing our toggle points from view. This solution is not particularly useful, and is likely to be annoying to users and unacceptable to the people who sign off on the solution.

The other possibility is to return false, but use the `href` in the link and focus on that navigational pane. If we do this, we'll allow screen reader users to continue reading in the correct place and ensure that we are not covering up our navigation or jumping all over the screen. This solution is implemented in the final files for this chapter.

Another screen reader issue is the close link. This may be confusing to screen reader users. In their minds, they have simply moved to another part of the page, so why would they need to close anything? This link makes sense only to someone who is visually looking at the page. To attempt to solve this, we use a close icon (the typical x graphic), with alt text that says "return to main navigation," with an appropriate `href`. Using the same strategy as applied for our main navigational links, we hijack the `href` to place the screen reader cursor in the next logical place.

Keyboard-only use

A keyboard-only user will experience many of the same issues as the screen reader user. In particular, placing the focus in the navigational pane will be critical to allowing a keyboard user to navigate properly.

One solution that may gain popularity over time is the use of an invalid value for the `tabindex` attribute. Assigning a `tabindex` value of -1 to an element allows that element to receive the focus programmatically, but does not add it to the natural tab order of the document. This solution is a bit controversial because of the invalid value—by specification, HTML requires `tabindex` to be a number between 0 and 32767 (see `www.w3.org/TR/REC-html40/interact/forms.html#adef-tabindex` for details).

Is the `tabindex` solution an acceptable one? IBM, Mozilla, and Microsoft all seem to think so, although representatives from IBM imply that they know this solution is not quite right (see `www.csun.edu/cod/conf/2005/proceedings/2524.htm`):

> *Keep in mind that this is not yet part of any W3C or other official standard. At this time it is necessary to bend the rules in order to have full keyboard accessibility.*

There may be unforeseen consequences for an invalid value, and manipulating the DOM to include a `tabindex` value on nodes where it is not a valid attribute seems a bit hackish. We're really using JavaScript only to camouflage the fact that we're doing something that is invalid per the HTML specification.

> *The -1* `tabindex` *strategy seems to have support within the industry. The Web Hypertext Application Technology Working Group (WHAT WG,* `www.whatwg.org`*), a group that is composed of web browser vendors and other interested parties, is working on producing HTML5. In that specification,* `tabindex` *is an attribute that will be allowed for any element, and will allow negative* `tabindex` *values.*

Conclusion

Is this the ultimate accessible solution? Maybe and maybe not. What we do know is that we've done our best to ensure we have a baseline of interoperability and accessibility in the solution by doing the following:

- Providing content and core functionality through simple HTML code
- Ensuring that we use unobtrusive scripting
- Ensuring our fonts are scalable and use both foreground and background colors together
- Using CSS in creative ways to modify the way things appear while maintaining a logical, semantic structure
- Using JavaScript such that we use links and `hrefs` to our advantage to lead a keyboard user or screen reader user through the page

We have done basic testing that allows us to address many of the issues a person with a disability will face when using this solution. Additional testing will tell you for sure whether or not this solution is usable and useful to all users with all levels of ability. It is imperative that you do your own accessibility testing with real users.

Try the techniques demonstrated here on your websites. This chapter has given you enough information to get started with your own accessible JavaScript solutions.

1-59059-543-2 $39.99 [US]

1-59059-518-1 $39.99 [US]

1-59059-542-4 $36.99 [US]

1-59059-517-3 $39.99 [US]

1-59059-651-X $44.99 [US]

EXPERIENCE THE
DESIGNER TO DESIGNER™
DIFFERENCE

1-59059-558-0 $49.99 [US]

1-59059-314-6 $59.99 [US]

1-59059-315-4 $59.99 [US]

1-59059-619-6 $44.99 [US]

1-59059-304-9 $49.99 [US]

1-59059-355-3 $24.99 [US]

1-59059-409-6 $39.99 [US]

1-59059-748-6 $49.99 [US]

1-59059-593-9 $49.99 [US]

1-59059-555-6 $44.99 [US]

1-59059-533-5 $34.99 [US]

1-59059-638-2 $49.99 [US]

1-59059-765-6 $34.99 [US]

1-59059-581-5 $39.99 [US]

1-59059-614-5 $34.99 [US]

1-59059-594-7 $39.99 [US]

1-59059-381-2 $34.99 [US]

1-59059-554-8 $24.99 [US]